Words that Change Minds

The 14 Patterns for Mastering the Language of Influence

Third Edition

Shelle Rose Charvet

Thank you for buying my book.

_____

Get a FREE version of the LAB Profile® when you join my mailing list.

Plus, get updates on new releases, deals, recommended reads, and more from Shelle Rose Charvet and The Institute for Influence.

GO TO THIS LINK TO STAY IN TOUCH:
bit.ly/WTCM-Paperback

Already a subscriber? Provide your email again so we can register your purchase and send you more of what you like to read - exclusive information in your inbox.

Use Words that Change Minds in Speaking & Writing

Strengthen your #1 skill for business – the ability to influence.

Do you know the **Influencing and Persuasion Principle?**

> "To get people to go somewhere with you, you need to meet them where they are… and not just pretend that they are already where you want them to be.
> Instead, go to *their* bus stop and from their bus stop, invite them on the bus."

Most people, particularly successful people, **use the same strategy with others that they used to convince themselves** to believe or do something, **but…. other people are different**!

Based on years of study and work with people and organizations, this book is packed with **practical applications for professionals who need to *predict and influence* behavior to succeed**. This is the first step to achieving your quantum leap in communication.

When you can easily **identify what is motivating people, how they think and how they make decisions,** you'll be able to:

- *establish a deep level of rapport and communicate effectively with anyone*
- *reduce conflicts and misunderstandings*
- *take the pain out of implementing organizational change*
- *shorten your sales cycle and guarantee customer satisfaction*
- *design powerful marketing and advertising campaigns*
- *recruit the right people who fit and perform*
- *dramatically improve your results in negotiations and presentations*
- *create your learning programs to satisfy diverse needs, increase self-knowledge and competence*

- *learn a whole new way to advance your coaching skills, and your coaching business*
- *lead high performance teams by managing your peoples' strengths, instead of suffering from their weaknesses*

The NEW 3rd edition of Words That Change Minds has more than **50% new material;** examples, research, advanced applications, with **7 completely new chapters,** including:

1. **How to Complete a LAB Profile®**
2. **Conversational Coaching with the LAB Profile®**
3. **Understanding and Working with Combination Patterns**
4. **Solving Communication Problems**
5. **Influencing Strategies and Techniques**
6. **The LAB Profile® of Conflict**
7. **LAB Profile® Inventions and Tools, and more.**

To my sons, Jason and Sam,
who give me much joy and keep on teaching me,
to my Mum and Dad, Betty and Frank Rose.
And to my Micha
for all your encouragement,
love and support.

Table of Contents

"*Words That Change Minds* is full of interesting tools for anyone who truly values good communication. This book will teach you how to understand people and how to speak to them. I highly recommend this book."

— Peter Urs Bender, author of *Secrets of Power Presentations*

"*Words That Change Minds* is a great self-help book, that will help you understand yourself and the people you work with."

— Joe Gaetan, Director of People and Improvement,
Monsanto Canada Inc., Mississauga, Ontario

"I had to laugh at the bookstore on Monday. Everyone that asked me if I knew any good books got an enthusiastic presentation on yours. I told them how much pain I would have avoided in personnel if only I had had your book nine months earlier."

— Gary E. Megal
Colorado Springs, Colorado

"Can you imagine your business profits increasing by 10-30%? That is what my company was able to immediately experience, as I used Ms. Rose Charvet's LAB Profile® to make improved hiring decisions."

— Edward Lund
Telecommunications Manager, California

"At last I got your book, and on the strength of its information I have my first decent commercial assignment helping a local employer do his own recruiting, as he is fed up with the standard of the local employment bureaux."

— Roger Phillip,
Personnel Trainer
Devon, United Kingdom

"*Words That Change Minds* provides a comprehensive overview of the fundamental differences in individual behavioral patterns, questions that reveal these patterns and the language most likely to influence people according to their dominant patterns."

— Joel P. Bowman, Professor
Haworth College of Business, Western Michigan University
Kalamazoo, Michigan

"The LAB Profile® was a fascinating discovery, which impacted the way I communicate with others, and transformed my consulting practice."

— Léon Tanguay,
Human Resource Development Consultant
Montréal, Québec

"The LAB Profile® and the book *Words That Change Minds*, written by Shelle Rose Charvet, have proven to be invaluable tools in my evaluation and hiring process. Candidates have been screened in to positions and screened out, far more appropriately, through the proper use of these techniques. I highly recommend these additions to your array of behavioural interviewing tools."

— Gordon I. Brown,
Vice-President, Executive Search
Corporate Consultants, Toronto, Ontario

"*Words That Change Minds* is a book of insight and inquiry. Shelle Rose Charvet offers a new way to think about relationships with ourselves and others. She provides a strategic language of influence to support lasting effective improvements in the building of our relationships. She describes the basic mental structures that we use to perceive, organize and act on our social world. *Words That Change Minds* is a unique reference framework for individual and family self-development. It is a landmark for leaders, executives and associates who are committed to improve, with integrity, the quality of life and the effectiveness of their enterprise."

"*Words That Change Minds* gave me a level of awareness and precision in communication that I did not think was possible. I used to get frustrated when I worked with others who had different communication patterns than my own. Now, I get curious. What a breakthrough!"

"I pull out *Words That Change Minds* whenever I am facing a situation where I am not connecting with an individual. By using Shelle's techniques I can understand them better and then establish a much higher level of rapport. As a sales professional there are times when I have to present to key decision makers. Shelle's book has helped me understand how to communicate with people on their terms and that has increased sales."

"*Words That Change Minds* belongs on the must-read list for everyone who interacts with other people. I have found it to be invaluable for understanding and communicating effectively with business associates, family and friends. It's the first book I have read that identifies various styles of communicating and outlines an easy-to-follow process to create an accurate exchange of information."

"Shelle's book, *Words That Change Minds,* is a helpful and practical reference tool and guide in preparation for management, negotiation, mediation or conflict resolution. Understanding and respecting people is at the core of good communications. I have found the LAB Profile® to be a useful and insightful tool. It helps you progress towards your desired outcome, while respecting the needs and pace of those with who you are working."

— Geneviève O'Sullivan,
Director Genera, Strategic & Corporate Relations,
Agriculture and Agri-food Canada, Ottawa, Ontario

"I read the book during a ski trip in New Zealand – it's easy reading, entertaining, and very practical. I've used the motivation traits questions to help a Malaysian friend clarify his career goals, a middle-age friend to build her résumé, and most interesting of all, a Chinese lady to decide whether or not she should buy a South Sea pearl necklace! And all the while, they didn't know I was using the standard questions because it was like natural conversation."

— Kenzie L. Kwong,
Director, Kenn & K Consulting Ltd.,
Hong Kong and Asia Pacific

"This book provides intriguing insights into what motivates people, how they make decisions and generally what makes them tick. I found this information very valuable."

— Juel Hogg
Marketing Program Manager,
Hewlett-Packard, (Canada) Ltd.,
Toronto, Ontario

"*Words That Change Minds* has greatly assisted our staff in honing their negotiating skills – I highly recommend this book to anyone who has to deal with high stakes communication."

— Harry Hynd
Director, District 6, United Steelworkers of America,
Toronto, Ontario

"Knowing the precise definitions of spoken or written words is not enough to understand the real intended meaning. The LAB Profile® solves this for each unique relationship and provides the influencing words that are most effective for that particular relationship."

— Chuck Watson
Corporate Accounts Vice President, Coulter Corporation,
Miami, Florida

"Excellent book – would recommend this book to anyone wanting to use NLP in the business world. Written in a down -to-earth, extremely readable, interesting style with useful real-world examples ... and with a great sense of humour!"

— David Kintler,
President, SalesWinners, Inc.
Coral Springs, Florida

"After reading Shelle's book, I asked her to train my management, customer service representatives, consultants and sales staff. Not only does it work in achieving bottom line results in business, she also taught my wife and I how to communicate at a new level. Shelle is the master of influential communication. I strongly urge all business leaders to read this book ... it could change your life!"

— Richard A. Grehalva,
Vice President, CSC Health Care Systems,
Birmingham, Alabama

Acknowledgements

I would like to thank my business partner, Stefan Irimia for thinking BIG, remembering what is important, for leading the team, and bringing out my best self, as a performer and as a writer. Also, I want to thank Ioana Ardelean for being the mid-wife of this book and many of the other elements that made this whole project fly. Thanks to Teo Calin for pushing all the moving parts ahead and making sure they got done. And to Silvia Truta for video editing and great makeup. Thanks to Elena Ion also for making me look great, and Monica Ion for great input to video content and many other things.

I'm also grateful to everyone who participated in inspiring conversations with me over the years.

Part 1: Introduction

Chapter I
Introduction

Introduction to the 3ʳᵈ Edition

A mutual fund company was generating leads for high-value new customers from their investment advice television program, but they were not happy with their closing rate.

Their high-value prospective clients (people who had $2 million or more to invest) would watch the TV program where the CEO handled phone-in inquiries about investing, and after several months of watching, would phone to find out about investing with the company. However, as the company had no formal sales process, the issue was that customers somehow got lost along the way and sales opportunities were missed.

They hired me to help them. I conducted LAB Profile® market research and interviewed prospective clients who phoned the company and said "yes" to investing and prospects who also phoned but didn't end up saying "yes". From these interviews, I uncovered the key LAB Profile® Motivation and Working Patterns for each group. Using that information, I then designed a sales process and proposed a series of keywords to use on their website and in the television program that they are still using today, 15 years later.

And the results? Their closing rate increased by 50%. Because of this, the CEO decided to come and train with me because he wanted to understand what was the difference that actually ... made the difference.

He registered for the 10-day LAB Profile® Consultant/Trainer Certification program with me but wouldn't commit to completing the entire program (even though he had paid for the whole thing). At the end of each day, we wondered whether he was coming back the next day. In the end, he stayed the full 10 days because he really wanted to learn.

Exciting and Scary Times

Since the first and second editions of *Words That Change Minds* were produced, much more has been discovered about how people think, get motivated, and make decisions. Many research studies about various aspects of human behavior, demonstrate the LAB Profile® Patterns in action. Neuroscience findings (including following live changes in the brain) also show how people's Motivation and Working Patterns shift, based on what someone is thinking about. The consulting and problem-solving work that both I and my students have conducted in over 30 countries, demonstrates the effectiveness of decoding what motivates people into sequences of combinations of LAB Profile® Patterns.

There is still so much to learn and work with how these Patterns show up in different Contexts, which is why I wrote my second book, **Words That Change Customers' Minds** and founded the **Institute for Influence,** which offers online training for women leaders and managers, and **SalesTrainerPlatform** with digital LAB Profile® for Sales training.

You can take almost any human attitude, quality or behavior, understand its components and figure out how to have an influence. Yes, this is scary. Since the publication of the previous edition of this book, many discoveries have been made that reveal much about people from their online behaviors and what they do in the real world. This information has unfortunately been used to manipulate and create more strife. As we have seen, elections have been influenced by organizations strong-arming voters by making use of their belief systems and deepest fears. The upshot is that people have become even more distrustful of institutions, journalists, national leaders and other people, often rightfully so.

But this is not the only way to have an impact. If you can truly understand others, go to their bus stop; their psychological, motivational bus stop and invite them on the bus, you are much more likely to have a positive impact, both for them and you.

I am writing this 3rd edition with the purpose of showing you how to have a positive impact in your world through understanding what motivates others, how they think and how they make decisions. My hope is that you will use it to create better, more ethical communication.

Introduction to the 2nd Edition

Cheryl walked into my office for her appointment looking frustrated and angry. A well-dressed, elegant professional, she did not waste a second on the customary niceties of a first encounter.

"I need to find a new job right away," she said. "I can't stand my boss and I heard that you do career profiles." After some discussion about what she wanted and what was important to her, we agreed to do a career profile. About halfway through the feedback on the profile she called a halt to the whole process. "Oh my God," she said. "My boss and I are obstinate in exactly the same way! We are constantly arguing. Neither of us will budge from our positions. No wonder we haven't been getting along! Can you show me how to communicate with him?" I took a few minutes and taught her the exact language to use and which language to avoid. Within two months she called to tell me of a major promotion she had just received. Today she is one of the highest-ranking women in her sector in the country.

Poor communication (or a lack of it altogether), is a huge problem in our times; at work, at home, and in the world at large. Discord among people is frequent, ranging from small annoyances like twenty-minute voicemail messages, lifelong parent-child resentments, to increasingly complex conflicts between nations and tribes. Finding solutions to communication problems has been the focus of much study and the development of many models.

Many psychometric assessments have been created to explain the differences that cause communication problems between people. Many of them stick people in boxes with labels, like round pegs into square holes. Often, they do not recognize people's inherent flexibility to shift thinking and behavior as situations change. It is not surprising that a great many individuals, while fascinated by questionnaires and profiling tools, tend to discount the sweeping generalizations these instruments produce. Instead some people prefer to rely solely on their intuition and gut feelings to make critical decisions such as hiring or choosing a spouse. I once told a CEO that if he hired his executive vice president because he liked the person, he would be in big trouble. The last thing he needed was to recruit someone who thought just like he did.

It is well-known that people communicate through a set of filters shaped by history, sense of identity, beliefs about what is true, and values about what is right, as well as perceptions and interpretations of what is going on. When someone else communicates with us, we squeeze the message through our own personal filtering system to understand. Of course, people from the same ethnic, cultural, gender, national, or geographic grouping have some common history and beliefs. That makes communication within those groups easier, than between people who come from different backgrounds.

Beyond these differences, each of us also has unique *ways* of thinking and processing. We pay attention to various aspects of reality, based on how we *individually* use our brains. Some of us think in detailed linear sequences, while others prefer to envision a larger whole. Some people are attracted to those things that are different and new, while others are drawn to what is the same (or at least similar) to what they already know.

But what if we *could* really understand what someone means when he or she talks to us? Even better, what if we could predict someone's behavior based simply on what was said? Best of all-what if we could *influence* that behavior by how we responded?

I investigated the field to find some answers to these complex questions of understanding, communicating, and influencing. I wanted to avoid easy solutions. Any good theory must be well-founded and verifiable by people's personal experience. It must also be applicable for a wide range of human activities, respectful of individual people and their differences, and learnable without a doctorate or engineering degree. Above all, it truly had to improve communication between people.

In 1983, while teaching communication seminars in Europe, I started to hear about some interesting work that came from (wouldn't you know it) California. I began to explore this approach, called Neuro-linguistic Programming (NLP). Despite its techno-babble name, it seemed to be designed to reach into people's minds and discover how specifically each person is unique. It was based on studying some of the great communicators and therapists of our time. It examined *how* they were able to accomplish what they did, without the usual investigation into the reasons *why* people have problems. It was about learning strategies that work, not about scrutinizing the failures that people experience.

I wanted to find out if these people were onto something. I took several in-depth courses and began to test their techniques in my work. The results were remarkable. I learned how to create rapport with anyone, to change beliefs that had been limiting me, and to help others do the same. Being a doubting Thomas, I liked the requirement that every intervention be tested for possible negative consequences prior to being completed with a person. If someone were to let go of the belief that rainy days make them sick, a practitioner would have to check first if getting sick on rainy days had some positive benefits that needed to be met in some other healthier way for that person, *before* helping them replace the belief.

In 1985, I encountered a specific tool developed from NLP that completely changed the way I communicate. It is both rigorous and flexible. It can be woven naturally into casual conversation. Since then, I have continued exploring its uses in a wide range of contexts. I have used it to:

- create powerful presentations for large groups of people
- redesign marketing and sales processes to help companies successfully reach their major customers
- attract and select only the right candidates for key executive positions
- help clients I have coached

- create *irresistible* influencing language for teenagers, and
- help organizations dramatically improve their communication about change with their own people.

While this tool was being widely taught and learned, I kept finding new ways of applying it and getting dramatic results. I wondered why no one had written a book on all the things you could do with it, provided you took the time to master the skill. This book is the result of testing it out for myself and with my clients.

During 1995 and 1996, I assisted in the supervision of two Master of Education theses. One thesis succeeded in establishing the reliability of the tool, and the other investigated whether there were predictable patterns in people who were able to make career decisions, compared with people who found it difficult or impossible to decide on a career. I have included the research abstracts in the appendices. Since then much more has been written and researched.

The Language and Behavior Profile (LAB Profile®)

The tool is called the **Language and Behavior Profile (LAB Profile®)**. It is a way of thinking about people and groups that allows you to notice and respond to how they get motivated, process information, and make decisions.

It is based on a set of about a dozen questions that you can feed into casual conversation or use, as a formal survey for groups. You pay attention to *how* people talk when they answer, rather than *what* they talk about. Even when a person does not answer the question directly, they will reveal their pattern by the manner in which they answer (or don't).

As you become familiar with the questions and the kind of responses people give, you will find that you can hear and pick up the patterns people use without having to actually ask the questions. You can immediately use the Influencing Language that is just right for the situation. People communicate with their particular patterns naturally as they speak, both in words and in their body language, and they respond immediately when you use *their* language.

Because the LAB Profile® can be used informally in conversation, I have included many example conversations in this book. To illustrate the kind of emphasis and inflection that we typically employ when we talk, I have made liberal use of **bold** and *italic* characters.

As you read this book, check it against your own experience, relating it to the people you know, recognizing yourself and others. I hope you will find some solutions to the challenges you face as you communicate with people on a daily basis. Even if you do not have specific communication problems, this book will provide you with useful information to consider and a vocabulary for describing what you are already doing-perhaps unconsciously.

I keep discovering new insights and uses for this material both in my personal life and in my work. I invite you to join me in exploring the possible applications of the LAB Profile®.

History of the LAB Profile®

Words That Change Minds was built on the Language and Behavior Profile, or LAB Profile®, created by Rodger Bailey. The LAB Profile® is based on specific applications from *Neuro-linguistic Programming*, a field developed by Richard Bandler, John Grinder, and others in the United States, beginning in the mid-70s. They created the original models of Neuro-linguistic Programming (or NLP) by examining and understanding the processes used by highly successful communicators.

The field of NLP has expanded exponentially since then, and is the subject of much research, with hundreds of books written on it around the world. This approach is now taught in several dozen countries across all five continents.

Let's start with Programming. Each person, through genetic makeup, environmental influences, and individual biochemistry, has managed to *program* herself or himself to be excellent at a certain number of things, mediocre at different things, and just awful in other areas.

If we observe and listen carefully to how a person behaves and communicates *linguistically*, we can glean an understanding of how, *neurologically*, a person puts his or her experience together to be excellent, mediocre, or awful at the things he or she does. Hence, this field is called Neuro-linguistic Programming.

The applications are enormous and mean that if someone is highly skilled at something, a person trained in certain NLP protocols can *model* them. Modeling is finding out how it is possible for that person to do what they do. And the person who models, searches for the answers to questions such as: "What are the absolute essentials?" or "What is that person paying attention to or ignoring, sequentially and/ or simultaneously, to be able to do it?" When the answers to these and other questions are found, then it becomes possible to teach that skill to other people, and even learn it oneself.

The Language and Behavior Profile is a model created by Rodger Bailey, an avid developer in the field of NLP. He created the LAB Profile® in the early 1980s. It is based on a set of patterns from NLP called, at the time they were developed, the *Meta Programs*. These Meta Programs are based on the filters that we use to make up our *model of the world*.

Creating Our Model of the World

Every person has a certain number of filters by which they let in certain parts of the real world. In Noam Chomsky's 1957 Ph.D. thesis, *Transformational Grammar*, he said there are three processes by which people create the filters of their individual Model of the World:

Deletion

The first process is called **deletion**. We delete lots of information from the environment around us as well as internally. In his 1956 paper entitled **Seven Plus or Minus Two**, George Miller, an American psychologist, said that our conscious minds can only handle seven plus-or-minus two bits of information at any one time, and that we delete the rest. That means on a good day we can deal with nine bits in total and on a bad day, maybe only five.

This explains why most telephone numbers are a maximum of seven digits. However, while I was living in Paris back in the 1980s, they changed the phone numbers to eight digits. Everyone then had to decide whether to remember phone numbers by groups of two, or four, or to simply add the new Paris code – the number four - onto the front of their old number. No one had an easy way of keeping eight digits in their head at once. Each person had to find their own way to break it down. People would give out their new phone numbers in their own peculiar manner. It created a great deal of confusion.

So, seven plus or minus two bits of information, is what we can comfortably be aware of at one time. Using the process of deletion, we filter lots of things out, either without being aware of them or consciously choosing to do so.

Distortion

The second process is called **distortion**. We distort things. Have you ever moved to a new place and gone into the living room before you moved your things in, and picturing what it was going to look like furnished? Well, you were hallucinating. Your furniture was not *actually* in the room, was it? So, you were distorting Reality.

Two examples of distortion are hallucination and creativity. They are both similar in that the external information is changed to something else. That is what the process of distortion is all about.

Generalization

Chomsky's third mental filtering process is called **generalization**. It is the opposite of Cartesian Logic (where you can go from a general rule to specific examples but not the other way around). Generalization is where you take a few examples and then create a general principle. This is how learning occurs. A small child learns to open one, two, or possibly three, doors and then she knows how to open them all. The child develops a Generalization about how to open doors. That is, until they have to enter a high-tech company and realize that, to open the door, there is a magnetic card that has to be slid down a slot in a certain way. The child has to relearn how to open doors to deal with those exceptions.

Generalization is about how we unconsciously generate rules, beliefs, and principles about what is true, untrue, possible, and impossible. Some women, for example, may have had several bad experiences with men and then come to the conclusion that men (i.e., *all* men) cannot be trusted. They develop the rule: *Never trust a man.* People have a certain number of experiences of a similar type and then make a rule or develop a belief.

With these three filters, Deletion, Distortion and Generalization, we each create our own model of the world.

Meta Programs

What is the link between these three processes: NLP, The Meta Programs, and the LAB Profile®? The co-originators of NLP used Chomsky's Deletion, Distortion and Generalization model to create a map for discovering and influencing a person's perceptions and interpretations of their experiences.

Leslie Cameron-Bandler (now Leslie Lebeau) took Chomsky's work even further. She postulated that each person makes specific kinds of Deletions, Distortions and Generalizations, which then show up in a person's behavior. From her work in therapeutic settings, she identified about sixty different Patterns, which she called Meta Programs.

Meta Programs are the specific filters we use to interact with the world. They edit and shape what we allow to come in from the outside world. They also mold what comes from inside ourselves as we communicate and behave in the world.

Meta Programs are like a door through which we interact with the world. This door has a particular shape and has the power to let only certain things in, or out. This may appear to be part of our individual nature, and therefore be permanent but in fact, the shape of the door itself can shift in response to changes in ourselves and our surrounding environment.

Rodger Bailey, who was a student of Leslie's, adapted her work for business settings. He created the LAB Profile® to be a practical, easy to use tool to help people understand what is motivating others when they communicate. He said that these Patterns are a status report on how a person responds to a given situation.

Most people would agree that our behavior is different when we are with different people, at work, or at home with our family. They are not, therefore, descriptions of our *personality*, but rather a picture of how we are interacting with different environments or contexts.

The LAB Profile® simply describes the form of our door, what specifically we let in and out in a given situation, or Context. **It is this recognition of our ability to change our motivations and behavior that sets this tool apart from the psychometric profiles that make sweeping generalizations about our personality**.

Language and Behavior Patterns

When I first learned about Meta Programs, there were about sixty patterns. We had to talk to the people we were studying with and *guess* what their patterns were. I spent a year and a half trying to guess what everyone's Meta Programs were, and needless to say, I was not very good at it.

To make detecting and using these patterns simpler, Rodger Bailey had the foresight to reduce the number of patterns from sixty to fourteen. (Do you really need to know sixty things about yourself or another person?) He also developed a small set of specific questions by which, regardless of what people answer, their unconscious patterns are revealed *in the structure* of the language they use. You pay attention to *how* people answer, instead of *what* they say. In this way, after asking a few simple questions, you can determine what will *trigger and maintain* someone's motivation and how they internally process information.

He identified two separate kinds of Meta Programs when he developed the LAB Profile®. He called the first set of categories **Motivation Traits**, and they are sometimes also called Motivation Patterns or Triggers. These are the Patterns that indicate what a person needs to get and stay motivated in a given Context, or conversely what will demotivate someone. Sometimes I call these the Motivation Triggers because they reveal what will *make* a person do something or *prevent* a person from acting in a certain way.

Rodger Bailey called the second set **Working Traits,** also known as Productivity Patterns. These categories describe the internal mental processing that a person uses in a specific situation. For example, we can determine if a person prefers an overview or sequential details, the environments in which they are most productive, whether a person attends to people or tasks, how they respond to stress, and the mechanics that lead them to become convinced about something.

And all this shows up in *how* a person talks.

Here is a table describing the difference between the original Meta Programs, developed by Leslie Cameron-Bandler and the LAB Profile®.

Original Meta Programs	Development	LAB Profile®	Benefit of LAB Profile®
60 patterns	Summarizing, concentrating on essentials	14 practical Categories	Easy to learn and remember
No methodology	Structured approach for detecting and utilizing	Questionnaire for eliciting patterns with clear indicators	Easy to use for research with groups, & for impact in conversation
No specific language for each Meta Program	Identification of specific language structures and behaviors for each Pattern	Influencing Language for each Pattern	Dramatically increases ability to persuade, because it fits language to internal mental structure
No particular practical applications at the time	On-going research and development	Used for mass & interpersonal communication, self-knowledge, psycho-metric profiles	Incredible potential for creating new applications. (See Resources chapter)

Influencing Language

He also developed the *Influencing Language*. Once you know a person's Patterns, you can then tailor your language so that it has *maximum impact* for that person.

Imagine for a moment that someone who did not master your mother tongue very well was attempting to get some ideas across to you. Chances are that you would spend a lot of energy translating it into terms that were more meaningful to you. When someone uses terms that you can *immediately* understand, none of your energy is lost in translating; the meaning just goes in. When you use the appropriate Influencing Language, the impact is powerful precisely because you are *speaking in someone's own personal style.*

You can choose exactly those **words that change minds**.

Reality

I need to make another point before we go on, just to avoid any confusion. From Noam Chomsky and many others, we know that people do not actually live in Reality. By deleting, distorting and generalizing, we inhabit our *perceptions* and *interpretations* of Reality. The LAB Profile® Patterns reflect a person's Model of the World. Because of this, I will NOT generally be dealing with Reality in this book, but rather the way we *perceive and interpret* it.

How the LAB Profile® Works in Communication

Let's say a person has an experience. When that person talks about his experience, they only communicate a minute portion of the actual event. They have to edit out the vast majority of what was going on, just to be able to communicate it in a reasonable time frame. It means that in order for you to tell someone about reading this book, you will need to eliminate most of what you experienced. You might say, "It was good," and nod your head, perhaps leaving out all the things this book made you think about, not mentioning whether you were physically comfortable at the time you were reading. Think of all those times when you did not grasp what someone was talking about because they left out elements you needed to fully understand.

People transform their actual experience, their opinions, and so on, in ways that correspond to their own particular Deletions, Distortions, and Generalizations.

Leslie Cameron-Bandler and Rodger Bailey determined that people who use the *same language patterns* in their speech have the *same behaviors*. The Language and Behavior Profile got its name from the connections between a person's language and how they behave.

The tools in this book will enable you to *understand, predict* and *influence* behavior. The LAB Profile® is a set of tools that can be learned as a skill. You will have the opportunity to train your eyes and ears to perceive certain things that you may not have paid attention to before. You will also learn some ways of describing and working with behavior patterns you may have already noticed.

Because the LAB Profile® is a set of skills, you will need to use it with rigor, paying attention to the shifts people make as they move from situation to situation. This is where the notion of Context comes in.

Context

The Context is the frame of reference a person puts around a situation. Since human beings are flexible by nature, they are able to behave differently at different times. Are we talking about you at work, in a romantic relationship, with your kids, with your peers, when you are on holiday, or when you are buying a house? Simply because a person has a certain pattern (or habit) in a given place and time does not indicate that they will have that same pattern in another Context.

When I run seminars in this material, people ask me: "Am I always that way?" The answer is no. We move, we grow, and our response to significant events in our lives can change how we function. These changes show up in the LAB Profile® patterns we use in conversation. Because our behavior can vary in different situations, you will need to make sure when using the LAB Profile® questions, that you have clearly and specifically identified the Context. What is the frame of reference (or Context) around the situation for the person you are speaking with? I will demonstrate how specifically to do this as we discuss each pattern.

If used with integrity and care, the LAB Profile® will enable you to improve your communication dramatically in many Contexts, so that you can adapt what you do to fit any situation.

To help you identify when someone is talking about or has switched Contexts, listen for:

- When?
- Where?
- With whom?
- and a verb.

When people use these cues, they are telling you what a Context is for them:

"When we are sitting in the living room with the kids, arguing about whether it's bedtime."

"In client meetings, doing a needs analysis."

As you practice noticing when people are switching Contexts, it will be easier to have a deep understanding of them, increase your impact and avoid inadvertently making blunders that harm relationships.

Chapter 2
LAB Profile® Applications[1]

Here are some examples of the LAB Profile® practical applications:

- **Market Research:** Since these Patterns vary by Context, several methodologies have been developed to empirically determine the different below-conscious motivations customers have for competing products and services. This is used to create multi-faceted communication strategies.

- **Sales and Marketing:** Understanding and speaking to your clients' unconscious Motivation Patterns.

- **Coaching:** The Conversational Coaching© methodology, where the coach elicits the client's LAB Profile® Patterns conversationally for their current situation and their desired state. The process enables the client to experience their desired state and develop their own solutions.[2]

- **Training for Behavior Change:** Using the LAB Profile®, you can choose activities which will create the desired behavior changes for any target group, first by decoding the Motivation Patterns for the group and then understanding which LAB Profile® Patterns are addressed by any given activity.

- **People Management:** You can train managers to identify the LAB Profile® Patterns and thereby the strengths of their team members, so they can adjust assignments to suit what team members naturally do best at work.

- **Recruitment:** Identify the LAB Profile® for a position and the corporate culture to create a job posting that will be irresistible to those who fit the role and discourage those who do not. You can then screen the selected short-listed candidates to find the best match. (Note: The LAB Profile® does not measure skills, knowledge or attitude; rather it measures whether the person has the Motivation and Productivity Patterns that are suited to the tasks and the environment; in other words, "fit".)

- **Skills Training:** Learning the LAB Profile® will enable people to develop finely-tuned abilities in the following areas: Influencing & Persuading, Negotiating, Leadership, Conflict Resolution, Sales and Customer Service.[3]
- **Consulting and Problem-Solving:** Use LAB Profile® methodology to diagnose and develop solutions to any communication problem. This is a favorite amongst business leaders and consultants.
- **Implementing Organizational Change:** Diagnose the present and desired organizational cultures in LAB Profile® terms and determine the appropriate change methodology for maximum sustainable results.
- **Team Building:** When you do a team LAB Profile®, you can determine the team's strengths and weaknesses with regards to their mandate. You can also identify communication patterns within the team and between this team and others, as well as determining the LAB Profile® Patterns of the next person to add to the team.
- **Teaching and Learning:** Teachers and students can identify the LAB Profile® Patterns which facilitate or cause difficulties in learning for individuals and whole groups. I gave a workshop to the National Indian Education Conference in Canada (for teachers on Native Indian Reservations) on how to prevent drop-outs using this methodology.
- **Modeling:** The LAB Profile® can be used to decode any strategy or any skill, by identifying the behaviors used and breaking them down into LAB Profile® Combinations.

---

[1] For more info (including a free LAB Profile®) see bit.ly/TheLabProfile
[2] Conversational Coaching with the LAB Profile®; one hour MP3: bit.ly/ConversationalCoaching
[3] For digital LAB Profile® for Sales training, see bit.ly/SalesTrainerPlatform or contact me directly to bring the digital training into your organization shelle@salestrainerplatform.com

Part 2: Motivation Patterns

Chapter 3
Motivation Patterns

Questions	Categories	Patterns: Indicators
(no question for Level)	**LEVEL** _____ _____	**Proactive:** *action, do it, short, crisp sentences* **Reactive:** *try, think about it, could, wait*
What do you want in your (work)**?**	**CRITERIA**	
Why is that (criteria) important? (ask up to 3 times)	**DIRECTION** _____ _____	**Toward:** *attain, gain, achieve, get, include* **Away From:** *avoid, exclude, recognize problems*
How do you know you have done a good job at ... ?	**SOURCE** _____ _____	**Internal:** *knows within self* **External:** *told by others, facts and figures*
Why did you choose (your current work)**?**	**REASON** _____ _____	**Options**: *criteria, choice, possibilities, variety* **Procedures:** *story, how, necessity, didn't choose*
What is the relationship between (your work this year and last year)**?**	**DECISION FACTORS** _____ _____ _____ _____	**Sameness:** *same, no change* **Sameness with Exception:** *more/ better, comparisons* **Difference:** *change, new, unique* **Sameness with Exception & Difference:** *new and comparisons*

Motivation Patterns

The first six categories in the LAB Profile® will show you how different people trigger their motivation and what language you will need to use to capture their interest. Each category is dealt with in a separate chapter.

For each category of Patterns, you will learn the questions to ask, how to detect the Patterns in ordinary conversation, what each person needs to get interested or excited about something, and conversely, what would put them off.

There are no good or bad ones to have. You can judge the appropriateness of each Pattern only in the Context of the activity that needs to be done. For each Pattern I have included ways to take advantage of the strengths and qualities inherent in each one.

While each category represents behavior on a *continuum* from one Pattern to another, **each Pattern is described in its pure form. Behavior predictions are only valid in the same Context in which the subject was profiled.**

After the behavior description for each Pattern you will find a section entitled **Influencing Language**. In these sections, you will find examples of the kind of language that has the greatest impact. For each category, the distribution of the Patterns is shown. The figures are from the research that Rodger Bailey conducted, and refer only to the Context of work. They will give you an idea of how frequently you can expect to find certain Patterns.

I will discuss the Patterns in different situations, with lots of examples to provide insight and illustrate the fine points of using *Words That Change Minds*.

At the end of both the Motivation Patterns and Productivity Patterns sections are **summary worksheets**, which can be used when profiling people. At the end of the book are complete profiling worksheets.

Level: Do it Now, or Have a Think About it?

Does a person take the initiative, or wait for others in order to act?

This category within the Motivation Patterns, is about what will get you going and what will make you think. What is your LEVEL of activity? There are two Patterns:

Proactive

People in a Proactive mode initiate. They tend to act with little or no consideration, to jump into situations without thinking or analyzing. They may upset some people because they can bulldoze ahead with what they want to do. They are good at going out and getting the job done. They do not wait for others to initiate.

Reactive

When in a Reactive mode, people tend to wait for others to initiate or until the situation is right before they act. They may consider and analyze without acting. They want to fully understand and assess the situation before they will act. They believe in chance and luck. They will spend a lot of time waiting. Some people may get upset with them because they do not *get started*. They will wait for others to initiate and then respond. In the extreme, they operate with extra caution and study situations endlessly. They make good analysts.

Distribution %	
(in the work Context, from Rodger Bailey)	
Mainly Proactive	15-20%
Equally Proactive & Reactive	60-65%
Mainly Reactive	15-20%

Since about 60 to 65 percent of the population in the work Context have an equally Proactive and Reactive Pattern, it is reasonable to assume that the person you are profiling is in the middle, unless they clearly demonstrate that they lean to one side or the other.

Identification

Since there is no specific question to ask for this category, you can pay attention to the person's sentence structure and body language, as they will be giving you their Pattern throughout your conversation:

Proactive: sentence structure

- short sentences: noun, active verb, tangible object
- speaks as if they are in control of their world
- crisp and clear sentence structure
- direct
- at the extreme, they "bulldoze"

Proactive: body language

- signs of impatience, speaking quickly, pencil tapping, lots of movement or inability to sit for long periods

Reactive: sentence structure

- incomplete sentences, subject or verb missing
- passive verbs or verbs transformed into nouns
- lots of infinitives
- speak as if the world controls them, things happen to them, believe in chance or luck
- long and convoluted sentences
- talks about thinking about, analyzing, understanding, or waiting, or the principle of the thing
- conditionals, would, could, might, may
- overly cautious, need to understand and analyze

Reactive: body language

- willingness to sit for long periods

Examples

Proactive:	*"I meet with my team every week."*
Mainly Proactive:	*"I meet with my team if it seems like we need it."*
Equally Proactive and Reactive:	*"I meet with my team to go over the current files. It is important to stay informed."*
Mainly Reactive:	*"Even though you might wonder if it is necessary to meet with the team every week, I do it because it is important that they feel they are being listened to."*
Reactive:	*"Even though everybody might wonder if it is really necessary to meet each week, it is important to consider the needs people have of being listened to."*

Influencing Language

If you think about it, matching someone's way of being is very important when communicating. Use these words and phrases to get people to jump into action:

Proactive

- go for it; just do it; jump in; why wait; now; right away; get it done; you'll get to do; take the initiative; take charge; run away with it; right now; what are you waiting for; let's hurry

Reactive

- let's think about it; now that you have analyzed it; you'll get to really understand; this will tell you why consider this; this will clarify it for you; think about your response; you might consider; could; the time is ripe; good luck is coming your way

Since most people have some Proactive and Reactive, you can use both sets of Influencing Language; considering and doing.

Recruitment

People who have a Proactive Pattern at work are suitable for those positions that require taking the initiative, going out and getting it done. They would work well in outside sales, in independent businesses, or the kind of work where having *chutzpah*[1] is an asset. If you are advertising for a highly Proactive person, ask the applicants to phone instead of sending in a résumé. (Reactive people will not phone.)

People who have a Reactive Pattern in the work Context are well suited to jobs that allow them to respond to requests. Representatives on customer service desks tend to be more Reactive. Many research and analytical jobs need someone who can spend a lot of time analyzing data.

Most people and most positions have a mixture of the two Patterns. When hiring, you will need to examine what proportion of the work to be done consists of Reactive or Proactive activities, to determine the kind of balance you need. It is appropriate to profile the others on the team to make sure you have a good balance.

There are some *key questions* to ask yourself regarding this category when profiling a position. To what degree will this person need to take the initiative? How much of the job consists of responding, analyzing, or depending on the actions of others? You might want to estimate the percentage of overall time in Proactive or Reactive activities.

Stepping on Toes: People Management

People who have a strong Proactive Pattern at work will be impatient with bureaucratic delays or internal politics, and may even go outside of their bounds, stepping on others' toes to get things done. They jump into activities and may go very far very fast, before you or they notice, when they are on the wrong track. As the manager of Proactive employees, you will need to channel their energy in appropriate directions. If they don't have opportunities to use their high level of energy, they will become frustrated or bored, and as a result may use their initiative in unproductive ways. You can motivate them by giving them a job to do and telling them to "Go for it." You may need to remind them to think before they jump. On the other hand, through my own experience, I discovered how to drive Proactive people crazy. Put them in a situation that they dislike intensely, then make sure that they can do nothing about it.

People with a Reactive Pattern at work will generally not take the initiative and will feel stressed or anxious when asked to do so. At the extreme, they will want to consider, analyze, and *be given* an understanding of situations almost to the exclusion of deciding or doing anything. In a team setting, Reactive people can contribute to the process by analyzing proposed solutions and slowing the process enough to consider ramifications and alternatives. You can motivate Reactive people by matching their Pattern. "Now that you have had enough time to consider and think about this, I'll need it on my desk by Monday at noon."

Fate and Destiny

When in a Reactive Pattern, people do not believe that they control their world. Chances are that they will be waiting for someone else to solve problems or make improvements for them. Do you remember Vladimir and Estragon in Samuel Beckett's *Waiting for Godot*? They spent the entire play waiting for the mythical Godot to appear and solve all their problems.

Since most people at work are somewhere in the middle, they will need to think and do, respond and initiate. The best kinds of work for these people are tasks and responsibilities that allow enough of each. To motivate these people, you would use both sets of Influencing Language. For example, "I would like you to think through what needs to be done and just go do it."

I have a friend who likes to go away for the weekend at the last minute. Guess what Pattern she has! She used to phone her brother up on a Thursday night and say "Hey I found a great deal to go to Majorca very cheap this weekend. Wanna go? Wanna go?" He usually refused and became annoyed. When she guessed he was more Reactive, she changed her approach: "I found some info about a cheap weekend getaway in Majorca and I was wondering if we might like to do it. I am sending you the information so you can think it over and let me know." He called back in an hour and said "Yes."

Sales and Marketing

Proactive purchasers want to buy right away. One day over coffee, I suggested doing a LAB Profile® to help a prospective client decide on a career change. I told her that the profile would show her immediately what kinds of activities would trigger and maintain her motivation. She enthusiastically agreed and wanted to do it right then. As we were walking back to my office she said: "Can we run?" She has an off-the-scale Proactive Pattern in that Context.

Reactive buyers on the other hand, need more time and may be more likely to buy when the product or service allows them to gain understanding. They will often be waiting for something to happen before making a decision. I went to see the CEO of a company that sells mutual funds, to talk about sales training for his sales representatives. At our *third* meeting, he told me that the company was completing a merger and he was "waiting for the situation to be clarified." As I was in a highly Proactive mode, the voice in my head exploded and said, "What do you want, a message from God? *Who* is going to clarify the situation, if not you?" I managed to control the impulse and asked: "Oh, and when is this likely to happen?" I used that phrase to match his belief that things happen *to* him. Reactive people will be more likely to buy if you suggest that this is what they have been waiting for, or "Haven't you waited long enough to get what you really want?" or "Once you have this, you'll understand why ..."

You will occasionally notice marketing campaigns that call to Proactive or Reactive people. These ads inadvertently may also be revealing aspects of the company's corporate culture. A large Canadian bank had a slogan: "Get us working for you." My interpretation was that I, as a potential customer, was going to have to wake them up and make them do something for me. But perhaps that way of looking at it is a result of my propensity for being Proactive. You may have noticed NIKE's slogan: *"Just do it.",* which is a call to action for Proactive folks.

When you are getting to know your prospective clients, who is the most ideal to get the most from what you are selling? People who jump and make decisions quickly or those who have thought it through? As we created the Advanced Business Influence program (see Resources), we realized that the ideal clients are those who get information and use it right away and make decisions quickly. Those who need to think things about for a longer time, tend not to be the ones who are likely to try out the communication and influencing strategies in the program and therefore won't get as much benefit.

However, if the product or service were investment opportunities, the ideal clients might need to thoroughly understand before buying. This would avoid buyer's remorse and unhappy customers because the Reactive clients are more likely to allow a financial advisor to take the initiative. More Proactive clients can become difficult to work with because as soon as they read, see or hear about something that interests them, or a problem, they want to jump on it right away, which may not be good for them in the long term.

Relationships and Communication

Communication between people who are Proactive and Reactive can be very problematic. One wants to go now and the other may not be ready. One wants to think things out carefully and check out every detail, while the other can't abide reading the user agreement. Ok, I don't know that many people who *want* to read a user agreement, but some folks need a thorough understanding before acting or deciding.

I remember when I had decided to have my kitchen remodeled. My husband and youngest son were to empty the cupboards, put everything into boxes and move it all to the garage. Shortly after the task had begun my husband came to me: "I can't work this way!" My son had been flinging as much into a box as he could and taking the box out and sticking it in the garage. My husband wanted to work out a plan whereby everything would end up in the right place, easy to locate, easy to unpack. This is the quintessential Proactive/Reactive conflict. Do it now vs. think about how to do it.

This is where I also have disagreements with my hubby. I often just want to get things done, or get out the door, while he needs time. The solution? We agree on a time to go out the door, and I find lots of things to get done, so I don't have the feeling that I'm spending my time just waiting.

Summary

Level

Question: There is no question for this category.

Proactive: Acts with little or no consideration. Motivated by doing.

Reactive: Motivated to wait, analyze, consider and react.

Distribution at Work:

15-20% Mainly Proactive

60-65% Equally Proactive and Reactive

15-20% Mainly Reactive
(in the work Context, from Rodger Bailey)

Influencing Language:

Proactive: do it; jump in; get it done; don't wait; just do it; now

Reactive: understand; think about; wait; analyze; consider; might; could; would

---

[1] A Yiddish word, meaning having a lot of nerve

Chapter 4
Criteria: Hot Buttons

What are the words and phrases that incite a physical and emotional response?

I asked Simone: "What do you want from your job?" She replied: "*A challenge*, something that allows me to *utilize my present skills* and *develop new ones, good remuneration* and *working with people*." Those are the things that are important to Simone in her work. But what does this mean? Simone has given me her Criteria for work.

Criteria is the term we use to describe a person's way of making distinctions about what is good, bad, awful, wrong, right, and so on. They are personal labels we give to our values; those things we value.

A person's Criteria are those words that *incite a physical and emotional reaction*: **HOT BUTTONS**. The words themselves are associated (or stuck in our memory) to a series of emotionally similar events that we have experienced through our lives. So, when a person hears one of their Criteria, *the word itself* will trigger the emotional response attached to it.

We each have our own definition for each Criterion. A single Criterion is composed of many elements, conscious and unconscious. You may never need to know a person's definition of their Criteria in those situations where you simply want to find out *what words* they use, to describe something they are excited about in a given Context.

In any family, each of you knows the others' negative hot buttons. The other members of your family know that if they say a particular word or phrase, you will react in a certain way.

Many people took interpersonal communication courses where they learned Active listening techniques, based on Carl Rogers' work. Active listening consists of paraphrasing what the other person said, *in your own words*, in order to show them what you understood. We can now appreciate that if Simone says that she wants "a challenge" and

I play back to her, "so you want something challenging," it does not *create* exactly the same experience for her. When I paraphrase into my own words, it has more to do with my reality than your reality, (and nothing whatever to do with Reality with a capital R). To solve this problem, and, to show someone you have understood them, play back *their* key words, their Criteria.

Other questions to elicit Criteria:

- What do you want in . . . (a job, a home, a spouse, etc.)?
- What's important to you?
- What counts?
- What *has* to be there?
- What would you like to have, be or do?
- What would have to happen in this project to meet all your needs?

Making Decisions, Hierarchy of Criteria

Knowing how to uncover and work with Criteria can give you a means of deciding what is more important and what is less important in a given Context. You can do this for yourself or with other people. I'll demonstrate with Simone. This technique is called making a **Hierarchy of Criteria.**

SRC:	Simone, you had a number of things that were important for you at work. Let's list them.
Simone:	A challenge, something that allows me to utilize my present skills and develop new ones, good remuneration, and working with people.

We have four Criteria here and we do not yet know which are essential, optional, or the most important for Simone. I, as the listener, may think one is more important than another for her, but that would be hallucinating.

SRC:	Simone, imagine for a moment that I have a couple of jobs that might fit your needs. In this hand over here (holding out my left hand, palm up), you will get a job with a *challenge*. And in this hand, (holding out my right hand, palm up, hands wide apart), this job allows you to *utilize your present skills and develop new ones*. Which one attracts you?
Simone:	A challenge.

If you observe carefully (which is *a challenge* to illustrate in a book) you can often see the choice being made before the person says anything. It is important to keep your hands wide apart so the person will perceive two *separate* choices. I do not know exactly how Simone is processing this choice, but by putting each option in a different hand, I am creating something more real or tangible for her.

How would I write down her choice if I were taking notes? An easy and quick way is to draw an arrow from *challenge* down to *allows me ...* to indicate that "challenge" was chosen over "allows me."

SRC:	In my right hand is a job that will offer you *a challenge*. In my left is one that has *good remuneration*. If you **had** to choose, which one would you want?
Simone:	Hmmm. A challenge.
SRC:	So, challenge is the most important so far. OK, in my left hand is a job with a *challenge* and in my right hand is a job where you'll be *working with people*. Which one would you prefer? (I keep switching the hand I put *challenge* in so as not create an association with one hand.)
Simone:	Still a challenge.

We now know that *a challenge* is the most important of these Criteria for Simone, in the Context of work. To complete the Hierarchy, we will need to compare all of the other options to each other as we just did.

SRC:	Simone, in my left hand is a job that allows you to *utilize your present skills and develop new ones*, and in my right hand is one with *good remuneration*. Which one would you like to take?
Simone:	Good remuneration.
SRC:	And in my left hand we have one with *good remuneration* and, in my right hand, one where you can be *working with people*?
Simone:	Good remuneration.
SRC:	And lastly, *working with people* in my left hand, and *allows you to utilize your present skills and develop new ones* in my right hand?
Simone:	Working with people.

Now we have Simone's Criteria in order of importance to her:

1. A challenge
2. Good remuneration
3. Working with people
4. Allows me to utilize my present skills and develop new ones

If you help people make decisions (e.g. in sales), this is a very useful process to take your customers through. It can also be used when coaching employees or clients. I use it for career coaching, where I would also need to get the client to define what would constitute each Criterion.

The easiest way to get someone to define their Criteria is to ask: "What is an example of something that was *a challenge*?" This works well because often people cannot give a straight definition of terms for something that is directly attached to a series of memories and emotions.

The Hierarchy of Criteria is also used to make some decision-making processes much shorter. This is a way of helping people get their mind, soul, and body to decide. When you create a tangible, forced-choice situation, people will feel magnetically attracted to one option or the other.

Can't Make Up Your Mind?

Sometimes a person has difficulty choosing between the two alternatives in your hands; you can confirm this by observing the vacillation in their body as they try to choose. What does this mean, and what do you do about it? I have identified five situations where this occurs:

1. The person did not accept the idea that they *have* to choose between two things they want.
2. One Criterion is a component of the other one.
3. The person has two labels for the same set of experiences.
4. One Criterion causes the other to occur (a cause-effect relationship for the person).
5. The person has a conflict between two values or Criteria.

In the first case, if the person cannot or will not choose, ask their permission to go through this activity. You can ask them to imagine that *if they **had** to choose* (knowing that in real life, they could actually have both), which one would attract them?

In working with the LAB Profile® in different countries and cultures, I have noticed some cultural differences that may make it hard for some people to play along and choose which Criterion attracts them. In a culture where there is a belief that you *can* have anything you truly want (i.e., the United States), there is no problem in choosing.

Many cultures, however, do not maintain this belief. In fact, many people do not believe that life is about getting what you want. Life is about doing what you are *supposed* to do. The reason they cannot choose between Criteria is they believe that what they may want is irrelevant to what they are supposed to do. The weight of outside considerations is greater than their desires. When this is an issue in a group, we discuss what makes for good decisions. If a person can be unburdened from their cares and obligations and, *just for a moment*, consider what appeals to them, they get the chance to sort out what is important to them. Then they can consider and negotiate with their external commitments.

Sometimes they cannot choose because one Criterion is a component of the other. In other words, one Criterion is *contained within* another Criterion. You can test for this by asking "Is *allows you to utilize your present skills and develop new ones,* part of a *challenge* for you? Or the other way around?" In that case you can include the component within the larger Criterion and only use the larger one. "So, when we're talking about *a challenge*, we know it includes *allows you to utilize your present skills and develop new ones.*"

Another possibility is that the person has two labels for the same set of experiences. If it means the same thing, he would have difficulty choosing between "it" and "itself." For example, let's say a person cannot choose between *interesting* and *a challenge*. To test for this, you can simply ask: "Are *interesting* and *a challenge* really the same thing for you?" If the person says: "Yes, it is always interesting when there's a challenge," you know that they are closely linked (in his mind anyway). In this case, you might want to use both labels to maintain a rapport with that person.

The fourth situation is when the person has the belief that one Criterion *causes* the other to occur in what is called a cause-effect relationship. You can check for this by asking: "For you, does having *a challenge* make you *utilize your present skills and develop new ones*?"

The fifth possibility for an unclear choice between two options presented in this manner is that the person has a conflict between two values or Criteria. They will waver back and forth and may say "yes, but" to themselves or out loud. You can predict, in this case, that the person will have difficulty making certain decisions in this Context and will feel in a "stuck" state. Remember Tevye in *Fiddler on the Roof*, "On one hand . . . on the other hand . . . ?"

Difficult to Satisfy?

What does it mean when you ask someone "What do you want?" or "What's important?" and the person lists fifteen or twenty things? This person may be difficult to satisfy. If she has fifteen or twenty Criteria and has no idea which ones are more important than the others, she may have a hard time making decisions or even being able to find all the things she wants. Can you imagine a woman finding the man of her dreams with fifteen Criteria?

What is a decision? Often making a decision, consists of choosing between two or more alternatives. One of the biggest favors you can do for a person who has many undifferentiated Criteria is to take them through a Hierarchy of Criteria, and then have them create a bottom-line cutoff point on what absolutely must be there and what is optional.

Uses for Criteria

If you are considering buying a product, for example, what *must* it have? If you are considering getting married, what are the most important things for you in the person and the relationship? Remember that, when you change Context, your Criteria may change. Most people do not want the same thing in a house that they want in a spouse.

In the process of goal-setting, you need to list the Criteria for success, and understand which are more important. We know that those people who have clearly defined Criteria for their goals are more likely to achieve them quickly. By defining your Criteria, you will have made them real and tangible to yourself.

One of the gentlemen I trained in this technique is a Real Estate Broker. When he hires people, he uses the Hierarchy of Criteria to find out whether the candidates have the priorities about work that he would like them to have. He asks them "What is important for you in your work?" He then casually asks: "If you **had** to choose between a job where you got to be a *team player* (putting out his left hand) and one where you could be *your own boss* (putting out his other hand), which one would you pick?"

If you are going to start a project with someone or select members of a team or task force, you might want to check out what is important to each prospective member. Do they have the values you are looking for? You can ask them these questions: What do you want from this project? What do you want in a company? What do you want in a team? What's more important to you? This (holding out one hand) or this? You will find that it is very easy to build this into ordinary conversation.

I was a member of the advisory board of the local YMCA. Our highest-ranking female staff member, quit the Association because she had been told that there was no possibility of a full-time executive director position at one of the local branches. As a result of her leaving, there was a reshuffle and suddenly a full-time executive director position was established. As a board member I hit the roof because of the unfairness of this situation.

The next thing I knew, I was in charge of a Committee that was to examine whether our Association had systemic barriers which prevented some employees from having the same opportunities as others. We were to make recommendations on how we could become a better employer.

We set some goals, defined the methodology, and then had to give the Committee a name. Some members suggested "The Employment Equity Committee," named after recently adopted legislation. I mentioned that many people (especially white males) had felt very threatened by this legislation and that, should we identify ourselves with it, we would get very little cooperation from the staff of the Y.

We named ourselves "The Fairness in Employment Committee" and got an 85 percent response rate when we distributed employee questionnaires. My point to the Committee was that we needed to call ourselves something with positive connotations for all staff, and make sure that we avoided any negative hot buttons.

The Brain and Strongly-Held Criteria, Values and Beliefs

Researchers conducted experiments involving strongly-held political beliefs to see what happens in the brain when evidence is presented that counters those beliefs[1]. When confronted with evidence that was counter to their beliefs, there was increased activity in the dorsomedial prefrontal cortex and amygdala. These are areas of the brain that correspond to self-identity and negative emotions; where we think about our identities and feel threatened. When I am teaching groups about Criteria, we often do an informal experiment where their Criteria are verbally taken Away From them and then given back. They are often surprised at the depth of physical and emotional discomfort and then relief that this causes. Related brain research is increasingly showing that the brain also negatively reacts to being confronted with information that runs counter to beliefs and values.

Influencing with Criteria

In the light of this research, how can anyone change anyone else's mind about anything? Confronting a person is probably counter-productive. As in the Influencing and Persuasion Principle, mentioned in the beginning, it is important to first go to the person's bus stop and acknowledge them and/or their Criteria without any caveats.

I was having a conversation with a client who was very frustrated that his online marketing efforts in North America weren't "getting the traction" he expected as compared with the results he typically got in the Eastern European market. I wanted to get him to try a new strategy from a well-known internet marketing expert, so I wrote him an email prior to our next meeting. I pre-framed my suggestion by saying that since he was concerned about not "getting the traction" he expected, perhaps we could discuss doing an A/B test (a comparison of the results of 2 marketing approaches) with the strategy I outlined for him, to which he responded with great enthusiasm.

When I wrote a blog post about the below-conscious gender-based metaphors in the controversy surrounding Judge Brett Kavanaugh's nomination to the American Supreme Court in 2018, and the sexual assault testimony of Dr. Christine Blasey Ford, I received many comments on my approach[2]. One person, who I am very fond of, but with whom I don't share most political opinions, objected to my blog. He wrote saying: "You might consider adding some of this information in your evaluation", and his email included an extensive number of clips from right-wing sources about the Democratic Party's war on Kavanaugh.

I responded by first acknowledging him as a person, how happy I was to hear from him after a long time with no contact, and a question about how he was doing. I followed this up with three of the most powerful words in human communication: "You are right" connected to a relevant statement we could both probably agree to. Then I simply explained what I was attempting to do in my blog and a warm salutation.

Here is my reply to him and his surprising response:

Hi xxx,

Nice to hear from you! How are you doing? I'm curious about all your projects that we discussed so long ago.

You are right - there are many more aspects to what is going on, and in this highly-politicized environment, everyone's motives are based on self-interest. I just wanted to share Suzette Haden Elgin's analysis based on metaphors.

Big hugs!

Shelle

Hi Shelle,

The last two years have been a whirlwind. (personal health update and progress on major professional projects.)

The family is doing well, and the grand-daughters soccer games are

great. Thanks for sending the analysis and I pray both sides can get back to working for a consensus to help everyone instead of trying to tear us apart. They seem to raise a lot of

money with that approach, so it may not change. The idea that there is only one view will never work out. I trust your long-distance marriage is still as great as you are.
Be safe
xxx

My approach was first to connect with him as person, avoid directly confronting his point of view, look for areas of agreement (Criteria), and explain myself without attempting to convert him to my viewpoint. I was delighted that he also zoomed out to look at the big picture with a wish for more consensus in the future. This dialogue is in stark contrast to typical conflicts of values on social media, where people end up calling each other Nazis, as in Godwin's Law[3], after descending into rounds of personal insults.

Sales and Marketing

The gathering of someone's Criteria is a necessary prerequisite for sales and any kind of influencing or persuading process. Unskilled sales people just *pitch their product* (usually using their own Criteria) without much regard to what their prospective customer actually wants. "Lady, this car has everything you want: good mileage, great handling, and flashy decals on the side!" This is what I call the "shot in the dark" approach. Who knows? They might actually hit something.

Many market researchers investigate people's Criteria so that the exact phrasing of an advertising campaign can match what is most important to the groups they wish to influence. If you want to get and keep someone's interest, you will need to link what you are proposing with their Criteria.

Before starting a presentation, I will often look for the chance to ask audience members "What's important to you about this topic?" or "If you knew how to understand, predict, and influence behavior, what would you want to use this ability for?" If someone tells me they want to "know how to present their proposals in a negotiation so that they will be accepted," then I make sure to link those Criteria with the points I am making.

Many people underestimate the power of matching someone's Criteria. Once, as a demonstration with a group, I told a woman about a job opportunity, using all her highly held Criteria. I did not tell her what the job *was*; I simply used her Criteria: "You'll really be needed, people will appreciate what you do for them, you'll be in charge of how you work, and the hours are regular." She said she would take the job, without even finding out what it was.

I know someone who moved from New England to California for a career opportunity that *matched* his Criteria, only to find that the work and the company did not at all meet his expectations. You will need to be careful to deliver what you promise when you use someone's Criteria to persuade them. Otherwise their disappointment and anger will most likely be directed at you. Criteria are verbal Triggers that bring up emotions, both positive and negative. When he was in Grade One, my son was having difficulties learning to read. We practiced at home and the teachers signed him up for the "Reading Club." Parent volunteers take members of the Reading Club out of class to help them with their reading skills. By the end of Grade One, my son had made some progress. He summed up his experience to me: "Only the stupid kids have to go to the reading club."

I met with the teachers at the beginning of Grade Two because they wanted him to join the club again. I explained to them what the *meaning* of the reading club was to my son and said that I didn't want him to join. After much discussion, they agreed, and I agreed to continue working with him. Two weeks later he said to me: "They didn't put me in the reading club this year. That's because I'm good at reading. And I'm not stupid." His reading skills picked up exceedingly quickly over the next few weeks.

Remember, in order to influence with Criteria, state them *exactly* as the other person expressed them. This is particularly important when working with potential customers and coaching clients. If you paraphrase in these situations, you will probably notice a reduction in the level of rapport and the feeling of connection. Conversely, when you use the other person's Criteria, they immediately confirm by nodding their head.

Summary

Criteria A person's labels for things are important to them in a given Context. They are *hot buttons* because they are attached to emotions and memories.

Question: *What do you want in a ...?*

What is important to you?.

Influencing Language:

Use the person's Criteria to attract and maintain interest. When a person hears their own Criteria, they will immediately feel the emotions attached to those words.

[1] Kaplan, Jonas T., Sarah I. Gimbel, and Sam Harris, Neural correlates of maintaining one's political beliefs in the face of counterevidence, *Scientific Reports* volume 6, Article number: 39589 (2016), bit.ly/ScientificReportsV6

[2] bit.ly/JudgeKavanaughandDrBlaseyFord

[3] "Godwin's Law asserts that as an online discussion grows longer, the probability of a comparison involving Nazis or Hitler approaches 1. That is, if an online discussion (regardless of topic or scope) goes on long enough, sooner or later someone will call the other person Adolf Hitler or a Nazi, the point at which effectively the discussion or thread often ends." adapted from: bit.ly/GodwinsLawWikipedia

Chapter 5
Direction: The Carrot or the Stick?

What will trigger a person into action? In what direction do they move? Do they move toward an objective, or Away From problems to be solved or prevented?

When you master this category, you will be able to prevent and avoid many problems and know how to reach your goals more effectively.

There are two Triggers in this category describing the *Direction* a person is moving in for a given Context. They are either moving **toward** a goal, or **away from** problems.

Toward

People with a Toward pattern in a given Context are focused on their goal. They think in terms of what they want, goals to be achieved. They are motivated to have, get, achieve, attain, and so on. Because of their concentration on the end goals to be accomplished, they tend to be good at managing priorities. Moreover, they are excited and energized by achieving their outcomes and getting what they want.

They may have trouble either noticing what should be avoided, or identifying problems. At the extreme, they can be perceived as naive by others because they do not take potential obstacles into account.

Away From

People who have an Away From pattern notice what should be avoided and gotten rid of, and otherwise not happen. Their motivation is triggered when there is a problem to be solved or when there is something to move away from. They can become energized by threats. A salesperson once told me: "If I don't get out there and sell, I won't be able to pay my bills at the end of the month." Deadlines, for example, get these people into action. People with an Away From pattern in a given Context are good at troubleshooting, solving problems, and pinpointing possible obstacles during planning, because they automatically pick up on what is or could be going wrong.

They may have trouble maintaining focus on their goals because they are easily distracted by and compelled to respond to negative situations. This is the kind of person who will drop everything to fix something. At the extreme they forget what the priorities are and only concentrate on dealing with crises. If this person is at the top of a department or an organization, the *entire organization may be run by crisis management.* They can have some difficulty managing priorities because whatever is wrong is likely to attract most of their attention. People who have a strong Away From orientation in a given Context can be perceived as jaded or cynical, particularly by Toward people.

Distribution %
(in the work Context, from Rodger Bailey)

Mainly Toward	40%
Equally Toward & Away From	20%
Mainly Away From	40%

Most people will have a mainly Toward or mainly Away From pattern on this continuum, in a given Context.

Identification

Question:
WHY IS HAVING THAT (THEIR CRITERIA) **IMPORTANT?**
(ask up to 3 times)

Toward: sentence structure

- talks about what they gain, achieve, get, have etc.

- inclusion
- what they want, goals

Toward: body language

- pointing toward something, head nodding, gestures of inclusion

Away From: sentence structure

- will mention situations to be avoided, gotten rid of
- exclusion of unwanted situations, things
- problems

Away From: body language

- gestures of exclusion, shaking head, arms indicating that something is to be avoided, gotten rid of

Note: Listen to what a person says after the word **because**. It will either be a Toward or an Away From statement.

Examples

Toward:	*I would get personal satisfaction and a promotion."*
Mainly Toward:	*I would get a promotion, personal satisfaction, make more money and not have to go on the road*
Equally Toward and Away From:	*"I would get personal satisfaction and not have to go on the road."*
Mainly Away From:	*"I would not have all this routine work, or be away from my family often, plus, I would get a promotion."*

Away From: *"I would get away from this boring work, all the deadlines, and my boss who keeps looking over my shoulder."*

Suggestion: Ask the questions in a series or laddering approach, as follows:

SRC: Adam, what do you want in your work? (Criteria)

Adam: **I want to be** effective, more proficient, fun and taken seriously.

SRC: All right, Adam, *why is having that important*?

Adam: To help people.

SRC: To help people. And why is that important?

Adam: Because I get satisfaction from helping people.

SRC: So why is *that* important?

Adam: Well, *that's what I want* from a job.

Here's a different example:

SRC: Joanne, what do you want in a job?

Joanne: I like to know what I have to do, and to be evaluated based on my own performance.

SRC: Why is that important?

Joanne: It gives me a sense of calm.

SRC: And why is *that* important?

Joanne: If I'm not calm with myself, I can't be calm with my kids.

SRC: And why is that important?

Joanne: *It keeps me from hitting my kids.*

Joanne wanted to have her Criteria met in order to prevent a certain outcome, while Adam was motivated to attain his Criteria in order to achieve an outcome.

The reason we ask the Motivation Direction questions several times is to get a more accurate sense of where the person puts their energy: *toward goals* or *away from* problems. In my experience, when we ask the question only once, we often get a one-line Toward answer, regardless of the person's actual pattern. I believe that is because many of us have subscribed to the "Power of Positive Thinking," and so devalue the importance of recognizing problems.

Ask the following questions about three times to find out what is triggering the person into action in that Context:

Alternate Questions:

- What's the point?
- Why bother?
- What's important about X?
- What's in that for you?

Changes in Context

So, why *did* you leave your last job? Because you couldn't stand it anymore? Or because there was something better on the burner? Why did you leave your last spouse? Because you were unhappy, or because there was someone else on the horizon? Why did you take your last vacation? Was it because you wanted a break from the grind or because you were interested in doing something in particular? You may have a Toward pattern in one Context and an Away From pattern in another Context.

Can your Direction change over time? Yes, it can. Your response to a single significant event may change your pattern. Let's say someone has a Toward pattern in a Context and has all kinds of habits that probably are not good for his health. Then he has a heart attack and what happens? Because the heart attack was a very nasty yet compelling experience, he may change Direction and begin moving *away from* health problems. He might change his behavior, quitting smoking, doing more exercise, changing his diet, and so on, because he *does not want* to have another heart attack. Some addiction treatment programs work on that basis.

Not motivated yet to change something? Sometimes people do not make changes in their lives because they have not yet hit rock bottom. A helpful question to ask might be: "Do you *feel bad enough now* to make some changes or would you rather wait until you feel *even worse*?"

Influencing Language

Using the Influencing Language appropriately will get you a person's complete attention. That will prevent you from having to repeat things several times. The rapport that you establish will be deeper because you have matched how the person thinks; you will not have to spend a lot of time to get on the same wavelength. Because you have established rapport, you can avoid a lot of misunderstandings.

Here are some typical expressions to use:

Toward

- attain; obtain; have; get; include; achieve; enable you to; benefits; advantages; here's what you would accomplish

Away From

- won't have to; solve; prevent; avoid; fix; prevent; not have to deal with; get rid of; it's not perfect; let's find out what's wrong; there'll be no problems

What Would Make You Set and Attain Goals?

For many decades people have been teaching and learning about the importance of setting goals. It has been proven many times that if you do not have goals, chances are you will not be able to find what you truly want. Was that last sentence a Toward statement or an Away From statement? It was Away From. The idea is that you don't get anywhere if you don't have goals.

When discussing a person's Motivation Direction, we are talking about what will **trigger** them into doing something, such as setting goals. Why do I personally set goals in my business? Because if I didn't, I would be totally disorganized. I do set goals, and I have an Away From Pattern at work. For me, this means that I can get distracted by whatever squeaks the loudest. In order to stay focused on what I need to achieve (and particularly so as *not* to become disorganized), I often ask myself: "What business am I in?" This helps me re-center on what I really need to be doing. Another useful question for Away From people to ask themselves is: "How does this activity fit in with what I want to accomplish?"

People with a Toward preference need to ask themselves: Are my plans going to work? What else do I need to predict? What haven't I thought of yet that may go wrong? They may need the services of a devil's advocate in order to make sure they are being realistic.

A good equilibrium between Toward and Away From on a team will help ensure that goals are set, well-laid contingency plans are made, and focus is kept on priorities.

Is It Fear of Success or Motivation Direction?

The Away From Pattern can impact goal achievement. John Overdurf, an excellent NLP trainer and coach I know, had a client who came to see him and said: "I'm very upset. My life is really going down the tubes. I've been a millionaire four times." At first glance you might say, "You've been a millionaire four times. So, what's the problem?" Let's think about it. If he has been a millionaire four times, that means he lost his money at least three times. So, let's look at what happened.

John asked him some questions and found out that he had an extreme Away From Pattern about work. He was motivated *to move away from poverty*. Let's put this on a graph to understand his pattern. On the vertical axis, we have his amount of motivation, or how motivated he is, from "not very motivated" at the bottom to "very motivated" at the top. Let's put revenue on the horizontal axis, zero revenue to one million dollars. If he is highly motivated away from poverty, at zero revenue, how motivated is he? Very motivated. As he earns money, what happens? His interest level declines as his revenue increases. Once poverty was not an issue, he would not finish work on contracts, or would forget to submit quotes to potential clients or procrastinate and not follow up. When the big contract would come that could push him over the million-dollar point, he would think, "Ahh, I'll do it when I get around to it," whereas when he threatened by poverty (whatever that means to him) he is highly motivated to do whatever it takes to generate revenue.

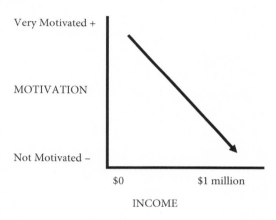

Although this is an extreme example, it explains why highly Away From people need to re-center at regular intervals on what they are trying to achieve.

If a person answers "freedom" in response to *Why is that important?* do not assume that it is either Toward or Away From. Probe further to find out if it is freedom *to* or freedom *from*.

Motivating Yourself

Sometimes people eagerly start on their goals and achieve them. Sometimes they start but don't complete them (think of New Year's Resolutions, January gym memberships, etc. And sometimes people just don't start, even when they say it's important to them. To increase your personal effectiveness, notice what happens when you are achieving your goals and when you are not.

For instance, do you have a hard time getting started on a long-term goal? Then you probably need to have something undesirable happening to kick-start you into action (Away From Motivation). This happens for me when I notice that my **jeans have shrunk.** This undesirable situation motivates me to get back into my personal fitness and eating programs. While this is a great way to get started, it won't enable me to maintain my motivation over the long term, as in the example where John's client wanted to 'move away from poverty'.

If you want to maintain your motivation over the long term, visualize what you want in front of yourself, i.e. I see a video of me fitting into my favorite skinny jeans, and feel the attraction of that image, drawing you towards it. This is how you can use both Away From and Toward Motivation, to help you get and stay motivated for achieving your long-term goals.

If you eagerly start on goals and projects, looking forward to achieving them (Toward Motivation) but tend to lose interest after a while, add in some Away From. What are the negative consequences if you don't finish? This is how deadlines can help. If there is a negative consequence for not meeting a deadline, this can help motivate you to stay on track.

I used this process when organizing the founding of an association. The volunteer board had to meet the deadline of the upcoming conference to get all the work of setting up the association BEFORE people showed up to the conference and the annual general meeting. That deadline kept us on track.

For more information on how to understand your own success strategies, check out my e-book and audio program, *Wishing, Wanting and Achieving*[1].

Positive or Negative Thinking?

When first acquainted with these tendencies, many categorize those with a Toward pattern as positive, while the Away From Pattern is seen as negative. This judgment comes from a certain interpretation of the words "positive thinking." Remember that **these patterns are simply triggers that will catapult someone into action.**

Mother Teresa was quoted as saying that she started her work when "I discovered there was a Hitler in my heart." Her Motivation Direction was Away From. Many lobby groups, are essentially motivated to move away from certain practices with which they do not agree. These groups, along with opposition parties (isn't the word "Opposition" by nature Away From?) tend to notice what is insufficient or wrong with government legislation to protect the environment, victim protection laws, nuclear safety regulations, welfare reform, and so on. Many journalists also have this Trigger.

In 2018, during the Brexit crisis in the UK, members of Prime Minister Theresa May's Conservative Party cabinet defected, lobbing criticisms at her and pointing out the problems with the current deal she had negotiated with the European Union, without proposing alternatives[2] . They were 'moving away from' what they did not want.

Conflicts of Language in Labor Relations

In the Context of labor relations and negotiations, conflict arises not only because of the often-contrary vested interests of labor and management. Conflict also arises because of the cultural differences between the two groups. If I can make a generalization, top management is often mainly Toward. Goals, business plans, objectives, and so on, are Toward activities. What is the primary reason for the existence of a union? To make another generalization, unions often exist to protect their members from disasters: poor pay, bad working conditions, layoffs, and the like.

Frequently, management and labor do not speak the same language. Management tends to negotiate in terms of moving toward its objectives, while labor attempts to prevent certain things from occurring.

In many labor-management conflicts there are clear examples of these patterns at work. The principal issue might be over employment security, retirement benefits, and other items that unions are determined to *prevent* the management from changing, particularly in the face of possible privatization, layoffs, or even factory closings. Management tends to be equally determined to modify contracts in order to *increase* competitiveness. In this example, each side is moving in a different Direction and, as is the case in labor disputes that escalate, each are operating out of different Criteria.

If labor and management can each learn to understand the Triggers and Criteria of the other side, and learn how to speak in their language, they could improve their chances of reaching agreement with less strife. Of course, in Reality, not all unions have an Away From motivation, nor do all employers have a Toward Trigger.

Innovation and Funding Start-Ups: Who Gets the Cash?

In a Scientific American article on raising venture capital, it was shown that above and beyond evaluating the business or idea, funders will "overwhelmingly finance entrepreneurs for whom they hold positive sentiments, regardless of their assessments of the business."[3] But how do investors determine their judgment of entrepreneurs? The authors' research showed that investors (both men and women) tended to ask questions of male entrepreneurs about how they "will win" and to ask female entrepreneurs questions about how they "will avoid losing". This means male entrepreneurs are asked Toward-oriented questions that highlight opportunities and promotion strategies while female entrepreneurs have to answer Away From-oriented questions that focused on potential limitations and problems. The authors concluded: "Men are more likely to be seen as the glamorous entrepreneurs who found companies that will become the likes of the Amazon, Google, or Uber. Women, on the other hand, are imagined as the heads of companies which manage only to keep their doors open: small businesses and lifestyle companies whose names are not recognizable."

The funding results indicate the Toward/Away From preferences of investors: They tend to be in Toward Mode with male entrepreneurs and Away From mode with female entrepreneurs. While female entrepreneurs own 38% of all businesses in the United States, they receive only 2% of all venture capital.

What to do? The authors noted that if entrepreneurs answered the Away From questions, they received much lower funding on average but if they shifted the focus to "Promotion" strategies and used goal-oriented (Toward) language, the results were very different.

A great hint for all entrepreneurs looking for funding: if asked a problem-focused question by investors, start briefly with how to avoid the problem and then quickly shift to how you will achieve your goals.

Political Divisions – a Matter of Toward and Away From?

While avoiding danger (Away From) is deeply imbedded in human DNA, research[4] over more than a decade, has shown that people with conservative views are much more sensitive to fear and physical threats, (starting in early childhood), than people who hold liberal views. Liberals become more conservative in their views when they have actually experienced threats of physical harm. An experiment was conducted that made conservatives feel safe and then their views became indistinguishable from liberals in the study group. Interesting, eh?

Professions Have Patterns

Some professions are inherently Toward or Away From. For example, medicine, as it is usually practiced in the West, is highly Away From. As a culture (as distinct from individual patterns) medical practitioners tend to focus on what is wrong with their patients. They move *away from sickness and dying.* I profiled all the pharmacists in a hospital and found that, out of seventeen pharmacists, fourteen had a mainly or highly Away From pattern at work. The other three were only slightly on the Toward side of the equation. As a culture, the medical professions are so Away From, that when the idea occurred to them that holistic health might be something worth considering, they called it *Preventive Medicine.*

The Away From orientation is appropriate for treating and curing (getting rid of) disease. Can you imagine rushing into your doctor about a medical emergency, and when you see her, she ignores your symptoms only to ask you about your health goals?

As you read about the different Patterns, you may find that you can deduce the cultural patterns of different professions.

Recruiting

If you are going to recruit someone, it would be useful to know whether the day-to-day activities of the job consist mainly of troubleshooting and problem-solving or rather concentrate on the attainment of objectives.

To assist a design and manufacturing firm in hiring a plant manager, I needed a list of responsibilities and tasks that this person would perform. The tasks included monitoring production reports and investigating causes of errors in production, shipping, and some data entry; ensuring that shipments are properly done; quality control; government compliance; negotiating with suppliers and facility maintenance. With the possible exception of negotiating with suppliers, most of the activities needed to meet these responsibilities required looking for, preventing, and solving problems. A Toward Plant Manager would have missed many of the potential errors and omissions while charging ahead to meet production targets. (I have noticed that many people who have an Away From Pattern call targets "deadlines.") I also profiled the senior management to ensure there would be a balance in the team, and someone would be looking out to make sure objectives were met.

If you want to hire someone motivated to perform the job at hand, determine whether the job is mainly goal-oriented or is mainly about troubleshooting. Do you need someone who is excited about working toward goals, or someone who delights in solving crises?

You can find out how to write career advertisements to only attract the "right" candidates in the Applications section of the book.

People Management and Task Assignment: The Carrot or the Stick

Since most managers already have a team of existing employees, they would be well-advised to discover what their strengths are, and to capitalize on those strengths instead of suffering from the weaknesses.

To get and keep Toward employees motivated, they need tasks that allow them to work toward something; to attain goals. You can tell them the benefits of doing a certain task, such as *improving* efficiency, *increasing* departmental revenue, or *receiving a bonus*. In meetings they will want to stay focused on the objective and will have little patience for discussions about what might go or is going wrong. They will consider such talk as off-topic. You will need to explain to them the benefits of discussing potential problems and make sure you do that in Toward terms: "If we discuss and plan for potential problems now we'll reach the objective that much sooner," is more appropriate than: "If we don't look at problems now, we'll be unprepared later."

If left to charge on to their goals, Toward employees (particularly when they also have a Proactive pattern), may get some nasty surprises later, due to inattention to potential hurdles or unforeseen negative consequences.

Away From employees will steer meetings into discussions of obstacles and what is wrong with proposals. To help them accept and support goal-setting in meetings, explain to them (in Away From terms) why keeping the goal in mind will *prevent the group from losing focus*, which could be a major *waste of resources* and allot them time for *disaster prevention*. For tasks, give them problems to solve and things to fix.

Impending disaster will energize them. "If this isn't out on time, they'll have our heads." The worst thing that you, as a manager, could do to an Away From employee is to take away all their problems. "Nothing's wrong, I'm worried." You, as a manager, also may not want to cope with the results of giving a Toward task to an Away From employee.

I also suggest that you do not ask a Toward employee to proofread a document. They are not likely to pick out the errors. If you notice mistakes in text as if they jumped out of the page, then you have an Away From pattern in the Context of reading. I gave the first draft of this book to a friend to read over, having forgotten about her Toward pattern. Apart from adding a couple of commas, she said, "It's just great," and went on to tell me all the things she liked about it.

The Cure to Writers' Block

When you write letters, reports, articles, or books, do you ever suffer from Writer's Block? If this happens regularly, then you may have an Away From Pattern in this Context. It is much easier, and more motivating, for Away From people to correct mistakes than it is for them to remain focused on the purpose of their text.

My philosophy is to work from my strengths, as opposed to suffering from my weaknesses. So, knowing about my Away From Pattern, I decided to write the first edition of this book by doing what I do best: fixing what's there. To do this, I had an audio program I had recorded on the same topic transcribed. I created a structure for the book and imported sections of the transcript. Lastly, I did the fun part. I corrected the text, turning spoken language into written text, looking for errors and omissions, needed updates, and new examples.

I told my sister-in-law, who is a writer, that I was able to produce about twenty-two pages per day. She found this to be incredible until I explained that: "I wasn't writing twenty-two pages, I was correcting twenty-two pages and adding in what was missing."

My advice to those of you who suffer from Writer's Block is to get *anything* down on paper (or up on the screen), even if you have to ask someone else to draft a letter, for example. Then fix it. It will be much less tedious, and you won't waste a lot of time wondering what to say.

A Very Toward dog!

Of course, this trick would not help you if you *really* had nothing to say.

Sales and Marketing

I asked the local Automobile Association: "Why do people buy your service?" They told me that 90 percent of their members join the club to avoid problems such as having their car break down and paying a fortune for a tow. In the Context of travel by car, the vast majority of their members therefore have an Away From pattern.

I worked with them on their member challenges. One issue was to get members to actually use the many travel services offered because they had found that those who had not used any services were less likely to renew. I explained what I meant by Toward and Away From and to give them a real sense of the difference, I took the management down to the front desk to eavesdrop on what members were saying. Person after person said that they *didn't want to have to deal with* breakdown problems, expensive alternatives, and so on. As a result, we redesigned their marketing, sales, and customer service processes to use mainly Away From language: "Your one-stop worry-free travel agency," "You won't have to deal with ...," "You needn't worry about ...," "No-fee travelers checks," "This will save you time," and the like. This helped them increase the percentage of members who renewed their membership, because more of them used more of the services.

Insurance is another Away From product. Most customers buy to avoid problems for themselves or their families. Investments, on the other hand, are inherently Toward. It is fascinating to observe the language used by insurance companies when offering investment opportunities. Often marketing campaigns reflect the culture of the company. I assisted the marketing department of a major pharmaceutical manufacturer in profiling its market. We also reviewed their print advertisements in light of our findings. One of their ads for a drug to prevent urinary incontinence had been particularly successful. It showed a smiling man in his sixties, swinging a golf club on a beautiful sunny day. The caption read: "18 holes and no accidents." Until we had diagnosed the Profile, they had assumed that the ad worked because of the positive scene in the picture. After they understood the nature of the product and the market in Away From terms, it was agreed that it was the caption that created the positive response.

As a salesperson or marketing director, there are several options you could take when planning your sales approach or marketing campaign. You can examine your product or service to discover if it is Toward or Away From by its very nature and design your process to attract more of the appropriate market segment. Alternatively, especially if your product or service could be both, you could design your strategy to adapt to either, based on your individual customer's triggers. Another option is simply to find out who is already buying your product or service regardless of the characteristics of the product, and gear everything to increase your market share within that group. Or, if you have already saturated that group, you may judge it appropriate to go after the other pattern by using the correct Influencing Language.

Many books on sales will tell you that a person will buy either to *gain a benefit* or to *avoid a problem*. Once you have asked the question *Why is that important,* to determine a Toward or Away From motivation, you can use the appropriate Influencing Language. If you want to sell a house to a Toward family, you might tell them (if it matches their Criteria) that this house *is close* to the schools, *has lots* of room, and *is near* public transport. For an Away From family, you could say that it *isn't far* from the schools, *isn't too small,* and you *don't have to walk miles* to get to public transport.

One real estate agent who studied and used the LAB Profile® found that he only had to work two-thirds of the year to keep his income at the level he wanted, and this during a recessionary period when many agents had been forced to leave the business.

Online Sales and Marketing

Having learned with some of the well-known online sales experts, and sold products online myself, the Away From Pattern is more likely to get the click but may not be enough to trigger a purchase. This means that while you can get your target market's attention by demonstrating you know their problem and their pain; prospective customers will also need to feel the pull toward a solution that fits for them. Of course, there is a lot more to it than that, but if you can set up the Away From their problem, then Toward the right solution process, you have already created movement in the client's mind.

Summary

Direction

Question: ***Why is that (Criteria) important?*** [Ask 3 times]

Toward: Motivated to achieve or attain goals.

Away From: Motivated to solve or avoid problems.

Distribution at Work:

    40% Mainly Away From

    20% Equally Toward and Away From

    40% Mainly Toward
    (in the work Context, from Rodger Bailey)

Influencing Language:

Toward: attain; obtain; have; get; include; achieve, etc.

Away From: avoid; prevent; eliminate; solve; get rid of, etc.

---

[1] Wishing, Wanting and Achieving e-book and audio recording by Shelle Rose Charvet: bit.ly/WishingWantingAndAchieving

[2] bit.ly/UkCabinetResign

[3] bit.ly/FemaleEntrepreneursHarderTime

[4] bit.ly/YaleExperiment

Chapter 6
Source: Can You Really Get Others to Do What You Want?

Where does a person find motivation? In external sources, or in internal standards and beliefs?

This category deals with the source of motivation, or in other words, its location. Where are judgments made, inside a person's body or from outside? These Patterns affect how you make judgments and decisions. As you try them out, you will be able to decide how best to use them, and others will notice your increased effectiveness.

Here are the two Patterns:

Internal

People with an Internal Pattern in a Context provide their own motivation from within themselves. They decide about the quality of their work. They have difficulty accepting other people's opinions and outside direction. When they get negative feedback on work they feel has been well done, they will question the opinion or judge the person giving the feedback. They prefer to decide for themselves, even when presented with compelling evidence.

They can *gather information* from outside sources and then *they decide* about it, based on internal standards. Because they *take orders as information*, they can be hard to supervise. "My boss wants this out by Tuesday? That's interesting."

Since they generally do not need external praise, they tend not to give much feedback as managers.

When in the Internal Pattern, people hold their standards somewhere within themselves, for the things that are important to them. Their motivation is triggered when they get to gather information from the outside, process it against their own standards, and make judgments about it.

External

People in External mode like other people's opinions, outside direction, and feedback from external sources to get and stay motivated. In the Context of work, if they do not get that feedback, they may not know how well they are doing. They take information as orders. "He said the green paper matches the decor. I'd better go get some." I made a stray statement about possibly thinking about getting a whiteboard for my "Idea Room" and then my hubby came home to show me 4 links with product analysis, to help me choose one.

They prefer when someone else decides. I got stuck in an External-External loop with one of my business partners. He asked me how I wanted the training room setup. Then I asked how he would like it. And he said: "I don't know, what do you think?" We did several rounds of this before we caught ourselves.

When in External mode, someone may have trouble starting or continuing an activity without outside encouragement, feedback or results of some kind. This is especially true of many people when they want to change a behavior or break a habit.

External people do not hold standards within themselves. They gather them from an outside source, including what they see on the internet. At work, if there is long absence of any external feedback or reaction to their work, they may experience something akin to sensory deprivation.

**Distribution %**	
(in the work Context, from Rodger Bailey)	
Mainly Internal	40%
Equally Internal & External	20%
Mainly External	40%

Identification

Question:

HOW DO YOU KNOW THAT YOU HAVE DONE A GOOD JOB?

(at work, at choosing a car, etc.)

Internal: sentence structure

- they decide or know themselves; "I know"
- they evaluate their own performance based on their own standards and Criteria
- they resist when someone tells them what to do, or decides for them
- outside instructions are taken as information

Internal: body language

- sitting upright, pointing to self, may pause before answering a judgment from someone else while they evaluate it, minimal gestures and facial expressions for their culture

External: sentence structure

- other people or external sources of information decide or judge for them; need to compare their work to an external norm or standard (i.e., a checklist or a quota outside information is taken as a decision or order).

External: body language

- leaning forward, watching for your response, facial expressions indicating they want to know from you if it was all right

Examples

Internal:	*"I know when I have done a good job."*
Mainly Internal:	*"I usually know. I appreciate it when my boss compliments me, but generally, I know when I have done well."*
Equally Internal and External:	*"Sometimes I know and sometimes my clients tell me."*
Mainly External:	*"Usually, when I meet the quotas set by my boss and my clients seem happy. And also, I can tell when I am working well."*
External:	*"My clients are happy. My boss is happy. I met my quota."*

Alternate Questions:

- How would you react to regular feedback from peers in (a specific Context)?
- Whom do you involve when you make a decision about ...?
- If you felt, you had done good work and someone you respect criticized your work, how would you react? (Listen if the person criticizes, judges, or attempts to persuade the other person (Internal), or if they question the value of their own work (External).)

Questioning and Testing:

Here are some examples to show you how to test if you are not sure from the answer to the first question:

SRC:	Can I ask you, Suzanne, how do you know you've done a good job at work?
Suzanne:	Feedback from other people plus knowing myself. (External & Internal)

This is an example of someone with both Patterns. Because we know that only about 20 percent are right in the middle, I would like to test to see if Suzanne falls on one side or the other:

SRC:	Let's say you thought you did a good job on something and you didn't get good feedback from the other people. How would you react?
Suzanne:	Well, I'd still *think* I did a good job but . . . something would be missing. I'd have to go check what they didn't like.

Here are two more examples:

SRC:	Louise, how do you know you've done a good job at work?
Louise:	I feel good about it.
SRC:	What happens if you feel good about it and nobody else appreciated it?
Louise:	They probably didn't see what I saw in it. (shrugging her shoulders)
SRC:	Robert, how do you know you've done a good job at work?
Robert:	I know I've done a good job when I get external feedback.
SRC:	What happens when there is no external feedback?
Robert:	I would feel, like, what's the point?

While Suzanne has both Patterns at work, she has more External than Internal, because when push comes to shove, she needs the feedback to really know if it is good enough. Both Louise and Robert fall firmly in the Internal and External camps, respectively.

Where Do You Know That?

Another question that will help you test in those cases where the answer to the first question is unclear. Ask: "*Where do you know that*?" An Internal person may point to a part of their body and an External person may either not understand the question or give a clear External answer.

Knowing Yourself: Recent Brain Studies

Recent research[1] suggests that "the brain is a large predictive machine, constantly comparing incoming sensory information and current experiences against stored knowledge and memories of previous experiences and predicting what will come next." Wow. That is a great description of what someone in Internal mode does! They do not ignore external stimuli, they evaluate them against what they already know. However, when someone has an extreme Internal Pattern, they tend to automatically discard any outside information that contradicts what they already believe. (See the Macho Test© below)

Influencing Language

You might want to consider choosing your words carefully, based on the information you have gathered about someone. As the most skilled professional communicators can tell you, the impact will be enormous.

Internal: The Language of Suggestion

- only you can decide; you might consider; it's up to you; I suggest you think about; try it out and decide what you think; here's some information so you can decide; what do you think; for all the information you need to decide, just call …

External: How others will react, or Command Language

- you'll get good feedback; others will notice; it has been approved by; well-respected; you will make quite an impact; so-and-so thinks; I would strongly recommend; the experts say; give references; scientific studies show; (if you have impeccable credibility with a person or group, you can also use "Command Language" such as "you should")

Command Language and the Language of Suggestion

When you have credibility with someone or a group, it means that they have become *External to you*. In this case telling someone what to do may be accepted as long as it's not too bossy. "This is how to do it." I call this *Command Language*, because you are being directive with someone.

When people are in Internal mode, clearly this will not work. In fact, they may just refuse to consider what you say because you were too definitive. At a below-conscious level, they perceive that you are trying to deprive them of the right to make up their own mind.

Instead you might want to use the *Language of Suggestion*, or a powerful alternative to the Feedback Sandwich, **The Suggestion Model©**:

There are 4 steps:

1. Make the suggestion (Using the Language of Suggestion for Internals)
2. State what problem it avoids or solves (Away From)
3. State the benefit (Toward)
4. Overall why it's easy to do (for Externals)

"When you are speaking with Ahmed, I suggest that you ask him what is important before showing him our solutions. (suggestion) That way you may avoid showing him things he won't like (problem avoided in Away From language), and you can go directly to the

solutions he is interested in (benefit expressed in Toward language). *This should be easy for you, since you already have a great rapport with him."* (encouraging comment)

Irresistible Language: Managing Your Boss

Some people are extremely hard to influence or convince, *until you know how.* Let's take an example of someone, perhaps your boss, who has the following combination: Internal and Away From. Chances are that this person has been making your life miserable by only noticing what you do wrong and disagreeing with every proposal. As Groucho Marx sang, "Whatever it is, I'm against it."

Some *irresistible* Influencing Language, tailor-made for this person could be helpful. Let's imagine that one day you enter her office with the report she asked you for and you say: "I've drafted the proposal you asked for to deal with the issues. *It's not perfect. Would you take a look at it?"* Your boss will likely grab the paper from your hand, correct it to her liking, and is more likely to accept it. You may have already done this!

Research confirms the power of inviting the other person to decide.[2] A Meta-Analysis of 42 studies concludes that when told "but you are free" to refuse a request, compliance rates increased in most contexts regardless of the type of request. The effect diminished however if the decision to agree or not was not immediate. Lesson learned! If you want someone to do something now, let them know: "but you are free to refuse". Hey, I'm going to try this out with my hubby!

Self-Awareness: Internal and External

According to researcher Tasha Eurich[3], who conducted a large-scale scientific study, self-awareness comes in two types:

Internal Self-Awareness, which is how clearly one sees one's "own values, passions, aspirations, fit with our environment, reactions (including thoughts, feelings, behaviors, strengths, and weaknesses), and impact on others."

External Self-Awareness, which refers to how well we know how others see our values, passions, fit with the environment etc., as above.

High Internal self-awareness is associated with high job and relationship satisfaction, and happiness and with lower anxiety, stress and depression. High External Self-Awareness is associated with empathy, taking others' perspectives and good relationships with one's employees. So far this dovetails nicely with the LAB Profile® Motivation Patterns Internal and External. The interesting part of her research shows that leaders need a balance of both in order to be effective.

Hyper Internals: The Macho Pattern[4]

Sometimes people can become extremely Internal; rejecting all opinions but their own. I have called this kind of behavior The Macho Pattern.

Do you know people who:

1. already know everything?
2. have no problems, everything is perfect?
3. if there are problems, they are of someone else's making?
4. are better, stronger, smarter, more knowledgeable, and more important than anyone else?

It can be very difficult to work and live with people who run this program. And it's not only men! Anyone can become Macho. Remember your reaction when one of your parents told you how to live your life?

How many times have major decisions been made to assuage someone's ego or simply to not lose face? Just listen to radio interviews. When the interviewer asks if a politician were surprised by the turn of events, rarely if ever will the person admit to being surprised. That would be saying that they did not already know everything there is to know. Once I sold a training program with optional follow-up coaching. No one took up the coaching offer because that would have meant conceding they needed help. Now the coaching is just part of the training program.

The Macho Test©

The Macho Test is an editing technique I developed to enable even the most Macho of people to listen and consider your ideas. It is now used around the world to check how you are presenting ideas to make sure you don't inadvertently trigger a Macho response.

But I suspect that much of this technique is already familiar to you – I have simply organized it into an easy procedure.

When you are writing something, or preparing a presentation and you want to make sure to be listened to and taken seriously without the other people feeling threatened, first prepare your draft.

Then, ask yourself if you have implied or stated the following:

1. There is something they don't already know,
2. I am telling them what to do,
3. They have a problem and I have the solution,
4. They are not perfect in some way, and/or
5. I am better than they are in some way.

If any of the above are stated or implied, it does not pass the Macho Test! You may wish to rephrase as follows:

1. *As you probably know....*(then state the thing you suspect they do not know)
2. Use the language of suggestion: *You may wish to consider...*
3. *I understand that other organizations have had this issue and what some of them have done is... How have you solved this problem?* (implies they have already solved all the problems)
4. *With your experience and knowledge in this area....*
5. *Your role is.... My role is...* (establishing different yet equal roles)

The Globe and Mail, a national Canadian newspaper published an article I wrote entitled: *"Ten Tips for Surviving the Health Care System."* The title passes the Macho Test as "tips" are only suggestions. It was reprinted in quite a few journals in several countries. It would not have received nearly as much attention had I entitled it: "Ten Rules for Getting Through the Health Care System."

Responding to Feedback and Criticism

When a person who is in External mode receives criticism or negative feedback, they question themselves. An Internal person in the same situation makes a judgment about the other person. "I must have done something wrong" (External) or "the customer is a jerk because he didn't appreciate what I did for him" (Internal).

If ten people told a highly Internal person: "Wow, your tie is ugly!" they might say "Gee, isn't that funny? There are ten people walking around here with bad taste." Whereas, a person who has an External Pattern about clothing would go home and change.

I had the advantages of being External driven home to me, when I bought a cheap bookcase, in a kit, which I had to assemble myself. As I was struggling to follow the instructions (my father used to say that if all else fails, read the instructions), I noticed that the top and bottom shelves did not fit properly onto the back board. "Cheap design," I grumbled to myself and I *made* it fit. When I set the bookcase up, I noticed that I had assembled the top and bottom shelves backward and the chipboard was showing! Had I been slightly more External, which is appropriate in Contexts one knows little about, I might have *questioned what I was doing* when I noticed the poor fit, instead of *criticizing the design.*

When following instructions, it may be more appropriate to be in an External mode. My twin brother confirmed this to me when we were discussing how the holes often seem to be in the wrong place in these sorts of kits, that is, until you figure out that *you* made the mistake!

I went out to supper with a friend. She suggested a restaurant where she had liked both the food and the ambiance. "Although," she said, "I've heard it's been taken over by new management, and that it's not nearly as good anymore." She then went on to insist that we go there anyway because she had to go see *for herself*. At the end of the evening she pronounced, "Well, they were right; the service was poor and so was the food. But I had to check it out for myself." Because she was highly Internal, someone else's word was not good enough. It remained an unresolved issue for her until she could decide for herself.

Many women tell me that their husbands often do not believe them, when they tell them there is something wrong with the car. The husbands need to determine that for themselves.

The easiest way to get an Internal person to listen and think about something is to phrase it as "information you might want to consider", or as a question. Otherwise they may simply judge you or the way you said it.

What Self-Esteem Is Not

Someone asked me about these Patterns. "Is it possible for a person to switch from Internal to External, or vice versa, depending on whether they receive positive or negative criticism?" As Rodger Bailey, the developer of the LAB Profile®, said: The LAB Profile® is a status report about how I (with my particular structural makeup) respond to Contexts." In a few of the profiles I have done, I noticed a Pattern that corresponds to the question above. One person was highly Internal when she thought she had done a bad job (one Context) and highly External when she thought she had done something well (a different Context for her). Nothing anyone would say could convince her that she had done a good job when she had decided otherwise. However, when she thought she had done something well, she had to check with others to make sure it was all right. I suspect that this has to do with low self-esteem and self-confidence. I would call this a self-handicapping strategy.

Do not, however, confuse an External Pattern with low self-esteem. It is not the same thing. When I am presenting to a group, for example, where do I get my motivational energy? Do I get it because the participants are smiling at me, or because I know I prepared my presentation well? (In that Context, if my goal is to present well and meet the audience's needs, it is appropriate to do some of each.)

A friend of mine once asked me: "Do you think I'm too External?" She then realized what she had said and began to laugh. My response was: "Too External for what?" I used to be influenced by peer pressure, but my friends talked me out of it.

Educational Design

I was working with a large group of high school principals in the province of New Brunswick and we were discussing the design of education programs. One of the participants made the comment that many of the programs are structured to create an Internal Pattern in the students. In my opinion, when you closely examine the structure and content of any educational program, you could probably do a LAB Profile® of its creator. Most programs will favor one or the other Pattern in each of the categories, probably based on the unconscious Patterns of the creators. The Principal's question was: "What about the kids who have an External Pattern in school and therefore need outside feedback to stay motivated and to know if they are doing well?"

I believe that it is fine to teach and encourage self-evaluation. However, when you want to *trigger motivation and keep the students interested* (which is a separate Context), some people will need ongoing encouragement, feedback or results to stay interested.

Recruiting

Does a job need someone who must *provide their own motivation and judge for themselves* the quality of their work? Or does it need someone to *adapt what they are doing based on outside requirements*? Sales and reception positions, or any job where meeting someone else's needs is crucial, generally need someone with an External Pattern. You would want to employ someone in these positions for whom feedback will determine what they do and how they behave. These people will need either to be closely supervised, or to have some external means of knowing if they are on track.

Many people-management positions require someone who has a mainly Internal Pattern with some External. Managers make decisions and set standards. You would have to have standards inside your body somewhere to do that. Frequently people say, however, when their boss is extremely Internal, that he or she does not listen or respond to suggestions. Also, free-lancers need to be mainly Internal to motivate themselves, but must also take into account client requirements.

For sales or customer service positions, you would need people with a good dose of External. Sales and customer service people must really care whether customers are happy in order to create and maintain great customer relationships. If a customer is not pleased with your product or service and your representative treats the customer indifferently or badly, it will not help you improve customer service. Customers have become much more Internal than they once were. They have high standards for value and service, and one bad experience is enough to turn them off.

One of the challenges that large Internal organizations face is how to incorporate spontaneous customer feedback into improving product design and service. I often find myself making suggestions to the person behind the desk, who sighs and says he can't do anything about it.

However, as relationships with customers shift, particularly between organizations, the sales people are more *long-term partners and consultants* to clients. If sales representatives do consulting, that presupposes that they have some expertise to impart, for example, on technical issues and standards. The salesperson or consultant, would therefore need to have some degree of Internal. They would need to be certain about what they know. You would not, however, want someone who has an extremely Internal Pattern, because ultimately their performance needs to be judged by the satisfaction of the client.

When you are profiling a job in preparation for recruitment or selection, determine whether the person's success at the position is based on meeting their own standards or adapting to someone else's.

People Management

Internal employees have trouble accepting being managed, and generally do not need praise to stay motivated. Working for a "micro-manager" would be torture. Their motivation comes from inside; they are self-starters. They need to make their own decisions and will do that even when they have not been given permission. They become demotivated when they do not get to decide anything. When you give them an instruction, they will consider that as a piece of information and then decide whether to follow it.

A friend recounted an intercultural incident between two people with an Internal Pattern, an English manager and an American employee. The English boss told his employee: "I'd reconsider that if I were you," intending to communicate that he thought it was a bad idea and it should not be done. The American took him literally; he reconsidered, decided it *was* a good idea, and went ahead and did it, much to the annoyance of his boss.

When two or more Internal people are on a team, they may have frequent arguments and conflicts because each will be operating from their own (usually unstated) internal standards (particularly if they also have an Away From Pattern). They can work more successfully together when they first negotiate and explicitly agree upon the Criteria, standards and measurements.

Employees with an Internal Pattern work best with little supervision. You can assign them a task and give them "carte blanche" to see it through. Give them decisions to make and, in cases where you are not sure of their judgment, get agreement on the standards to be met first. Make sure you know their Criteria and attach them to the job to be done. "Here's a *challenge* for you."

When giving them instructions, preface them with "Only you can decide to . . . or, "Here is the information on this; the end goal is to achieve that. You get to decide the best way."

External employees will look to their manager for guidance and encouragement. You will need to be explicit about what you expect them to do, as they tend to interpret information as instructions. If you said to an External employee: "The order forms are now available," they would drop what they were doing and go get them.

In the absence of regular feedback, they can become demotivated and unsure of themselves. Where the manager is highly External, they may end up looking to the employees for approval. External employees need to have clear goals and some external means of knowing if they are on track, in the form of regular feedback sessions, checklists, quotas, or examples to follow.

Annual performance appraisals are insufficient feedback for people who have an External Pattern. Many will work themselves into a lather before their performance appraisal, because they have no idea themselves of how well they have been performing.

When assigning a task to an External person, let them know how much it will be appreciated (if his or her Organization Pattern is Person) or what the impact will be (if his or her Organization Pattern is Thing). "You will get lots of good feedback," or "This will make a noticeable difference to our work" are phrases you could use to get their interest. The tasks that will play to their strengths are those that demand that they adapt to and meet someone else's expectations, provided that those expectations are clear.

Joke Alert!

How many External folks does it take to change a lightbulb?

"I don't know, what do you think?"

How many Internal folks does it take to change a lightbulb?

"It looks okay to me. It doesn't need changing."

Selling in a Buyer's Market:
Adapting to the Shift in Customers' Patterns

Customers can be very difficult to deal with. They demand products of perfect quality, resist complicated purchasing processes, and want anything that breaks to be fixed immediately at no cost to them. They quickly jump on any mistakes made, give customer service staff a very hard time, and even play one supplier off another to get the best deal. And they want more for less. They will ask questions in a retail store, and then go home and buy on the internet.[5]

In other words, customers have become highly Internal to their suppliers. Suppliers beware! Spending time and money developing the best products and services for your clients is clearly no longer enough. Language and processes need to be adapted to meet the needs of people who take everything you say only as information to consider. Notice the skepticism with which clients scoff at your claims to be the best. "Prove it," they insist (to *their* satisfaction).

TD (a Canadian financial group) responded to the change in the mortgage market. Their slogan was highly appropriate: "The best mortgage package in Canada? You be the judge." Great language for Internals.

CIBC, a large Canadian bank, switched its online strategy from:

to:

Their language in the second ad is much more inviting, suggesting an invitation to talk, rather than the Command Language of the first ad. This strategy, using language for Internals is very appropriate in a culture where the population tends to dislike or distrust the banks.

In another example, the sales approach of a career coaching outfit consisted of booking an appointment with prospective clients, showing them the process they use, and then sending the person away to think about it and decide if they needed it. Upon questioning, it turned out that about 80 percent of their clients had an Internal Pattern; so did the founder and majority of staff. When I suggested that they *might consider* using an approach for External people to attract more clients, the founder thought about it and decided against it. He felt that External clients would take up too much time in counseling sessions.

To sell to people who have an Internal Pattern, you need to give them information and let them decide.

"You may want to try it out and let me know what you think. The only way to know if this is the one for you is to test it out for yourself." That is why car dealerships insist that their sales people get the prospective buyer behind the wheel.

Buying Online:
The Sequence of Internal and External Buying Patterns

When customers make purchases online, they go through sequences of being Internal and External. Let's say you want to book a hotel in Paris. You know the area, price range and facilities you would like, and you do a search. (Internal) You get many options and look through them to see which one fits the best (Internal). But before you hit the button, chances are you will read the reviews just to be sure. (External)

I have worked with large companies to help them decode their customers' (business and consumer) buying processes into sequences of LAB Profile® Patterns, so that they can increase their sales effectiveness. With this process, marketers can figure out the sequences their business and consumer customers go through and help them through the buying process by offering information that is visually and verbally matched to the customers' sequence.

Intimate Relationships

At some levels, we could say that each person in a relationship has their own Patterns; Internal, External etc. But some of the research shows that at a more fundamental level, each of us is fairly External to our partners. When John Gottman researched couples' interactions[6], he explained that one partner makes a 'bid' to the other, such as "Look at that beautiful bird outside." What the partner is looking for, is a sign of interest, recognition or support from their partner. "The husband thought the bid was important enough to bring it up in conversation and the question is whether his partner recognizes and respects that."

This is an example of External (needing a response indicating respect, support etc). The partner either "Turns Toward" or "Turns Away From" the bid. (Hmmm, this language sounds familiar!) Gottman found that couples who were divorced after a six-year follow-up, had only a 33% of Turn Toward responses, while those still married had an 87% Turn Toward rate.

Gottman also found that showing contempt for a partner is the number one reason for breakups. Again, the reaction to us from our partner is an essential factor in the success of the relationship. (External) Showing kindness even when in a fight is what binds people together. (External)

So even if we have trouble convincing our partners to do what we want them to do (because they seem so Internal to us) maybe deep down, what we say and do really does matter. If you want help convincing your husband to do something, you may wish to try out my HusbandMotivator™ app. (And yes, it also works with wives, bosses and others!)

Doctors and Patients

In France, I read a study that pronounced that 80 percent of patients do not finish taking their prescriptions. Doctors have told me that about the same percentage applies in other countries too. Many people simply forget to take their medicine when their symptoms disappear.

We can use the LAB Profile® to explain this. Many people have Internal and Away From Patterns in the Context of bodily ailments. We tend to go to the doctor when we *feel* sick, not when someone else says we look unwell. I notice a problem myself – Internal and Away From.

Doctors would therefore need to sell their patients on complying with instructions. "*You need to decide for yourself* if you want to *really get rid of this illness*. If you do, take all of this medicine, as prescribed" (Internal and Away From). Even though many people are External to doctors and other authority figures, once they get home, they shift back into an Internal mode with regards to feeling unwell.

Doctors can recognize the implications of the fact that many of their patients shift into a highly External Pattern while they are in the doctor's office. Patients tend to believe whatever the doctor tells them because they have accepted the doctor as a knowledgeable authority figure. This means that doctors need to be very careful about what they say and imply.

My mother broke her wrist during an icy winter. I took her back to the hospital to have her cast replaced because the first one was too tight. The doctor fitted her new cast on and made a joke: "There, that'll keep you for *this time*." This time?! Right before my eyes I watched my mother nod to acknowledge the implicit presupposition that if he was talking about *this time*, there was going to be a *next time*! "No!" I shouted, "This is the last time!" But my mother didn't have an External Pattern with regards to me; I was her daughter. Three months later, she tripped in her garden and broke the other wrist.

Just to contradict what I said above, there is also another trend. Millions of people are now consulting practitioners of complementary medicine and consuming nutritional supplements that they research on their own. When asked why, many say either that the doctor has not been able to cure a particular problem or that they do not believe the approach used by the doctor can help them. These people have developed Internal standards for what they want and don't want.

Selling in Other Contexts

The approach for getting patients to take their medicine could also work for Internals in other Contexts. "You need to decide if you really want *(customer's desired outcome)*. If you do, then you might want to try out *(our product or service)*."

External people need references. They need to know who else has bought. The advertisements where a famous person is flogging a product, attract the attention of people who are External to that famous person, in that Context.

It can be easier selling to people provided you can get them to be External to you. This entails establishing credibility as well as rapport. One client of mine asked me: "Do you think I need it?" Proof that I had established credibility and that they had become External to me. Appearance also counts. You look more credible when you are wearing clothes that are one notch more formal than your client's, showing credentials and references, and slipping in expressions such as "In my experience", or "one thing I learned the hard way was …."

External buyers will also purchase something for how it will make them look or the impact it will have on others. Why *do* people buy Jaguars? Because the leather seats are comfortable? A market researcher who worked on the Jaguar account told me that people buy luxury cars more for the perceived value these cars offer than the status they confer. Then he stopped and thought. "Maybe," he snorted, "they are buying because they want to *be seen* as buying for value."

If you want to attract both groups, or if your client pays attention to both Internal standards and External feedback, use both Patterns. "It's up to you, but many folks buy the blue one." For those cases where you are not sure, use one Pattern and observe. If you do not get a positive response, try the other one.

Closet Externals and Closet Internals

As in the Jaguar example above, the potential buyer *seems* to have an Internal Trigger, but the real motivator was External. Bill Huckabee, the researcher who pioneered the field of LAB Profile® market research called this the "Closet External". In other words, the External aspect is hidden in the closet.

To convince someone with this Pattern, you need to appeal to both sides at once – if you are too overtly speaking the External side by telling them what to do or saying what everyone else is doing, your input is likely to be rejected. Instead, you might try, "Only you can know what you want, although most people are getting this one." This is using the Language of Suggestion (for Internals) and then adding in what everyone else is doing (for the External part). This has proven the most successful strategy according to the feedback I've had.

In a study quoted by the Scientific American Mind [7], the people who rated their level of knowledge of a subject as high, were also likely to "over claim" the extent of their knowledge. This effect was enhanced when they were given an easy test to do before being asked what their level of knowledge was. Getting this External feedback that they were knowledgeable (while two other groups had to do a difficult test or no test at all), they rated themselves as much more knowledgeable than the other two groups. Closet External in action! Donald Trump's behavior as president in the face of criticism, was typical of someone who was often in Closet External mode. For example, when Trump's supporters criticized his tweet about compromising on the financing for his wall to end the government shutdown at the end of 2018, he immediately hardened his stance, in line with what his supporters demanded. When celebrities, Democrats, or main-stream media criticized him, he would spend hours or days attacking them on Twitter. He was incredibly sensitive to outside negative feedback and tended to respond immediately, all while appearing to be the tough Internal guy on the outside.

At other times, he exhibited typical Internal behavior, such as when he ignored advice from experts who were against withdrawing the US troops from Syria in early 2019. He stuck to his own inclination to bring them home. His cabinet was hard-pressed to get him to agree to bring them home slowly over several months. Both of his tendencies,

Closet External and High Internal, demonstrate just how Contextual the LAB Profile® Patterns are.

People who are "Closet Internals" tend to look and sound like they want and need your input, but then they go away and do what they want. Using the Language of Suggestion for Internals seems to work best with these folks. What do you think?

Some Things Are Contagious

According to an article in the Scientific American Mind[8], some things are socially contagious. Weight changes, eating disorders, emotions, psychogenic illness, suicidal thoughts, and perhaps even mass shootings. For this to be possible, it means one group of people must have become External to the group with the behavior in question.

I imagine that positive behaviors are also socially contagious – a good reason to *establish your credibility* when you wish to be a *role model for behaviors* that you would like others to adopt. If your audience becomes External to you, they are more likely to pick up and replicate what you do.

Joke Alert!

How might a person in Internal mode say: "I don't know something."?

"I haven't decided yet."

"How might someone in External mode say: "I don't know something."?

"What do you think?

How might a person in Internal mode say: "I was wrong."?

"I've changed my mind."

How might someone in External mode say: "I was wrong."?

"Was that a mistake?"

Summary

Influencing Language:

Internal:	only you can decide; you might want to consider; it's up to you; what do you think?, etc.
External:	others will notice; the feedback you'll get; results; give references; so-and-so thinks, etc.

Source

Question:	***How do you know that you have done a good job at . . . ?***
Internal:	They are motivated to decide based on their own internal standards.
External:	They need outside feedback to know how well they are doing and to stay motivated.

Distribution at Work:

40% Mainly Internal

20% Equally Internal and External

40% Mainly External
(in the work Context, from Rodger Bailey)

[1] Van Mulukom, Valerie, Is it Rational to Trust Your Gut? bit.ly/IsItRationaltoTrustYourGut, 20180516

[2] Carpenter, Christopher J., A Meta-Analysis of the "But you are free" Compliance-Gaining Technique; Communication Studies; Vol 64, No 1, January-March, 2013, pp. 6-17

[3] Eurich, Tasha, What Self-Awareness Really Is (and How to Cultivate It); bit.ly/WhatSelfAwarenessReallyIs. This article is well-worth reading as it also reveals surprises with regards to how experience and power can negatively affect self-awareness.

[4] Adapted from my article The Macho Test, see bit.ly/MachoTestArticle. And you can also find out how Macho you are here with the Macho Factor Quiz: bit.ly/MachoTest

[5] See also my book on Customers and the LAB Profile®: Words That Change Customer's Minds.

[6] Gottman's research was explained in this article by Emily Esfahani Smith of The Atlantic, quoted here: bit.ly/LastingRelationships

[7] Schmerler, Jessica, You Don't Know as Much as You Think: bit.ly/FalseExpertise

[8] Long, Kat and Victoria Stern, Mass Shootings are Contagious: bit.ly/MassShootingsAreContagious

Chapter 7
Reason: The Right Way or A Way to Do It?

> *How does a person reason? Is there a continual quest to finding alternatives, or a preference to follow established procedures?*

This category will lead you to unlimited possibilities and show you the right way to get there. There are two Patterns:

Options

People with an Options Pattern in a given Context are motivated by opportunities and possibilities to do something in a different way. There is always another better way to do things. They love to create procedures and systems but are not so keen on following them. If you give an Options person a guaranteed way to make a million dollars, he will try to improve it.

They are thrilled by unlimited possibilities and ideas. The thing that is irresistible to people in an Options mode, is breaking or bending the rules.

They like to start a new idea or a new project. However, they do not necessarily feel compelled to finish it. They much prefer to do development and setup rather than maintenance activities. Sometimes they will have difficulty committing themselves because they believe this will reduce their options. At the extreme, they might avoid deciding anything (particularly if they also have a Reactive Pattern). Alternatively, they can be totally committed to an idea or project, until the next new idea comes along.

Procedures

People with a Procedures Pattern like to follow a step by step process. They believe there is a "right" way to do things. Once they have a procedure, they can follow it over and over again. They are interested in *how* to do things, not in *why* things are the way they are.

A procedure has a beginning and an end. It may have choice points at which you gather more information and make a decision. Without one, someone who needs a procedure may feel lost or get stuck. When they commence a procedure, the most important thing for them is to get to the end of the procedure. They are the ones who tend to complete and finish what they start.

They can feel personally violated when it is suggested to them to break, or go around, the rules. Once they know the procedure to follow, they can be quite happy doing that.

Distribution % (in the work Context, from Rodger Bailey)	
Mainly Options	40%
Equally Options & Procedures	20%
Mainly Procedures	40%

Identification

Question:
WHY DID YOU CHOOSE YOUR PRESENT WORK?
(*or house, vacation, car, etc.*)

You may recall that in the introduction to this book we discussed Reality. Noam Chomsky stated that in order for people to create their own models of reality, they use three processes called Deletion, Distortion, and Generalization. This category deals with Distortion. The question we ask for this Pattern is: "Why did you choose ..." and the rest refers to a particular Context.

For someone with an Options Pattern, when they hear the question **Why did you choose,** they hear the question **why** and answer this question with a list of Criteria for their answer.

When someone with a Procedures preference hears the question, they delete the word **why** and substitute **how did it happen?** They answer the question: "How?" Sometimes, the first thing they say is, "Well, I didn't choose." They tell you a story or series of events that led them to getting the job. "I was working at my brother-in-law's and there was an opening in this other company at the time I finished a contract, so I took it."

Options

- list of Criteria
- opportunities, possibilities
- expanding options and choice

Procedures

- did not choose
- answers the question "why" by telling "how" it happened
- the facts, events leading to, a story

How you recognize someone who has an equally Options and Procedures Pattern is interesting. They might tell you a story with Criteria imbedded in it. I happen to be quite in the middle on this Pattern with regards to some of my work, and if someone asked me why I chose to set up my own company after I returned to Canada, I tend to say: "After I came back, I looked around for what to do, and became a partner in a small training company. After a while I became **dissatisfied**. And **being organized** is important to me. I realized that I could probably make **more money** in my own company and **decrease expenses** and **be independent**. So, I set up my company, Success Strategies." I have used both Patterns in the answer. (Criteria in **bold**)

Examples

Options:	*"I thought it would be stimulating, interesting, and challenging."*
Mainly Options:	*"It was more interesting and had more responsibility and better pay. A friend of mine told me about it."*
Equally Options and Procedures:	*"A friend told me about it and it looked more interesting."*
Mainly Procedures:	*"I had been with the same company for ten years. A friend told me they were hiring in her company, so I applied and was hired. The job is more interesting and I make more money."*
Procedures:	*"I didn't really choose. I met my boss through my brother-in-law who worked with her. They needed a technician and I was just completing a contract."*

Influencing Language

The possibilities are endless for finding the right thing to say.

Options

- opportunity; choice; break the rules just for you; another better way; unlimited possibilities; an alternative is; that's one way; here are the options; there has got to be a way; the sky's the limit, ways and means

Procedures

- the right way; speak in procedures: first . . . then . . . after which . . . the last step; tried and true; reliable; how to use this; just follow the procedure; the procedure is; proven methodology

Sales and Marketing

I wrote and performed a keynote speech entitled, "Sex, Diets and Success"[1] to debunk the sales strategies of unethical self-help gurus. They promise amazing results and tell you how easy it is to succeed (except in the fine print). In other words, they get you to dream (LAB Profile® Patterns, Reactive and Options), which means you are passively visualizing your mansion, fancy car, piles of money and so on. Bitcoin and cryptocurrencies have been promoted the same way, as are a lot of scams. But if someone is in Reactive and Options mode, they are not Proactively and consistently following the Procedures needed to succeed. They are just thinking about their dreams. So, they buy the program, don't follow it, feel like a failure (because they believe that success is up to them personally) and then purchase the next product, hoping that will be the one that will *do it for them*. Unfortunately, no program will "do it **for** you", since you need to do the work to succeed. In my article, I also demonstrated how to sell and buy personal development in a way that motivates people to get into the mode that will actually help them succeed.

Sometimes getting someone who is in an Options mode to make a decision can be hard, since choosing means eliminating options, which they don't like to do. They are motivated to have possibilities, so give them alternatives, but not so many that it is even more difficult to choose. They want to know *why* they should buy. I remember having a sales appointment with someone who was grappling with a problem. As I left, I inadvertently used an irresistible Pattern. I said "There's *gotta be a way* to find what you're looking for." By the time I had returned to my office, the phone was ringing off the hook. She said: "You're right. There's gotta be a way. And you're the one who can help me."

Sometimes they will decide immediately (particularly if they are also Proactive) if you break the normal procedure, just for them. My carpet cleaner told me: "The office says we have to charge $50 to clean the sofa, but since I'm already here, I can do that for you for $30."

More recently, I discovered that sometimes being in Options mode is simply part of a person's buying procedure and it may be an indication that they are not yet ready to choose. When someone is ready to buy, they unconsciously shift into Procedures mode. As a sales professional, you can test to see if your client is ready by asking:

"Are you ready to look at the next step?" (Procedures Language)

If they are ready, they will go with you. This is how you can find out if they are ready to buy now, before your clients become consciously aware of this themselves. If they are not yet ready, they are likely to show you that they are still in Options Mode:

"What else do you have?", or *"I'd like to check some other things out."*

The right way to sell to someone who prefers Procedures, is to get them started on a procedure because once started, they feel compelled to finish it. Tell them that this product or service is the tried and true, right way to do things. They will be more interested in knowing *how* to buy it or use it than why they should buy it:

"The first step, I'll show you the products. Then you can look at them. I will show you how to use them and you can try one out. You can then decide which one suits you best. After that, we'll cover how the payment plan works and set it up for you to sign. Lastly, you can take your product home right away."

If the product meets their Criteria (and other factors do not interfere), they are likely to complete the procedure. It is preferable to have the client going away happy with the product as the last step of the procedure, rather than paying the bill as the last step.

Certain kinds of stores naturally attract one or the other Pattern. Some people (me, for example) can be overwhelmed by the large amount of choice one has in retail book stores. Others are thrilled.

IKEA, the Swedish home furnishings put-it-together-yourself, store has a mainly Procedures store design. When you walk into IKEA you cannot get out until you have gone through the entire store (short of pulling the fire alarm). I know; I have tried. They have a procedure for doing everything. They have procedures for walking through the store, measuring, deciding, ordering, lining up, paying, parking, loading, and assembling the furniture once you get home.

Recruitment

You can see that for recruiting, and for managing one's own career, the Options and Procedures Patterns are quite important. In fact, this is one category where it really pays to get it right. When you profile a position, ask whether the job mainly consists of *following procedures* or *creating and designing systems and procedures*? Is it setup and development, or maintenance? When you know what the balance is, you can write your advertisement to attract the right people and turn off the ones who would not fit. (See also the section on writing advertisements for jobs.)

When you are in the right job, it can make all the difference. If you like to create and develop processes, find alternatives and color outside of the lines, Options positions are for you. If you prefer to complete and finish what you start and have a step by step process to follow, then Procedures jobs are for you. When I was writing the 3rd edition of this book, I first created a procedure to follow and then followed it! (Options to create the process but most of the time, I just followed it. Occasionally I would get a great idea and explore the ways it would fit into the book.)

Multilevel marketing companies or MLM's, such as Mary Kay, Amway, and all the health and wellness companies work by recruiting sales people (a downline) to sell their products. According to Robert FitzPatrick of Pyramid Scheme Alert, the vast majority of people involved in these kinds of businesses actually lose money. Very few succeed at making a full-time living at multilevel sales. They target the wrong people. The multilevel marketing companies try to recruit new distributors by telling them about *unlimited income possibilities*. This is Options language. Unlimited choice or possibilities, or the sky's the limit, are *irresistible* to Options people.

When people become distributors, they usually find that the companies have already worked out the procedures for selling the product. All you have to do is **proactively and consistently follow the procedure** to make your *sky's the limit* income, which most of them are incapable of doing. The irony is that if they used Procedures Influencing Language in their promotional packages, recruits would be more likely to make their unlimited income.

When you look at the success strategies proposed for telemarketers, and this would apply to other kinds of salespeople, one Pattern is striking. They need to follow a process; a Procedure. Therefore, telemarketers who have a Procedures Pattern will likely sell much more than the ones who prefer Options.

The reason for this is simple. Sales involves being Proactive and mainly following a procedure. You contact prospective customers, establish rapport, do a needs analysis, present something that matches the needs, and lastly help the person make a decision. That's a procedure. If I prefer Options, this time I will do it one way; another time I will try another way. Options sales people tend to have an up and down performance, because occasionally they will get a brilliant idea and strike gold. They do not, however, hone their procedure until it works well. And they often "forget" to follow up. People with a Procedures Pattern will continue to follow the same process over and over again because it feels comfortable and right. This is ideal for sales (although in changing sales situations, they would need to be taught a new procedure).

Certain kinds of jobs are inherently Options or Procedures. Piloting an airplane, for example, is quite clearly a procedure. Can you imagine a commercial airline pilot who has an Options Pattern? "Let's go over the North Pole this time." Anything to do with safety and security needs a Procedures person. Emergency procedures need to be memorized and followed to the letter. Someone who has Internal and Procedures would do very well at that kind of work. On the other hand, you would want an Options person to develop and test a safety procedure, preferably one who also has an Away From Pattern to avoid mistakes.

Architecture would need someone with lots of Options and an understanding of Procedures. A building contractor would have a much heavier dose of Procedures to ensure compliance to regulations. You might want to test for this if you are going to do renovations.

Options people excel in situations where there is a need to develop creative solutions or alternatives to the present systems. Business process engineers, for example, would need a heavy dose of Options.

In a training company in France I worked closely with my boss, who had high Options and Internal Patterns in his work. I learned much from him about creative seminar design. We were frequently asked to lead the same seminar several times over in the same large organizations. We would meet before each one to prepare and he would insist that we redesign each one. I would object: "But Pierre, it worked well last time, it was really good, and they liked it." He would say: "No, no, there has to be a better way to do this." I had the feeling we were constantly throwing the baby out with the bath water. You can see the conflict between Options and Procedures.

In fact, to design training you need to develop Options, but in order to perfect the delivery of training you need to repeat enough Procedures to be able to reproduce processes that work. The best professional speakers have well-honed routines, which necessitates doing both Options and Procedures. I know some creative professional speakers and trainers who have excellent ideas and programs, but who don't shift into Proactive and Procedures to market and sell themselves. They wait for customers! Or go off and create another program that they don't sell.

There are often mismatches in professions between which Patterns are needed, and who tends to be attracted to the position. When I have asked nurses: "Why did you choose to become a nurse?" the answer often is something like: "I want to help people," or "Once I got my certificate, I could travel." These are Criteria, Options answers. Many people attracted to nursing are interested because of the *possibilities* nursing has to offer. They are people with an Options preference. After they decide to become nurses, they go to nursing college. Who teaches in the nursing schools? People who did not find what they wanted in hospital work. So the nursing students get their certificates and go to work in the hospitals. What are hospitals all about? Procedures, and often very tight ones with little choice.

As many health care systems adjust to older populations and tighter budgets, there is increasingly an emphasis on home-based care. There are an expanding number of private nursing services. You can be a nurse, care for people, and do it your own way, getting a chance to develop alternatives. Hospitals themselves are also having to change, necessitating a more flexible workforce.

A Little Variety

Clashes at Work

One of the things I noticed when participating in change operations in corporations is the internal culture clash between different departments. Let's take software design and marketing, for example. If you are a software engineer, you may have a mainly Options Pattern. You develop and design software. Marketing tends to be mainly Procedures because there are steps to follow to take a product to market (aside from the "creative" step where the messages, visuals and slogans, are developed). The software engineers create software and often they drop one project to work on another. They may keep changing, adapting, making the program better, as well as coming up with alternative solutions. The marketing department will be screaming at them: "Stop fixing it! Just give it to us so we can get it out on the market." Why are there so many upgrades to your favorite software package? A consultant friend summed up the software problem: "Not enough time to do it right once, but all the time in the world to fix it."

The same thing can happen between design engineers and the plant. What do design engineers do? They create systems and design products. What does the plant do? It makes them. Production managers get furious when Engineering keeps changing the specs.

Inter-Team Effectiveness

In order to work more effectively together and reduce the number of conflicts among Options and Procedures departments, each need to understand the role of the other and how they function. Options-oriented teams need to explore possibilities creatively in order to invent solutions. Procedures teams need to know that the fruit of these deliberations will actually arrive completed at the right time and place. Many companies would do well to have a Project Manager who handles Options and Procedures equally well to coordinate the work between these two departments.

Terminal Options

The Latest Revision!

Technology Providers and Users

Have you ever noticed that when you ask a "techie" how to do something, they give you lots and lots of possible ways to do it? It is a continuing challenge for end users to find simple procedures for using software, devices, and even the TV remote controls. I'm speaking about myself here, of course! I am often overwhelmed by the number of ways, choices and decisions needed to use technology.

Have you ever been directed to find some information on a webpage, only to discover that you can't find it when you look on the page? And then the person who directed you there insists that it is there, and you still can't find it? Creators and users of technology approach technology quite differently. Eye tracking studies[2] show that most users still use the "F-shape" when they are scanning a webpage, which is a visual Procedure. Developers, who are not typical end users, tend to scan all over the page at high speed, in a movement more like this:

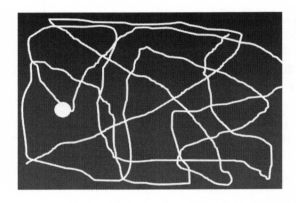

The problem happens when developers favoring the above Options-like movement patterns design webpages and other technology for people who unconsciously follow the same Procedure over and over. End-users who follow the F-shaped visual scan cannot find elements that are outside of their usual scanning pattern. If this Options-Procedures dichotomy is still happening with simple web-page design, imagine the difficulty it poses for typical end-users of everyday apps and products when an upgrade appears that changes the Procedure they knew well.

I consulted with a large software developer to determine the LAB Profile® Patterns of both the end users and the corporate purchasers. End-users tended to have Procedures and Sameness Patterns (you will find more on this Sameness Pattern in the following chapter), while the corporate purchasers of their software tended to have Options and

Difference (want NEW things) Patterns. (More on Difference Pattern in the next chapter)

Who Controls the TV Remote?

People who are in Procedures mode don't like flipping between channels. Once they get involved in a program, they want to follow it to the end. Options TV/Netflix/Prime/YouTube etc., watchers often flit from program to program. I suspect the folks who developed "picture in picture" TV had Options Patterns or had a commitment problem! Rumor has it that women like to watch a program to the end and men like to flit. Jerry Seinfeld said: "Men don't care what's on TV. They only care what else is on TV"[3].

People Management

People with an Options Pattern work best in situations where they get to develop or set up new systems and procedures. They will invariably find a way around standard operating procedures, so you need to decide how best to benefit from their creativity. They are motivated by tasks that involve creating something from scratch, particularly where the end result will increase choices. To motivate them, you can tell them to think of the possibilities or to find an alternative to what we do now.

You can motivate Procedures people by telling them that this is the *right way* to do something. They feel comfortable doing the same thing over and over. Let them know how important the finished result is.

For employees who have both Options and Procedures Patterns when at work, give them opportunities to both follow and develop or improve the procedures. You can use the Influencing Language for both Patterns. "You will get to develop a better way to do this. You can make sure it is right (Internal and Procedures), and then you can use it from now on." For someone who has an External Pattern, you could substitute: "Check with me to make sure it is right...."

Reorganizations and Employee Engagement

Many organizations reorganize often, looking for ways to have more engaged employees and increase creativity and innovation. They are aiming to get employees into new ways of thinking in order to respond to constantly changing environments. Great idea! When you look inside these programs for Patterns, what are they designed to create? Often they give the message that it's better to have an Options Pattern. You ought to be able to turn on a dime, totally change what you are doing, develop alternatives, and create new systems to anticipate and respond to changes.

What would actually happen in the corporate world, the helping professions, the education system, or any other sector, if no one finished or completed procedures? Imagine that for a moment. And of course, many of the purely Procedure-type positions have been automated or done with artificial intelligence.

I have found many biases against the idea of the Procedures Pattern. People resist being called "Procedural." I believe it is important to honor Procedures people for what they contribute, instead of pointing out to them how rigid this makes them. They get things done. We need Options people to think of new choices and alternatives, and we need Procedures people to see that they get implemented. Building a high-performance team depends on how well you use the different strengths in the team to accomplish what needs to be done.

Learning New Skills (or ...Why Some of Us Can't Understand Computer Nerds)

Learning is a specific Context. People have different learning styles; knowing your Profile in that Context (or that of the people you are teaching) is useful for accelerating the speed at which new material can be integrated.

When I got my very first computer, I had quite a few different software packages with it. The person from whom I bought it was an experienced computer user, and he spent a lot of time teaching me. He would say, "I'd like you to *understand why* it's set up this way." I would say: "No, I don't want to understand why it's set up this way. Tell me *how* to turn it on." "Well," he would continue, "You need to *understand a few of the concepts* behind this particular program." "No I don't. I want to know *how you make* and *print* a document." Or he would say, in response to a how-to question: "There are *several ways* you can do this." And I would answer, feeling my blood pressure rise: "I don't want to know several ways. Just tell me *one way. The right way!*"

I needed the procedure to follow. It was only after I had mastered some needed procedures that I was the least bit interested in why things were set up the way they were. In that circumstance he could have matched my style by telling me: "I'm going to show you the *basic procedure* for making and printing a document. Once you've got that down, I'll explain *how it* works so that you can master the other things you'll need to do. Then *you will be able* to figure it out for yourself." An Options person would be motivated by all the possibilities the software has to offer. However, I suspect that many computer neophytes, and others learning new skills, simply want the procedure to follow.

When faced with a new app or piece of technology, some people only learn what they need to know and get easily frustrated, while others play with it until they discover all the ways to use it (Options). When I realized the second strategy is more fun and more efficient for mastering new technologies, it changed my approach. I still get frustrated though, when there isn't a clear process to follow and too many choices to make.

This is still an issue today, also in many learning programs and seminars, where experts give beginners so many Options the learners get overwhelmed. On the other hand, I remember attending a seminar on creativity where the facilitator gave us the Procedure for being creative.

Delegation and Working with Groups

When a group of people is learning something new, they need a step by step Procedure so they can follow a process to master a skill. Don't give them options, choices or alternatives at the beginning. Similarly, if you are giving instructions to a group to follow, or delegating, if you give them options, they may become paralyzed and not know what to do. If you give them a clear step by step process when giving instructions to a group, they will more easily get into action. I was giving an introductory workshop on the LAB Profile® at a conference in Montreal and we did not finish all the Patterns we wanted to do in the allotted time. The group seemed frustrated and wanted to continue. I said, "Okay, well there are some options. We could break for lunch now and come back early and do the last Pattern, or we could keep going now and have lunch later, or we could just forget it. What would you prefer?" Everybody went um, ah, um. No answer.

I said "I have a suggestion. Let's break for lunch now. Those of you who want to, can come back a half an hour early and meet in this room and we'll do it." They said great, and everyone left for lunch.

When explaining an exercise or assigning a task to a group, you need to give them explicitly the step-by-step procedure.

Coaching

When we are coaching people, we often try to help them have more choice about what they do. If your client needs a Procedure and you give them too many choices, you may inadvertently put them into sensory overload. Not deprivation, overload. Too much choice. A step by step process is more helpful for them.

Options coaching clients love to explore the alternatives but may be hesitant to commit to a course of action. One way to motivate them to do this is, to remind them of their Criteria and demonstrate that choosing and following through enables them to have all these Criteria.

(Criteria as Options) *"Once you choose an alternative and put it into place, you'll have many more possibilities to spend time with your family, or explore new hobbies etc."* (Options and Toward)

"Once you choose an alternative and put it into place, you won't have to worry about all the things that prevent you from spending time with your family or exploring new hobbies." (Options and Away From)

Summary

Reason

Question: ***Why did you choose your current work (or house, etc.)?***

Options: Compelled to develop and create systems and procedures. Have difficulty following set procedures.

Procedures: Prefer to follow tried-and-true set ways. Get stumped when they have no procedures to follow.

Distribution at Work:

     40% Mainly Options

     20% Equally Options and Procedure

     40% Mainly Procedures
     (in the work Context, from Rodger Bailey)

Influencing Language:

Options: opportunities; variety; unlimited possibilities; lots of choices; options; break the rules just for them

Procedures: the right way; how to; tried and true; speak in procedures: first . . . then . . . lastly

---

[1] Here's my article on how unethical self-help gurus sell failure to their clients and an alternative for promoting personal development programs ethically: bit.ly/SexDietsAndSuccess

[2] Pernice, Karen; F-Shaped Pattern of Reading on the Web: Misunderstood, But Still Relevant (Even on Mobile); bit.ly/FShapedPattern; 2017 11 12

[3] bit.ly/SeinfeldScripts

Chapter 8
Decision Factors: To Change or Not to Change

How does a person react to change and what frequency of change is needed? Does the motivation come from a search for "difference" or "sameness"?

The Decision Factors category is about your internal time clock and how often the *bell rings* for change. Are you motivated by evolution, revolution, both, or stability? There are four Patterns:

Sameness

People with a Sameness Pattern want their situation in a given Context to stay the same. They do not like change and may refuse to adapt. They may accept a major change once every ten years, but they will provoke change only once every fifteen to twenty-five years.

Sameness with Exception

Sameness with Exception people like a given Context to stay mainly the same but progress. They will accept change if the change is not too drastic. They prefer their situations to evolve slowly over time. They tend to resist major changes except when they are perceived to be progressive or gradual. They need major change once every five to seven years. This is by far the largest category in the work Context, and probably in many other Contexts as well.

Difference

People with a Difference Pattern love change; they thrive on it and want it to be constant and major. They will resist static or stable situations. They need drastic change about every one to two years, and if they do not get it, they may leave. They like change to be revolutionary, dramatically different.

Sameness with Exception and Difference
(the Double Pattern)

People who have both Patterns like change and revolutionary shifts, as well as situations where things are evolving. They are happy with both revolution and evolution. They need major change every three to four years, on average.

Distribution %	
(in the work Context, from Rodger Bailey)	
Sameness	5%
Sameness with Exception	65%
Difference	20%
Sameness with Exception and Difference	10%

Identification

Question:
WHAT IS THE RELATIONSHIP BETWEEN YOUR WORK THIS YEAR AND LAST YEAR?
(vacation, this home and the last one, etc.)

Or

WHAT IS THE RELATIONSHIP BETWEEN THIS JOB AND YOUR LAST ONE?

The question asks: "What is the relationship between . . .?" In this situation, the word *relationship* implies sameness, similarity, or some kind of link. People will either naturally understand the word and tell you how it is the same or similar, or alternatively they will not know what you mean, or reinterpret it to mean how is it *different*.

Sameness

- how they are the same, identical
- what they have in common
- how it has not changed

Sameness with Exception

- how it has evolved over time
- it is the same except more; less; better; worse; improving; etc. (comparisons on a sliding scale)
- focus on the trip more than arriving at the destination

Difference

- may not understand the word *relationship*
- will describe how it is completely different
- new, different, changed, transformed, revolutionary
- language points to an immediate switch
- focus on the destination, ignore the trip

Difference and Sameness with Exception

- use *both* Difference and Sameness with Exception responses

Examples

Sameness:	*"It is exactly the same. I'm still crunching numbers."*
Sameness with Exception:	*"It's the same but I have more responsibility and less time."*
Difference:	*"It's totally different. Now I do outside sales."*

Difference and Sameness with Exception:	*"There have been big changes this year and my performance has improved greatly."*

To test your diagnosis in the work Context, ask the person how often they changed what they were doing on the job. They may have had the same job title, but what we are looking for is *how often* they changed responsibilities. Their answers will usually match the change clocks for their Pattern. In other Contexts, you could check by asking how often they have moved homes, what they do for a vacation each year, whether they go to the same summer home each time or do different things, and so on.

Be especially clear in identifying the Context when you ask this question, because people's Patterns often change depending upon what they are talking about. I profiled a man in several Contexts. Regarding work, he said, "Well it's *basically the same*: I have *more* responsibility, I've got *more* people to supervise, and *more* accounts." Sameness with Exception. Then I said, "OK, what's the relationship between the last holiday you took and the holiday before that?" He said "Relationship! What do you mean by relationship?" Two minutes after answering the first *relationship* question, he was suddenly unable to understand the word *relationship*, simply because we had switched Contexts.

Influencing Language

Here are some totally new ways to improve communication and maintain rapport.

Sameness:

- same as; in common; as you always do; like before; unchanged; as you already know; maintaining; totally the same; exactly as before; identical

Sameness with Exception:

- more; better; less; the same except; advanced; upgrade; progression; gradual improvement; similar but even better; moving up; growth; improvement

Difference:

- new; totally different; unlike anything else; unique; one of a kind; completely changed; unrecognizable; shift; switch; a complete turnaround; brand new; unheard of; the only one

Sameness with Exception & Difference:

- better and new; a totally different approach to improve; gradually making changes; shift to a more relaxed state; it's completely new and so much better than before

Making Your Change Pattern Work for You

Since people may have different Patterns from Context to Context, it is important not to generalize about someone. A friend of mine, while he makes frequent changes in his work, always wants to go to the same restaurant to order the same thing. People who have a Difference Pattern in the Context of reading may have four or five books on the go at any time. Some people have cottages where they spend their vacation every year; others would not consider going to the same place twice.

When I looked at my own history, I discovered that in the past I had a habit of moving residences about every eighteen months. I subsequently also discovered that if you do that, banks and other financial institutions will think you are a flake and be hesitant to give you a mortgage. Guess what Pattern they have?

Knowing your own Pattern can help you understand and predict what is happening in your life. When my change bell rang one fall, suddenly I started to notice all the things that were wrong with the place I was living. I was itching to move. I told myself that since I was working on a number of business projects and I needed cooperation from the bank, I would need them to perceive me as a steady, *normal* type. So, I had my living room painted, bought some new furniture, moved around the old stuff, and made the whole place *feel different*. After I received the financial backing I needed, I cracked and bought a new place. I managed to stay in that last home for 16 years, by making lots of changes & renovating. Plus, I travel a lot, so in *theory* I didn't really live there for the whole 16 years.

I have a friend who has a combination of high Options and high Difference Patterns in the Contexts of work and study. She had started and had not completed three different master's programs at three universities in different cities. She adopted three children from different backgrounds. After her first undergraduate degree, she went back to school and became a nurse. Every so often she would go back to hospital work because she really liked to take care of people. She would usually stay for a bit, get frustrated by the procedures, and leave. Her change Pattern is an average of one to two years, and for some Contexts it is as short as six months.

As a student, it was very difficult for her, because if she read a book once, she could not stand the idea of reading it again. She wanted to read something different. She did a LAB Profile® with me and decided, "I'm doing this master's program and I am finishing it." (She also has an Internal Pattern.) This was the third attempt, and she managed to build in many different projects towards her Master's degree. For her thesis, she conducted a research project in Asia to complete her degree, while her husband was there on sabbatical. She found a way to *build her need for Difference into her activities*. She has since completed her Ph.D. and changed jobs twice in 3 years.

"Hamster migration: every seven years."

Her husband has a Sameness with Exception Pattern in several Contexts. He is motivated by evolution and progression, while she prefers to have things changing all the time. How can this work in a marriage? Since none of us is actually living in Reality, maybe it doesn't matter what your spouse's Patterns may be as long as he *thinks it is getting better* and she thinks it is totally different? And so long as he does not bang his shins on the furniture when she moves it around.

For couples with different Patterns, I would suggest that you understand your own need for change, as well as your spouse's, and make sure you each feel your needs are being met.

Revolutions and Evolutions: Recruitment

There are several things to think about when doing a Job Profile in preparation for recruiting someone. Does the job require a great number of different tasks? How long does each task remain the same? Does the successful fulfillment of the objectives demand creating a revolution (Difference), building upon what is already there (Sameness with Exception), or maintaining the status quo (Sameness)? How much of each?

You can predict that people with a high Difference Pattern are likely to create revolutions around them, especially if they also have Proactive and Options Patterns. In fact, someone with a combination of Options and Difference can be a compulsive change-artist. I wanted to call on a client with this Pattern after not seeing him for two years. I tried the company where he had been working. He had, of course, left and gone somewhere else. Thank goodness for social media which makes it easier to find people who move around a lot.

I profiled a man and told him about his Difference Pattern and what that meant for his career. He retorted that he had been a high school teacher and principal for thirty years. I asked him in how many schools had he worked. He had been in *seventeen different schools*. Knowing this Pattern will allow you to predict someone's past, which is a great party trick to have up your sleeve.

Since the majority of people (65%) in the work Context have a Sameness with Exception Pattern, you will be more likely to find those candidates. Many jobs need someone who can build and progress. A fewer number of positions actually require revolutionaries.

To attract candidates with a Sameness Pattern, talk about maintaining, security, stability etc. To attract someone with a Sameness with Exception preference, mention developing, improving, growing, enhancing. For a position with many different, short projects, use language such as new, different, short projects, unique working situation.

Some professions naturally attract people with certain preferences. Start-ups attract people who like to be doing something new and different. Teaching in the public school system (state schools in the UK) tends to attract those who prefer Sameness in their work. They spend about 12 years in the school system, then go to university (another kind of school) and then back into the school system. There are exceptions to this though, one reason why it can be challenging to introduce changes to the curriculum, testing procedures, teacher evaluation procedures, etc.

People Management

Employees with a Sameness Pattern do not respond well to change. They are well-suited to tasks that do not change, such as many administrative or production tasks. Managers with this Pattern strive to keep standards up and want to provide continuity. This attribute is also appropriate for maintaining a long-term rapport with clients. To motivate Sameness employees, talk about what this task has in common with what they already know.

Sameness with Exception employees will accept change once a year as long as it is not too drastic. They will feel stressed if placed in high-change environments. It is more motivating when they perceive a *progression* in their work. To get them interested in a task, tell them how it will make things better or will build on what they are already doing.

To capture the interest of someone with a Difference Pattern, give them lots of different things to work on. Get them to change things (if they are also Proactive) or create changes for them to respond to (if they are Reactive). For some companies, this happens frequently anyway.

Difference people need to hear how what they are doing is totally different. Each time I update (Sameness with Exception) or put out a new version (Difference) of this book, many people ask me what is new about it. That is a hint as to what they really want to find!

Taking the Pain Out of Organizational Change

Once upon a time, (and very long ago), large companies had work groups that were called typing pools. Many of the people who worked in typing pools stayed there long term, sometimes fifteen, twenty or twenty-five years, typing documents all day long. Then a miracle occurred. Word processors were invented. The agents of change were very excited by all the *different possibilities* these wonderful new machines could offer. They heralded the arrival of the miraculous machines by announcing to the people working in the typing pools: "We have bought some *totally new machines* which are going to *revolutionize* how you do your work." Many people resigned. Countless more panicked and said "I'm too old to learn this. I can't do this. I am a failure." It wasn't long before typing pools completely disappeared from the workplace.

The moral of the story has little to do with the revolutionary machines. If you had been typing for over fifteen years, would you really be interested in revolution? The **language** of change created much unnecessary stress and resistance in the workplace.

Forget the word *new*. Forget the word *revolution*. A more appropriate language for populations with Sameness and Procedures Patterns would be: "We have bought some machines which are *exactly like* a typewriter. They have the *same* keyboard. They have a *few* extra keys which allow you to go *faster*, work *better*, correct mistakes *easier*, but *essentially, they're the same*. And we'll *teach you the procedure* for using them."

Organizations began to notice that large numbers of their workforce balked at frequent changes. Many introduced "Continuous Improvement" programs. They were not called "Dramatic Difference" programs.

But this lesson needs to be relearned over and over. Many firms seem to be constantly re-organizing, re-engineering, shifting technologies and introducing new software, without taking into account the Patterns of their employees. It is important to prepare the groundwork for major technological and organizational changes by knowing your workforce and planning your announcements and implementation. Matching the language you use with the people affected, can *dramatically improve* the chances of making the change stick. Stress and resistance are not a necessary outcome of change programs.

I have noticed that those responsible for introducing or implementing change in organizations frequently have a high personal need for change. They are often mismatched with their environment, and so, *do not speak the same language* as the people they wish to influence.

How to De-stress a Workforce Overwhelmed With Too Many Changes

To reduce stress-related illnesses and engage employees in high-change, high-stress environments, it is important to send out and implement strategies using Procedures and Sameness influencing language. This gives people a sense of familiarity and knowing what is expected of them. "*As we are introducing this process* (avoid saying "new"), *you will notice that you will see that we are maintaining the current priorities that you know and have always been doing* (Sameness), *and that as we take each step, one at a time* (Procedures), *we will teach you the procedure to use* (Procedures), *so that it will be easier to keep everything running smoothly.* (Mainly Sameness and Procedures)" Sameness and Procedures language and implementation can really help de-stress a workforce that is overwhelmed.

Why New Coke Didn't Make It

Once again, there is no substitute for good market research. Here's an old but very telling marketing fiasco. Do you remember *New Coke*; the new formula for the much-loved soft drink that was introduced for a very short time between April and July 1985? Apparently, when they tested the taste of New Coke, the results were conclusive: New Coke tasted better than the old Coke. However, they could not have tested the *name*. Here is how the Coca-Cola Company describes what went wrong: "The fabled secret formula for Coca-Cola was changed, adopting a formula preferred in taste tests of nearly 200,000 consumers. What these tests didn't show, of course, was the bond consumers felt with their Coca-Cola: something they didn't want anyone, including The Coca-Cola Company, tampering with."[1]

Let's consider the distribution of the Patterns in this category. Only a maximum of 30 percent of the population *in the work Context* is interested in *new*, according to Rodger Bailey's work. But this was the soft drink Context. How many people do you think would want to drink something new in soft drinks, as opposed to what they know, trust, and buy consistently? Apparently, not very many. Coca Cola responded and returned old Coke to the market. They called it Coke Classic, which is Sameness language. And of course, when they introduce new products such as Coke Zero (diet Coke for men), etc., there is no mention of anything new.

Labatt Blue, a Canadian beer, apparently understood the Pattern. They produced a billboard campaign with the slogan: "Tired of the same, old thing? Neither are we." I suspect that consumers of the large, well-known brands of beer have a Sameness Pattern, while folks who prefer the micro-breweries have a frequent hankering for new tastes.

In the US, Marshall's and in Canada, Winners, attracts women to their clothing and home accessories stores with Difference slogans; "*A different kind of store.*" or "*At Marshalls there's always a new deal to find and love.*"

When your market has mainly a Sameness Pattern, you need to demonstrate how the product will give them something they know. It must look, sound, and feel like old *reliable*. "You can always count on us" or "We'll always be there." This can be a creative challenge for new products and services. How about: "Remember when you . . .? It's back, just the same, and better than ever before."

Sameness with Exception customers want improvements. Show them how your product or service is better than the competition or what they had before, how it will make their lives easier (Toward), with fewer hassles (Away From). End users may prefer to buy *upgrades* rather than different software packages.

Difference people want something totally new and different from everyone else: "*You'll be the only one in your neighborhood*" (External) or "*You can see for yourself how unique this is*" (Internal).

If you want to attract everyone, you will need an updated version of *new* and *improved*, since that slogan is now old hat.

Sales and Marketing

In sales and marketing, there are two Contexts which are important. First, getting your potential customers' attention, and second getting them started on the buying process. To get just about anyone's attention online, on the street, in a shopping center etc., you need to stand out from the crowd. That means being Different somehow. Online advertising goes to extreme lengths to grab attention with colors, movements, provocative headlines. This Difference Pattern is essential. But once you have gotten attention, then match the Decision Factors Pattern of your audience.

With regards to banking, many customers want a feeling of Sameness with regards to their account managers, how to use the website, forms and procedures to follow etc., even if they are looking for better service or products.

In the consulting and training field, we often encounter clients who have the "shiny new object" syndrome. They are totally enthusiastic about a new tool, a new consultant, a new methodology and promise to have the whole organization learn and implement the system. Consultants often find that once the first round is done, their clients stop responding to them because the clients are off working with the next shiny new object to come their way. The solution? Get a commitment (and payment!) for a project that will actually make a positive difference to the people and organization, (i.e. not a small pilot project, but something significant) and make sure that you charge what it's worth.

Purchasers and Users of Software

Software purchasing and using presents an interesting Context. From my work with some major software companies, my clients and I happened on an interesting conflict of Patterns. With regards to the corporate purchasers of software, we have noticed that they seem to have an Options and Difference combination. They often want upgrades and new software to look and be totally different, with many more possible applications, even if they do not need them right away. Contrast this with the poor end-user, who suffers through each new installation, having to learn everything all over again. End-users tend to have a Sameness and Procedures combination. (As I do when it comes to software. I hate it when my usual software changes because I'm afraid I'll have to spend hours and hours learning how to use it - *again!*)

For my software clients, we have developed marketing materials and sales processes to reflect the Patterns of the purchasers as they go through the phases of the buying process, as well as the end-users. Part of the process includes educating the purchasers on how to get more enthusiasm from the end-users, and less resistance to new upgrades.

Summary

Decision Factors

Question: *What is the relationship between (your work this year and last year)?*

Sameness: They like things to stay the same. They will provoke change only every 15 to 25 years.

Sameness with Exception:
They prefer situations to evolve over time. They want major change about every 5 to 7 years.

Difference: They want change to be constant and drastic. They will initiate change every 1 to 2 years.

Sameness with Exception and Difference: They like both evolution and revolution. Major change averages every 3 to 4 years.

Summary

Distribution at Work:

       5% Sameness

       65% Sameness with Exception

       20% Difference

       10% Sameness with Exception and Difference
       (in the work Context, from Rodger Bailey)

Influencing Language:

Sameness:	the same as; as you already know; like before; identical
Sameness with Exception:	more; better; less; the same except; evolving; progress; gradual improvement; upgrade
Difference:	new; totally different; completely changed; switch; shift; unique; one of a kind; brand new
Sameness with Exception and Difference:	better and new; a totally different approach to improve; gradually making changes; shift to a more relaxed state; it's completely new and so much better than before

---

[1] quoted from bit.ly/TheRealStoryOfNewCoke

Chapter 9
Using the Profiling Worksheet: Motivation Patterns

On the following page is the Motivation Patterns Worksheet to help you master both asking the LAB Profile® questions and recognizing the patterns of the person you are interviewing. A similar worksheet can be found at the end of the Productivity Patterns section. The full profiling sheet (for both the Motivation and Productivity Patterns) is included near the end of the book.

On the left side of the page are the questions to ask. I have emphasized in **bold** the basic questions, while the Context is in *script*. Remember that for LEVEL (Proactive and Reactive), there are no questions to ask. You simply listen for the patterns while the person is talking.

On the right side of the chart are the patterns and a summary of each of the clues for recognizing the patterns.

When I am interviewing someone, I usually start off by putting one check mark each on Proactive and Reactive, since 60 to 65 percent of the population is right in the middle. Subsequently during the interview, if they use mostly one pattern or the other, I add check marks in the appropriate place.

With regards to Decision Factors, if someone has the Sameness with Exception and Difference pattern, I usually put check marks for each example of Sameness with Exception in that place and the same for Difference, so that I can get a sense of how much of each pattern a person has.

I will often write down the expressions that indicate a particular pattern, so that I can verify them when I review the results with the person.

Giving Feedback

When sharing their results of the LAB Profile® with someone, avoid using jargon such as *Toward* or Away From. It will be more meaningful if you simply describe the behaviors of each pattern. For example: "You

149

prefer to solve problems and do troubleshooting rather than working toward goals. What triggers you into action is when there is a problem to be solved or prevented."

I have included a pattern summary in the Appendix to help you use layperson's terminology when speaking to the uninitiated.

The LAB Profile® Worksheet: Motivation Patterns

Name: _____   Company: _____

Profiler: _____   Position: _____

Date: _____   Context: _____

Questions	Categories	Patterns: Indicators
(no question for Level)	**LEVEL** _____ _____	**Proactive:** *action, do it, short, crisp sentences* **Reactive:** *try, think about it, could, wait*
What do you want in your (work)**?**	**CRITERIA**	
Why is that (criteria) important? (ask up to 3 times)	**DIRECTION** _____ _____	**Toward:** *attain, gain, achieve, get, include* **Away From:** *avoid, exclude, recognize problems*
How do you know you have done a good job at ... ?	**SOURCE** _____ _____	**Internal:** *knows within self* **External:** *told by others, facts and figures*
Why did you choose (your current work)**?**	**REASON** _____ _____	**Options**: *criteria, choice, possibilities, variety* **Procedures:** *story, how, necessity, didn't choose*
What is the relationship between (your work this year and last year)**?**	**DECISION FACTORS** _____ _____ _____ _____	**Sameness:** *same, no change* **Sameness with Exception:** *more/ better, comparisons* **Difference:** *change, new, unique* **Sameness with Exception & Difference:** *new and comparisons*

Part 3:
Productivity Patterns

Chapter 10
Productivity Patterns

Questions	Categories	Patterns: Indicators
(no questions for Scope and Attention Direction)	**SCOPE** _____ _____	**Specific:** *details, sequences, exactly* **General:** *overview, big picture, random order*
	ATTENTION DIRECTION _____ _____	**Self:** *short monotone responses* **Other:** *animated, expressive, automatic responses*
Tell me about a (work situation) that gave you trouble.	**STRESS RESPONSE** _____ _____ _____	**Feeling:** *goes in and stays in feelings* **Choice:** *goes in and out of feelings* **Thinking:** *doesn't go into feelings*
Tell me about a (work situation) that was (Criteria). **(wait for answer)** **What did you like about it?**	**STYLE** _____ _____ _____ **ORGANIZATION** _____ _____	**Independent:** *alone, I, sole responsibility* **Proximity:** *in control, others around* **Cooperative:** *we, team, share responsibility* **Person:** *people, feelings, reactions* **Thing:** *tools, tasks, ideas*
What is a good way for you to increase your success at (your work)? **What is a good way for someone else to increase their success at (their work)?**	**RULE STRUCTURE** _____ _____ _____ _____	**My/My:** *My rules for me/My rules for you* **My/. (period):** *My rules for me/ Who cares?* **No/My:** *No rules for me/My rules for you* **My/Your:** *My rules for me/Your rules for you*
How do you know that someone else (an equal of yours) is good at their (work)? **How many times do you have to (see, hear, read, do) that to be convinced they are good?**	**CONVINCER** _____ _____ _____ _____	See ____ **# of Examples:** *give number* Hear ____ **Automatic:** *benefit of the doubt* Read ____ **Consistent:** *not completely convinced* Do ____ **Period of Time:** *give time period*

Productivity Patterns

The next eight categories of the LAB Profile® will tell you how people deal with information, what type of tasks and environment they need to be most productive in a given Context, and how they get convinced about something.

These categories will help you learn how to analyze people, in terms of how they are most productive and what they need.

At the end of this section, is another Summary Profiling Worksheet to help you master asking the Productivity Patterns questions, identifying and working with the Patterns.

Chapter 11
Scope: The Forest and the Trees

> *What size pieces of information does a person handle best? The big picture or specific details?*

Using the Scope category, you can determine whether someone can handle overviews and grand designs, or whether the details make more sense. There are two Patterns in this category:

Specific

People who have a Specific Pattern in a Context handle small pieces of information well. At the extreme, they cannot perceive or create an overview. They treat information in linear *sequences*, step by step, in all its detail. A Specific person perceives the trees, branches, and twigs, rather than the forest. They may have difficulty prioritizing as a result. If they are interrupted in the middle of a sequence, they tend to either start over at the beginning or resume the telling from the point at which they were interrupted. Specific people work well where details must be attended to, in tasks such as organizing events or handling logistics.

General

People with a General Pattern in any given Context prefer to work on the overview, or at the conceptual level, though they can concentrate on details for finite periods of time. Because they see the big picture all at once, they may present ideas in a random order without stating the link between one thought and another. They concentrate on the forest; having to deal with the trees for long periods of time irritates them.

Distribution %
(in the work Context, from Rodger Bailey)

Mainly Specific	15%
Equally Specific & General	25%
Mainly General	60%

Identification

While there are no specific questions for this category, you can recognize the Patterns within virtually each sentence spoken.

Hint: One simple way you can know for sure is to time your LAB Profile® interview. On average, a full interview takes about 5 to 8 minutes to complete, not including giving the person your feedback. With a Specific person, the interview will be much longer.

There are no questions for this category.

Here's how to recognize these Patterns in conversation:

Specific

- speak in sequences, step-by-step
- *lots* of modifiers, adverbs, adjectives
- proper nouns for people, places, and things
- if they lose the sequence, they may start over again or continue from where they left off
- only seem to be aware of the step before and after the one they are on; not much perception of the overview

General

- may present things in random order

- overview, summaries
- concepts, abstracts
- simple sentences, few modifiers or details
- few words

Examples

Specific:	*"Yesterday at 10 A.M. George and I met with Mr. Vivaldi, our big client from Rome, who spoke about renewing our shipping contract for the third year in a row. He now wants the price of the cardboard packaging to be included with the total price next year."*
Mainly Specific:	*"Yesterday at 10 A.M. George and I met with Mr. Vivaldi, our client from Rome, to discuss renewing our shipping contract. He wants to include the packaging in the total deal."*
Equally Specific and General:	*"Yesterday, Mr. Vivaldi told George and me that he wants to include the cardboard packaging in the price next year."*
Mainly General:	*"Next year Mr. Vivaldi wants to renegotiate our contract."*
General:	*"Rome wants to renegotiate."*

Combinations

I am often asked, when someone is answering the Reason question from the Motivation Patterns, how one would know if they were Specific or Procedures, if they are telling a story. The Reason question is: "Why did you choose your current work?" To distinguish between a Procedure Pattern and a sequence, which is Specific, you will need to pay attention to the amount of detail given.

Here are some examples. The first one is a response from a Procedures person who has a mainly General Pattern in this Context. "I didn't really choose this kind of work. I was working in another company and they laid off a lot of people. I didn't have a job when this one came up. I applied and got it." Procedures, mainly General.

Here is an example of Procedures with Mainly Specific. "I was working for the Whoofed Cookies Beverage Company as a field engineer from 2001 to 2010. Then the company went into a period of financial difficulties, so in order to stop themselves from going under, they had to let 250 people go. They closed my department and then I spent eight and a half months unemployed. I had made thirty applications in each of three geographical areas. Then Stephanie Slobdonovich from the Miracle Cure Cleaning Company called me; I had an interview the following day at 10 A.M. and was hired." (Lots of detail but no Criteria for why the job was chosen.)

Here is what Specific and Options would sound like. "It was exactly the kind of thing I was looking for. I get to work with people. Different kinds of people. I get to work with tall people, short people, fat people, thin people. People with curly hair and people with thin hair and people with no hair on the top of their heads ...etc." This is not a story; it is all Criteria (therefore Options), and described in what I would call, excruciating detail. (If I have characterized that example as *excruciating*, what does that tell you about my own Pattern?)

Here's another general hint:

As you become increasingly familiar with recognizing the Patterns in everyday conversation, you will find yourself noticing and hearing many Patterns at once, sometimes within a single sentence.

Influencing Language

Generally speaking, it is important to match a person's Pattern in exactly the way they talk to you when in conversation.

Specific

- exactly; precisely; specifically; details; use sequences and lots of qualifiers

General

- the big picture; the main idea; essentially; the important thing is; in general; concepts

When Bad Communication Happens to Good People

When a person with a General Pattern is communicating, negotiating, or problem-solving with a Specific person, you may notice many misunderstandings. The person in a Specific mode may be concentrating on each separate example of a problem, for example, and listing what happened in chronological order, while the General person just wants to get to the point. There is a huge difference in the size of pieces of information each is treating; one is dealing with each item in great detail, while the other is trying to get at the big picture.

Several things can happen:

1. While the General person will be able to follow the specifics for a while, he will quickly get bored or feel drowned in detail and want to quit, leave or yell, depending on his preferences.
2. The Specific person will insist on giving ever more details of information in an attempt to make things precise for the other person and may not understand the attempts of the General person to summarize the situation.
3. The General person may speak in such vague terms that she does not give enough information for others to understand what she is actually talking about. She may then lose credibility with the Specific person, who may suspect her of bad intentions.

So, what is the cure? There are several options. (Wouldn't you know it?) First, you will need to realize that this situation may take some time to resolve, because of one party's need for detail. This can be an advantage where the specifics of a contractual agreement need to be sorted out properly, and will save time later, as they will not be overlooked. (You would have to have somewhat of a General and a Toward Pattern to *overlook* something.)

You could ask a person who has both Specific and General to mediate between the two, essentially *translating* back and forth. If you are mediating, you will need to reassure both parties that their respective approaches are important and relevant, however different they may be.

For the Specific person, you will need to play back their issues and Criteria, and then describe the sequence by which you will proceed, which includes translating items into General terms. For the General person, give them the big picture. "The main thing is making sure you both can understand each other; I'll help by facilitating that process."

Other alternatives include getting the specific person to make a list of the important issues on one page, in order to facilitate the General person's understanding. To help a General person be clearer to a Specific person, ask them sensory-specific questions such as "How would you know when it's right?" or "Can you give me a tangible example?" or "What specifically would have to happen?"

To capitalize on the strengths of each one, have the Specific person check the details of any agreement (especially if they are also Away From, so they can pick out errors and omissions). The General person will be able to determine whether the process is generally on track to achieving an agreement.

The key is making sure that each understand how they themselves and the other person are functioning. They can use these complementary differences to mutual benefit, provided they accept them and adjust the process, as mentioned above, to take into account each person's needs and strengths.

When someone is highly Specific, how can you interact with them to help speed them through to the end of their sequence? One of the things you can do is ask them what happens at the end. This may be perceived as a sort of violation, but at least it is not an interruption.

Patent and other Lawyers

When my software company, weongozi, applied for patents for our Libretta® software, we engaged a great lawyer. He had a mixture of Specific and General Patterns, which was perfect for the complicated task at hand, as well as mainly Procedures with a good dose of Options. He was able to zoom out and determine the overall strategy as well as attend to the details in each claim. Our meetings were lengthy as he would go step by step through each item with us. I had a hard time listening to all the detail as it went way over my attention threshold, but it was important, so I made myself do it.

Why Do All the Songs I Know End in La, La, La?

Here is an analogy to illustrate how someone with a Specific Pattern processes information. When people want to remember the words to a song, they usually start singing the song from the beginning, because the words are stored in their brain sequentially. If you interrupt them, they lose their train of thought, and will have to go back to the beginning to pick it up again. Simply talking and responding will not make them go back; it is *being interrupted* that makes them start over. Asking them "then what happened?" may help them to get to the next item. By doing that, you are respecting the sequence and moving them on to the next step. The word "then" presupposes that something happened before, and something happened after. Another suggestion, if they do not have an off-the-scale Specific Pattern, is to ask them to fast-forward, almost as if they had recorded their thoughts on tape.

Recruitment

Does a job require close attention to specific, sequential details for extended periods of time, or is detailed work of this kind only a small part of the overall responsibilities? Bookkeeping requires someone who can concentrate on specifics for long stretches at a time; deciding financial strategies is much more an overview kind of task. People and project management tend to be mainly General functions.

Many positions in manufacturing are Specific in nature, such as assembly-line work. General people would make many mistakes through inattention to detail in this kind of work. Quality control necessitates a Mainly Specific Pattern as well as Procedures and Away From.

The essential question to answer when profiling a position is, to *what extent is attention to detail necessary*? You would not want a pharmacist to generally get the dosage right when dispensing a prescription. But they have machines for that now!

Difficult Bosses

If a manager has equal preference for Specific and General, they can be very difficult to work for. This kind of manager not only knows *what* needs to be done, but tends to become very specific in telling employees exactly *how* to do it. Because they, as managers, have a handle on both aspects of the work, they often do not delegate, believing that it is easier to just do it themselves, or that they can do a *better* job themselves. When combined with a Cooperative Pattern (please refer to Working Style), they do not leave any territory for their employees to deal with on their own.

One of the advantages of having an equal aptitude for the detail and the big picture is that this person can handle complex tasks and analyses. They can attend to any level or the whole thing.

The Leadership Challenge

One of the most important things leaders do, including for you if you are a self-leader, is to decide which level of detail to focus on right now (today, next week, for the next month etc.) in order to meet goals. If a leader gets stuck in the detail when they shouldn't be, they can miss what is critical to getting the important jobs done and moving to the next level. I spoke with the principal of a new school, with ambitions to grow quickly and advised him to make sure that the tasks he was doing actually needed his skills; otherwise to delegate them.

Employees also need to make sure they are working on the right things: the right level of detail vs. the big picture. Gabriela's boss complained to me that he doesn't know what to do with her. While each of her tasks were being executed in an excellent manner, she was not helping the department as a whole. She was the sales manager and sales targets were not being reached.

Gabriela was unhappy because of the negative feedback from her boss. While he agreed that she completed her tasks in an excellent way, he kept repeating that she just doesn't get it. She was not working on the important things that will make the difference. She was focusing on the details; not zooming out to the big picture to identify where to put her effort and time. I also had an employee once who did this too. She didn't have a sense of which of her tasks should be the priority.

I recommend keeping your goals and targets in mind, as well as the issues and problems you need to address, and regularly check in to see if you are meeting them and if what you are doing (this month, this week, today, this hour etc.) will do the most to move you ahead. To do this, zoom out and imagine having an overview of your work, your role as if you were in a helicopter hovering high enough to see the past, the present and the future. This will enable to make better decisions about what to focus on.

Sales, Marketing, and Submitting Bids

Prospective purchasers who have a General Pattern will want broad descriptions that match their Criteria. As can be expected, Specific people want all the facts, listed in order. Print advertisements for technical products or software often contain a lot of specifics right in the ad. These ads could be accompanied by another one for General purchasers, with a compelling image and a few words.

Many companies, when submitting a bid, do not know whether the purchasing group consists of mainly Specific or General people or both. Why take a chance on either giving too much information or not enough? Bids *must* contain a lot of detail. The *Executive Overview* will be read by the Generals, with an occasional peek in the Index to find the specific bits they need to complete the picture. The Specifics and people with a mixed Pattern will need the full text to make their decision.

As is often the case when you are submitting a bid for work with a government agency or large corporation, you don't know the LAB Profile® Patterns of the people who will decide. That's why I developed the Proposal Template[1], which will help you with a structure that appeals to the main Patterns.

Life, the Universe, and Everything

In Douglas Adams' much-loved wacky science fiction novel, *The Hitchhikers Guide to the Galaxy*, the great question of life, the universe, and everything was asked of the biggest computer ever built. After centuries of computation, and much speculation on the part of Galaxy philosophers, the wonderful computer submitted its answer to the waiting populations. The answer was: 42. *Well, what can you expect when you address a General question to a Specific entity?*

Too General?

When you are planning, it is important to be able to move from mainly General into the specific steps. I spoke with a man in his late 30's who had been very unhappy in his work, to the point of becoming depressed and taking sick leave.

When we discussed what his goals were and how to go about reaching them, he found it difficult to move beyond generalities such as "I want to be happy in my work," or "I don't want to work by myself." He would also talk about needing to find the right job, since he had wasted so much time in the wrong profession. He was putting immense pressure on himself and became stuck as he was struggling to find the nature of the tasks and environment that he would find motivating.

He was in the following combination of Patterns: Reactive, General, Away From, Options, Stress Response Feelings. With this combination, he found himself going around in circles because, he was waiting and thinking about (Reactive), general ideas to consider (Options and General), noticing what was wrong with the ideas (Away From), and feeling very stressed (Feelings).

It can take time to help someone with this issue. If the person in question becomes sufficiently fed up with their current situation, this can help them become motivated to do whatever is needed. That is Away From motivation. We have all been motivated this way at some time – fed up enough to change the situation. "Are you sufficiently fed up to change the situation now, or would you prefer to wait until it gets worse?"

The Toward approach is to work with them to discover elements from different aspects of their life where they were very motivated and fulfilled that are relevant for their work. But to do this, first make sure they are in a resourceful, playful state and able to focus. Both approaches would need much more information than I can give here, but essentially the person needs to move from Reactive, General and Options, to more Proactive, Specific and Procedures. (For more on how to do this, please see the chapter on Conversational Coaching© with the LAB Profile®).

People who are very General may present things in random order (how's that for an oxymoron?), because they are looking at the big picture. They sometimes do not bother specifying the link between items, since they can see the whole relationship. As a result, some people will not know what they are talking about. Someone who is in very Specific mode tends to give more details than most people can tolerate. I love it when I give a keynote after the Chief Financial Officer has spoken to an audience, as many of them give too much detail for most audience members.

How can you know if you have been too General when you are communicating? Look at the people listening, do they look confused? Do they appear to want more from you? You can ask if they would like more information? About which part? It's useful to notice the response you are getting! If your tendency is to be very general, be prepared for questions and ask yourself what else they might like to know.

If you have the tendency to give too much information, the **Two Sentence Principle** might be for you. Speak two sentences and then observe or listen to your audience (whether one person or many). Do they want more? Do they look bored or want to leave?

Summary

Scope

Question:	There is no question for this category.
Specific:	Deals with details and sequences. Cannot see the overview.
General:	Prefers the overview, big picture. Can handle details for short periods.

Distribution at Work:

15% Mainly Specific

25% Equally Specific and General

60% Mainly General

(in the work Context, from Rodger Bailey)

Influencing Language:

Specific:	exactly; precisely; specifically; gives lots of details
General:	understand; think about; wait; analyze; consider; the big picture; essentially; the point is; in general

---

[1] The LAB Profile® Proposal Template (bit.ly/LabProfileProposalTemplate), which I developed as a generic template which can be adapted, to help people win bids, even when the LAB Profile® Patterns of the decision makers are unknown.

Chapter 12
Attention Direction: When Hinting Won't Work

Does a person pay attention to the nonverbal behavior of others, or to their own internal experience?

The Attention Direction category reveals whether and when a person perceives, and responds automatically to, the body language and voice tone of other people or not. There are two Patterns:

Self

People in a Self mode do not show many emotions, although they do have feelings. There is sometimes a time gap between when they receive a stimulus and when they respond to it. They respond based on what *they* consider to be appropriate. These people are convinced only by the *content* of what people say, rather than the accompanying tone, body language, or level of rapport. They have difficulty establishing rapport because they do not notice other people's body language, and therefore they miss many clues. People with this Pattern simply do not pick up hints.

They know how well the communication is going, based only on their own feelings. As a result, they tend not to be adept at interpersonal communication. At work, many Self people become technical experts in fields where communication skills are not essential.

Other

When in Other mode, people have Automatic reflex reactions to people's behaviors. They are animated (for their culture) and respond to others with facial expressions, body movements, and shifts in voice tone. They know how the communication is going based on the *responses* they *consciously or unconsciously* observe from the other person. These people are good at creating and maintaining rapport, provided they also have the other appropriate Patterns.

Distribution %	
(in the work Context, from Rodger Bailey)	
Self	7%
Other	93%

One in Fourteen People

According to Rodger Bailey's studies in the work Context, approximately one in every fourteen people you will meet will have a mainly Self Pattern, if these statistics also hold true for the general population. From my experience, I believe that you will find more who are somewhere in the middle between the two Patterns.

Identification

There is no verbal test for this Pattern, as it shows up in body language or the absence thereof. To test for Attention Direction, I usually drop a pencil accidentally on purpose. People with an Other Pattern will spontaneously bend down and pick it up, provided they have seen it or heard it drop. Self people will not pick it up. When speaking to someone on the phone, I will sneeze or have a coughing fit in the middle of a sentence. Does the person say their cultural equivalent of 'Gesundheit' or continue as if nothing had happened?

The following clues will also be apparent throughout the conversation:

Self

- Absence of culturally appropriate behavioral responses such as head nodding, saying "uh-huh," etc.
- reacts only to the content of what you say

- doesn't "pick up the pencil"
- **doesn't notice or respond to your voice tone**
- **little or no facial expression or voice variation**

Other

- responds to both content and nonverbal aspects of the communication
- will nod head, move body, say "uh-huh", etc., as a response
- animated (for their culture)

Let's say I were speaking to someone who had a Self Pattern and I, with my shoulders drooped, my bottom lip sticking out, and a whiny tone of voice, said: "I'm really happy to be here." She or he would think that I *was* really happy to be here. For this kind of person, unless you actually say: "I am annoyed and irritated" explicitly, they do not pick it up. Hinting will not work, nor will sarcasm as a method of communication.

While only 7 percent of the population at work are Self; probably many more are borderline; that is, they have some of the Self Pattern. You can recognize those people when you drop the pencil. They look at the pencil, they look at you, they look at the pencil, and then they may eventually decide to pick it up. It is not spontaneous, not a reflex. A reflex action is something outside of voluntary control. Sometimes you can also recognize these borderline people because, although they may exhibit little nonverbal behavior themselves (i.e., facial expressions, gestures, and voice variation), they may be able to notice and respond to the nonverbal behavior of others.

Examples

There are no word examples for this category. Only behavior observation will allow you to identify "Self" and "Other" Patterns.

While leading a communication and conflict resolution seminar at CERN (European Centre for Nuclear Research) in Geneva, there was an engineer who had a strong Self Pattern. Much to the annoyance of other participants, he kept stopping the discussion to ask for more explicit definitions of terms. He was filtering for the *content* of what was being said. I asked the participants to do an exercise in groups where they were going to practice some confrontation techniques. One person was supposed to observe and give feedback while they each took turns role-playing. When I went into his group, he was practically in tears because, although he had understood that there was something to be observed, he just could not see or hear anything. I had to do some on-the-spot counselling to help him focus on what *was* possible for him to do.

The definition of a good host or hostess is knowing what your guests want before they become aware of it themselves. For example, when you are in someone's home and cannot find your salad fork, without your having to ask, does one of your hosts notice your dilemma and go get you one? A Self person would not have noticed that you needed one. You would have had to ask for it.

Communication

Some people have asked me if someone is in a Self Pattern, would they feel uncomfortable in social situations. How does a person with a Self Pattern usually know if the communication is going well? They will focus on what is being said, and how they themselves feel about it, without noticing the nuances of nonverbal communication, and so may feel quite comfortable. Whereas, an Other person can evaluate the communication, by unconsciously picking up body-language cues and listening to tone of voice. What is more likely is that the Other people, in communication with a Self person, might feel more uncomfortable because of the absence of the nonverbal responses by which they normally get feedback.

When communicating with an Other person, the quality of the rapport that you established is just as important to them as the substance of what you are communicating. People in a Self mode tend not to notice the level of rapport you have with them, so you will need to be absolutely rigorous in the presentation of your arguments or explanations.

Recruitment

Self people do not usually succeed in work that requires the ability to create and maintain rapport. They are not suited for customer-service work or dealing with angry customers. Self people do well where technical expertise is required.

Other people, provided they also have the Choice Pattern from the Stress Response category, have the ability to empathize with others.

Once a Self, Always a Self?

Some people have this Pattern across several Contexts and others can be Self in only one Context and not in another. One student told me about her husband, who "never seemed to notice what was going on." She felt she always had to *tell* him. If you are concentrating so hard on what you are doing, such as texting, that you don't notice what is going on around you, then you are in Self mode.

It is more rigorous to test in different Contexts, rather than just assuming that someone who has a Self Pattern will always have that Pattern.

Influencing Language

Pay attention to both the level of rapport you have established and make sure that your propositions hold water logically. Remember Sheldon from the Big Bang Theory television program?

Self

- keep the communication focused on the content
- match their Criteria and Convincer Channel and Mode

Other

- they are influenced by the depth of rapport

There is no specific Influencing Language for Self people. Pay attention to your content because the relationship is not what they filter for. Be totally rigorous in what you say. Define your terms properly. If they also have an Away From Pattern, they will cut your argument to pieces, if it does not completely hold water. There is no point in taking it personally; that is just how they function.

If You Have a Self Pattern

If you have a Self Pattern at work, it means you focus more on what you are doing and may not notice someone's tone of voice or their facial expression, or if you do notice, you may misread what they are feeling. Others may also misinterpret what you mean because you don't tend to use a wide range of expressions or tone changes or give many non-verbal cues. You like to concentrate on the content of your work and master it. It might be helpful for you to invite colleagues with whom you have a good relationship, to let you know verbally what they are feeling in cases where you might have missed something important.

Self and the Autism Spectrum

Self behaviors overlap with typical behaviors from the Autism Spectrum such as some difficulties with gestures, eye contact, facial expressions and tone of voice. This does not mean that someone who is in a Self mode is necessarily on the spectrum; they are just in a Self mode.

Summary

Attention Direction

Question:	There is no question for this category.
Self:	Attends to own experience. Doesn't notice nonverbal behavior or voice tone.
Other:	Has Automatic reflex responses to nonverbal behavior.

Distribution at Work:

7% Self

93% Other

(in the work Context, from Rodger Bailey)

Influencing Language:

Self:	Focus on the content, match their Criteria and Convincer Channel and Mode.
Other:	They are influenced by the depth of rapport.

Chapter 13
Stress Response:
Freaked Out or Cool as a Cucumber?

How does a person react to stress in the work Context?

The Stress Response category examines how you respond to the pressures, at work or elsewhere, that are *typical* for the Context you are in. This is not about how someone would respond to major life dramas, since almost everyone would have an emotional response in those situations. People respond to these "normal" pressures in the following three ways:

Feeling

People with a Feeling Pattern have emotional responses to the *normal* levels of stress at work. They go into their emotions and *stay there*. High-stress jobs can therefore be difficult for them to handle over the long term. To many other people, they seem to overreact to situations or be hypersensitive. They are well suited for artistic or creative work, where emotion provides the juice. As salespeople, they find it difficult to handle rejection and may not, as a result, prospect for new customers as often as they should.

Choice

People with a Choice Pattern first have an emotional response to the normal stresses at work and then either return to an unemotional state or not, as they desire, in any given situation. *They have choice.* Because they feel emotions themselves, they can empathize with others, or choose not to. They tend to perform well as people-managers, as they can combine the personal side of the job and distance themselves when necessary.

Thinking

People with a Thinking Pattern tend not to have emotional responses to the *normal* stressful situations for a given Context. They may have trouble empathizing with others, as they themselves do not go into emotional states. They will not panic in most emergencies, but keep a cool head. They are reliable performers in high-stress jobs.

Distribution %	
(in the work Context, from Rodger Bailey)	
Feeling	15%
Choice	70%
Thinking	15%

Identification

Question:

TELL ME ABOUT A WORK SITUATION THAT CAUSED YOU TROUBLE.

For Contexts other than work, simply substitute the Context for "work situation." That is, tell me about a buying decision that caused you trouble.

When you are asking this question, avoid having the person tell you about *all* the times they had a particular kind of problem. "Whenever a customer is unhappy with our service, I get nervous." Make sure the person picks one specific troublesome (not catastrophic) situation that he remembers. What you are to determine, as they review that situation, is if they go into an emotional state and get stuck there, have an emotional response and come out of it, or have no emotional reaction at all.

Nonverbal Indicators

For the Stress Response category, there are no specific language Patterns to listen for. To recognize the Pattern, you will need to observe and listen for nonverbal cues, changes in how the person behaves. This means that you will need to compare the person's nonverbal behavior before and after you ask the Stress Response question.

Feeling

- they visibly and vocally have an emotional response while describing a difficult situation
- changes in 3 or more of the following are indicators of a change in emotional state:
    - body posture,
    - gestures facial muscle tension
    - eyes drop
    - voice will change in timbre, tone, speed and volume
- will stay in their emotional state throughout their recital

Choice

- will go into their emotions initially and return at least once

Thinking

- will not go into their emotions

Warning: It is possible, when you ask this question, that the person may go into a highly negative or painful emotional state, if they have a Feeling Pattern or if they *choose* to talk about a major catastrophe. For this reason, make sure that you ask the Stress Response question before the Style and Organization questions: "Tell me about a working experience that was (*your positive Criteria*). What did you like about it?" It is important to ensure that you do not leave someone in a negative state. Reminding them of situations associated with their positive Criteria will help shift them into a more positive frame of mind. If they seem to still be distressed, you may also have them change seats to help them get out of the negative state.

Examples

These Patterns can only be recognized by observing and listening to those behaviour changes listed above, not in the language structure.

For a demonstration of the three Patterns, please refer to my LAB Profile® Online Program or audio program *Understanding and Triggering Motivation: The LAB Profile®*.

Recruitment

It is very useful to pay attention to Stress Response, because people with each of these Patterns have varying abilities to handle stressful work situations. For example, the Thinking Pattern would be most appropriate for an airline pilot or an air traffic controller. Remember Captain Sullenberger landing Flight US 1549 in the Hudson River back in 2009? Could you imagine what would happen if a high Feeling airline pilot were in the same situation? Air traffic controllers whom I trained told me that you usually can tell if the person beside you is having a *close incident*. The heat energy apparently *just pours out*.

If rapport and empathy are important in a job, then Choice is the best Pattern to have. People with the Choice Patterns have feelings and can also come out of an emotional state, if appropriate, to look at the situation or take action. When you regularly experience emotions yourself, you can more easily recognize that other people also have feelings. If Harry stays on the analytical, thinking level as a response to Sally's feelings, he probably will not acknowledge the importance of Sally's feelings to her, or even sympathize with them. *And he probably won't have what she is having!*

Many people in artistic careers have the Feeling Pattern, because art is often an expression of feelings and emotions. I discovered that the principal activity of the staff in many fine dining establishments (especially in Europe) is not customer service, but trying to keep the chef happy. Many chefs are highly emotional people. When they go over the edge about something, all hell breaks loose.

Incompetency Attacks

In sales positions, Feeling people may become demoralized when faced with rejection from prospective customers, because they may take it personally. It means that they would often feel stressed in that kind of function and may even be prone to what a friend of mine calls *Incompetency Attacks*. An Incompetency Attack has nothing to do with one's real level of competence, which may be excellent. It is a strong, emotionally-based belief of one's incompetence, usually felt by someone with a Feeling Pattern in that Context.

Career Coaching

When I am coaching someone about career choices, I pay close attention to this Pattern, because it gives an indication of how much stress the person can handle.

Passion

There are some other issues to consider. While a high Feeling person may be prone to suffering from stress, they also have a *need* for passion and intensity. When a person has both Feeling and Options Patterns in a Context, they are highly passionate about developing alternatives, a very creative combination.

Emotional Outbursts

In Berlin, I participated in a workshop on Integral Facilitation (a Zen approach to running groups) and accidentally blew it up. The American facilitator had an international group of participants and she wanted us to learn how to use this approach, even with difficult issues. In one subgroup, we were discussing the contentious question of immigration in Germany as an example.

I was feeling that this group was being overly nice and agreeable with one another and wanted to find out what was the Integral approach for dealing with dissent in groups, so I piped up and said: "I think we should throw out all the immigrants and lock the door." The facilitator didn't really integrate this point of view to the discussion, but ended up reframing it as "a need to relook at how we integrate immigrants." I was prepared to let it go, but another participant decided to stick up for me and insisted that my point of view wasn't being respected. When we returned to the larger group, she confronted the main facilitator with the fact that my point of view had been ignored. When the facilitator attempted to answer this person, she got up and left the room, which clearly was frustrating for the facilitator.

When we returned after lunch the facilitator took the woman aside, and in full view of the entire group, screamed at her for what seemed like a very long time. One person intervened to try to explain and the facilitator told her to shut up. I waited and then intervened to mediate, since the situation was clearly deteriorating. I had to raise my voice to get the facilitator's attention, to enable them both to be heard and to create an acceptable summary of the disagreement. It eventually calmed down.

That night I realized that while I had calmed them both down, I had become very upset myself at what had occurred. We debriefed the episode in the wider group the next day. The facilitator explained that she had reacted because of an ancient negative hot button that gotten pushed, but I mentioned that I was still upset about her freaking out and mistreating a participant. I felt her reaction was completely unacceptable for a professional facilitator, especially someone who was there to model a Zen approach. It took me a couple of days to deal with my own Feeling pattern!

If you have emotional outbursts that you would like to manage better, first be aware of *what* your typical negative hot buttons are. Secondly, notice your reaction in the moment as it's happening (yes you CAN do this). Thirdly, get out of the situation without drawing attention if possible so that you can do what you need to calm down. And fourthly, if it is not possible to leave, breathe deeply and smile, knowing that you can come back later when you are emotionally ready to handle the situation.

I recently set myself the goal of being a nicer person, by going to the other person's bus stop before reacting, particularly with my husband, family and certain work colleagues. (You know, practicing what I preach!) The above process helps me do this.

Managing Stress and People

According to Rodger Bailey, most of the population at work has the Choice Pattern (70%). This means that when faced with a difficult or troublesome situation they will first have an emotional response. As a manager you can assist by helping these people *disassociate* themselves from their feelings, if appropriate, by helping them change perspectives.

There are a couple of ways to do this. You can distort time by asking them: "Can you imagine what we'll think about this situation two years from now?" You can have them see it from someone else's viewpoint: "I don't think our customers will care much about this." Or you can have them view the whole thing from the outside: "If you were a fly on the wall when this happened, what would you notice?"

With Feeling people, you will probably have to practice your conflict resolution and mediation skills. To maintain their motivation, give them tasks that they can get passionate about. As they are working, watch for signs of distress and overload of tension. These people are the most likely to suffer from stress-related illnesses because they feel stressed more often than people with the other Patterns. Feeling people may overreact, particularly in tense or conflictual circumstances. It would be useful for them to learn how to dissociate or cool off. I would guess that President Trump has a Feeling Pattern, since he has a tendency to immediately go on the attack from his Twitter account when criticized or slighted by other high-profile people. He is not known for just "letting it go".

When faced with a highly intense reaction from an employee, create rapport by raising your tone to almost the same level as his while saying something positive or surprising: "I'm so upset about you being upset, that I am ready to tear my hair out!" Saying something like that will get their attention, so that you can then channel their energy toward a more productive path.

People with a Thinking Pattern are highly appreciated where there is need for someone with a cool head. These people spend much time already disassociated from their feelings and can be called on when a rational approach is needed. Do not expect them, however, to create rapport with others who are in an emotional state, because it is unlikely that they will feel empathy. Thinking people, particularly if they have a combination with Internal, can, however, take the heat and be able to stay in the kitchen!

Post-Traumatic Stress Disorder Can Be Contagious

An article in the Scientific American discussed research on how 10 to 20% of therapists working with patients who have PTSD, can develop the symptoms of PTSD without any first-hand contact with the traumatic events. Symptoms can include nightmares, flashbacks and images. But not all therapists (or family members, and caregivers) have this issue. The article quoted a study which found that therapists and family members "who exhibited greater emotional empathy were more apt to experience secondary trauma at the time of follow-up."[1]

What are the LAB Profile® Patterns inherent in emotional empathy, if we define this trait as Daniel Goldman does: "feel physically along with the other person, as though their emotions were contagious"? Probably External (being open to letting in information from the person with PTSD), Away From (noticing what is wrong), Other (focused on the other person's non-verbal communication), Stress Response Feeling (gets into a negative emotional state and stays there), Person (priority on people, relationships, and emotions), and Convincer Channel See (uses the visual channel to input info when becoming convinced). With this combination of Patterns, a person has no boundaries between them self and others and can easily become "infected". This would make a great topic for research. Could you predict that therapists with this combination of LAB Profile® Patterns, would be more likely to get 2nd hand PTSD? If so, processes could be developed, specific to them, to prevent and treat PTSD.

New more effective protocols for treating PTSD have been developed and are being validated as I write, including one called the RTM Protocol, which has had an astounding rate of over 90% of US Veterans being symptom and diagnosis free at two-week, six-week, and twelve-month follow-ups, with five or fewer treatment sessions.[2]

Influencing Language

You can *rouse* and motivate people in an extraordinary way by simply *being there* and making *rational sense* of it all.

Feeling

- get them excited about something and focus on the emotion, using words such as:
- intense; exciting; mind-boggling; extraordinary; this is fantastic; amazing, etc.

Choice

- speak in terms that indicate you can go in and out of an emotional state (i.e., "You can get excited about this, and then realize that it makes good sense too.").

Thinking

- present the *logical* facts:
- the cold reality; hard facts; clear thinking; statistics

Language Range and Culture

The use of highly emotional words is not necessarily an indicator of a Feeling Pattern. Some cultures use superlatives as the usual way of speaking, while others avoid them as much as possible.

For example, I suspect that the use of superlatives is another difference between American and English Canadian cultures. You may have noticed that, in comparison to other English-speaking cultures, Americans tend to use vocabulary that hovers at the extremes, from the *COMPLETE DISASTER*, on one end, to the *AMAZINGLY WONDERFUL*, on the other. The French and the Québécois also tend to do this.

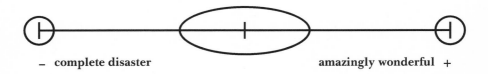

– **complete disaster**   **amazingly wonderful** +

English Canadians (and, in my experience, French Canadians from outside Québec) tend to linger closer to the middle, in a range that goes from the *PRETTY BAD* to the *PRETTY GOOD*.

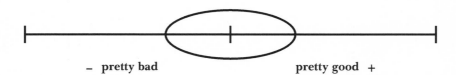

– **pretty bad**   **pretty good** +

I've heard Americans talk about how difficult it is to get English Canadians excited about something. My advice to Canadians, when listening to Americans describe something, is to apply the Monty Python rule of thumb and divide whatever they say by ten.[3]

By comparison, the English (particularly the upper classes) seem to have an even smaller linguistic range; they go from *NOT GOOD* on the negative side, to *NOT BAD* on the positive side.

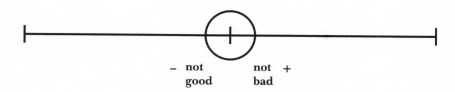

To influence someone using the Stress Response Influencing Language, you will need to choose the kind of language appropriate to the culture.

Summary

Stress Response

Question:	***Tell me about (a work situation) that gave you trouble.***
Feeling:	Emotional responses to "normal" levels of stress. Stays in feelings.
Choice:	Can move in and out of feelings voluntarily. Good at empathy.
Thinking:	Do not go into feeling at normal levels of stress. Poor at showing empathy. Keep cool in high-stress work.

Distribution at Work:

15% Feeling

70% Choice

15% Thinking

(in the work Context, from Rodger Bailey)

Influencing Language:

Feeling:	intense; exciting; mind-boggling; wonderful
Choice:	empathy; appropriate; makes good sense and feels right
Thinking:	clear thinking; logical; rational; cold reality; hard facts; statistics

---

[1] Christian Wolf, Post-Traumatic Stress Disorder Can be Contagious; Oct 3, 2018; bit.ly/PostTraumaticStressDisorderCanBeContagious

[2] For more info on PTSD treatment research: bit.ly/ResearchAndRecognition

[3] This "dividing by 10" is from the British classic comedy television series: Monty Python's Flying Circus.

Chapter 14
Style: Environment and Productivity

What kind of environment allows the person to be most productive: working alone, with others around or sharing responsibility?

The Style category allows you to discover (or confirm) how you can be at your best; whether you want to share your work with other people, do it yourself while involving others, or work all on your own.

In this category, particularly in the work Context, many people have more than one Pattern, a dominant and a secondary Style. Your LAB Profile® Style preferences, as for the other categories, can change, depending on the Context.

There are three Patterns:

Independent

People who have an Independent Pattern in the work Context want to *work alone* and have *sole responsibility*. Their productivity suffers if others are around or if they have to share responsibility. When interrupted, they may lose their train of thought. They prefer to work in an office with the door closed. At the extreme, they may forget to consult with others (especially if they are also Internal). At work, they can go for long periods of time without craving contact with others.

The expression, "A camel is a horse designed by a committee," was probably authored by someone with this Pattern. As a manager, an Independent person will do most of the work by himself and probably not establish rapport easily.

Proximity

Proximity people want a *clear territory of responsibility* but need to have *others involved* or around, in proximity. They need well-defined responsibilities; to be productive and stay motivated, and their tasks must involve other people. Their productivity will fall if others share responsibility and authority, or if they have to work totally alone.

Of the three Patterns, this one is most suited for people and project management positions. They will make sure that everyone knows what they are responsible for. Proximity people do well as the boss, or when they have a boss, because they are most productive when territories are well established.

Cooperative

People with a Cooperative Pattern want to work and *share responsibility with others*. They believe in 2+2=5, the whole is greater than the sum of its parts, Synergy Principle. They may have trouble with deadlines and finishing tasks if they have to work on their own. They do not need a personal territory to be in charge of, and as managers, will want to do everything *with* their employees.

The very old Californian light bulb joke describes these people. How many Californians does it take to change a light bulb? It takes six: one to change the light bulb, and five to *share the experience.*

Cooperative does not necessarily mean that the person cooperates, in the usual sense of the term, just that they need to do an activity *with* someone else. When my oldest son Jason was about five years old, he spent an hour building a Lego boat. My youngest son Sam, then about two and a half, came down from his nap and kicked the boat to pieces. Jason was very upset, but from Sam's point of view, Jason had *the nerve to do it all by himself*. He did not wait for Sam to do it *with him*. This was intolerable for Sam, who usually did not go off by himself and play. He was sometimes disruptive when he played, but he needed the company.

Distribution %	
(in the work Context, from Rodger Bailey)	
Independent	20%
Proximity	60%
Cooperative	20%

Identification

Questions:

TELL ME ABOUT A WORK EXPERIENCE THAT WAS (their Criteria).

- wait for their answer

WHAT DID YOU LIKE ABOUT IT?

For Contexts other than work, you can simply insert the Context into the question: "Tell me about an experience in a relationship that was...."

Make sure the person you are profiling picks a *specific example* of a situation that meets their Criteria. If they have numerous Criteria for the Context you are discussing, simply use one Criterion. Some people may never have had an experience that meets all of their Criteria.

For this category, listen carefully to what the person talks about. Write down the answer for the first question and then ask the second question. Does the person talk about doing something *totally alone, in charge with others around,* or *together with others*?

Note: The answer to the first question is the most relevant for detecting the Pattern in the Style category.

Independent

- says I, I did it, myself, my responsibility
- won't talk about or mention other people
- the activity presupposes that they did it on their own

Proximity

- other people are present but "I did it"
- may or may not mention others, but the *nature* of the activity necessitates the presence of others (i.e. sales or teaching)

Cooperative

- will say: we, us, our job, together, etc.
- includes other people and shares responsibility

Here is how to ask the above questions:

SRC: Sara, what was one of your Criteria for work?

Sara: Challenge.

SRC: So can you tell me about a work situation that had challenge?

Sara: It was a performance issue. There was a question whether a *particular group of people* were performing at the level they were supposed to. *I had to define who was responsible and what to do about it* because the performance wasn't adequate. *I* had to pool that together in different departments and the challenge was to come up with the solution.

SRC: What did you like about that situation?

Sara: I used creativity, it was stimulating, there was a challenge.

In the example that Sara chose to mention, we know that others were involved so it cannot be Independent. Sara says "I" and clearly demonstrates an awareness of who is responsible for what. Her Pattern is Proximity.

Examples

Independent:	*"I designed the new software and debugged it."*
Independent and Proximity:	*"I designed the new software and then with my team I got all the bugs out."*
Proximity:	*"I designed the new software with my team."*
Proximity and Cooperative:	*"I designed the new software with my team and then together we ironed out the bugs."*
Cooperative:	*"We designed the new software and debugged it. It was a great team effort."*
Independent and Cooperative:	*"I designed the new software and then we all sat down and debugged the thing together."*

Alternate Question:

HOW LONG CAN YOU WORK ALONE IN YOUR OFFICE WITHOUT PHONING OR GOING TO SEE SOMEONE?

Influencing Language

You can figure this out all by yourself, and use it with other people, so that you will all work well together.

Independent

- do it alone; by yourself; you alone; without interruption; you'll have total responsibility and control; just close your door and reroute your phone

Proximity

- you will be in charge; others will be involved but this is your baby; you will direct; lead; your responsibility is X and theirs is Y

Cooperative

- us; we; together; all of us; team; group; share responsibility; do it together; you won't be alone in this (Away From); let's; we could do that

Recruitment and Management

Many management and professional positions advertise for "team players," but what does this really mean? Most management positions require someone who can harness energy, orchestrate activities and create a vision for their team. These activities need a good dose of Proximity with only some Cooperative.

To understand what is needed in a position, look at the activities and the proportion of time spent in each one. Which ones are *do-it-aloners*? (To do a complete LAB Profile® of a position, check the chapter on recruitment.) Which activities involve being responsible for the outcome with others involved, and which demand working together at the same time to accomplish the objectives? If the job requires a high degree of proficiency in all three, you are unlikely to find an ideal candidate and may need to redefine the position.

Many years ago, I was Assistant Human Resources Director in a national youth-development organization for a region that included the provinces of Manitoba, Saskatchewan, and Alberta as well as the North West Territories. My boss had a mainly Cooperative Pattern and I had Proximity and Independent Patterns at work. She had us decide everything together and I just wanted my *own files*. I needed to have a territory, something that I could be in charge of. She was highly satisfied by our working relationship and I was frustrated.

People who have a mainly Independent Pattern at work need space and time to themselves. They excel in those situations that call for someone to keep plugging away by themselves, even when all hell is breaking loose around them. They can concentrate for long periods by blocking out peripheral activities. They do not fare well where constant communication and creating consensus are an integral part of the job. Think of the people you know who need a private space and no noise to be able to concentrate.

Since about 60 percent of the population at work has a mainly Proximity Pattern, most jobs have been designed to give people their own territory as well as necessitating interaction with others. Where the division of tasks has been masterminded by a Cooperative person, there is little mention of individual responsibility, and this confuses and frustrates many employees. I suspect that the brief experiment with "open concept" design of offices was created by Cooperative types. Some companies experimented with the "Virtual Office" concept, where no one has a designated workspace to call their own. You simply reserve a space, depending on the nature of your activity. Most people are not productive without their own physical space (digital nomads being an exception, of course).

Where an Independent person has had a hand in job design, they may have left out defining how people will interact and communicate with each other. This is great for programmers, who for the most part need to be left alone to code. This may lead to "the left hand doesn't know what the right hand is doing" situation between individuals and departments, common in many organizations. For positions where you need to consult with colleagues, cubicles with lower walls so that it is possible to catch someone's eye can work.

I was asked by Great Universal Shopping (GUS), which was a major catalogue retailer in the UK, to help them with recruiting and keeping staff in their contact center. Their employees were part time, mainly women, on the phone following the automated script, calling customers to confirm their orders and upsell them. I modelled their top performers, watching them work. When I walked into the call center, there were hundreds of people working at their desks, and interestingly, most of them noticed me (looked up, said hi to me with their eyes or waved) with an air of curiosity. Their call center design had cubicles which were low enough for everyone to see over the top. This supported the Style they wanted for their work; Proximity!

How do you need to set up work spaces and atmosphere to support the people and the work that needs to be done, so that people feel great and are productive?

What about the interior design of your home? Is it open space (Cooperative)? Does it have separate spaces for different activities (Proximity), or lots of rooms with doors that can be closed for privacy (Independent), or some combination of all this?

Holidays can be a stressful time for families if they don't get the "Style" right. Do you want to be alone, with family members who each contribute something and have a role (parents & kids -organizer – organize - Proximity), or all just hang out together (Cooperative)? I once profiled a man in the Context of family holidays and he had an Independent Pattern. Imagine his family's response!

Pattern Combinations

I am often asked if there are relationships between two or more Patterns in the LAB Profile® such as, whether there is *a relationship between Independent and Internal*? These Patterns do not necessarily go together. You could want to work all by yourself, not know if your work is good enough, and have to ask, "Maureen, I've just finished this; can you tell me what you think about it?" (Independent and External), or I could publish a report and decide that it was done well, without bothering to get any feedback (Independent and Internal). Most of the Patterns can go with any of the other Patterns. The important thing about Combination Patterns, is that you can predict behavior and influence more effectively when you understand how the individual Patterns combine to create whole attitudes and behaviors. For more on this, see the chapter on Combination Patterns.

The Loneliness Epidemic

More and more people live their lives surgically attached to their mobile devices, texting or on calls (even when around others in social settings) and more people are working alone, either in their home office, or alone in co-working spaces and cafés. Many seniors live on their own, with few daily contacts with others. And there are many young people who spend much of their lives online and are reluctant to go "offline" to deal with their real lives. (How did this word come to mean normal waking reality??)

Each of these examples are very much like being in Independent mode. All alone. Texting, phoning, binge watching programs, playing games etc., is not like being with other people. A man told me he was working in a café near a woman with whom he wanted to speak, and it took him well over 30 minutes to work up the courage to even strike up a conversation. A national survey found that nearly half of Americans feel lonely or left out. Only 53% report having meaningful conversations with others, and Generation Z, (born between 1996 and 2012) is the loneliest generation and is in the poorest health.[1]

Even if these statistics are only partially true, this is an epidemic which will have huge repercussions on health worldwide. At work, only 20% of the population has an Independent Pattern. I'm not sure about other Contexts but as we know, the human environment affects our productivity and clearly, our happiness. We need more communities where people can live, work and play either together (Cooperative) or "in conjunction with one another" (Proximity). A sponsor at an event I spoke at, was from a national Canadian provider of seniors' residences and care facilities. Their representative made the case that we all used to tell Grandma that she was better off being independent and staying by herself in her house, when we probably all know Grandmas, Grandpas, and other seniors who are having a great time in a caring community with lots of interesting people and activities. Subsidizing communities for seniors would be a great way to reduce their health care costs and increase their quality of life.

Summary

Style

Question: ***Tell me about a (work) experience where you had (Criteria). What did you like about it?***

Independent: Likes to work alone with sole responsibility.

Proximity: Prefers to have own territory with others around.

Cooperative: Productive when sharing responsibility with others.

Distribution at Work:

20% Independent

60% Proximity

20% Cooperative

(in the work Context, from Rodger Bailey)

Influencing Language:

Independent: you get to do it by yourself; you alone; total responsibility

Proximity: you'll be in charge; with others around, you'll direct; lead

Cooperative: us; we; all together; share responsibility; let's; do it together

---

[1] Cigna, a global health services company released a survey in May 2018; bit.ly/LonelinessStudyNC

Chapter 15
Organization: People and Things

> *How do people organize their work? Do they concentrate more on thoughts and feelings, or on ideas, systems, tools, and tasks?*

The Organization Category is about how people organize their work, either by getting the job done or focusing on people and feelings. There are two Patterns in this category:

Person

Individuals with a Person Pattern pay attention to the feelings and thoughts of either themselves or others. Relationships and experiences with people take on such an importance that **they become the task itself.** They will organize their work so that they can focus on people and their feelings. They are good at establishing rapport.

Thing

Thing people concentrate on products, ideas, tools, tasks, and systems (things). They may treat people and ideas as objects, and believe that emotions have no place in the world of work. They want to *get things done*, and are strongly *task-oriented*.

Distribution % (in the work Context, from Rodger Bailey)	
Mainly Person	15%
Equally Person and Thing	30%
Mainly Thing	55%

Identification

Since 55 percent of the population have a mainly Thing preference at work, you will hear this Pattern more commonly in the workplace, although specific professions will have their own cultural Pattern (i.e., many people in the human services professions have a Person Pattern).

The questions are *the same as for the Style category*. In other words, when you ask the questions below, you will receive both the Style and Organization categories of information simultaneously. For the Organization category, pay particular attention to the answer of the second question: What did you like about it?

Questions:

TELL ME ABOUT A WORK EXPERIENCE THAT WAS … (their Criteria).

- listen to the answer

WHAT DID YOU LIKE ABOUT IT?

Person

- speak about people, emotions, feelings
- will name people, use personal pronouns
- people are the object of their sentences

Thing

- talk about processes, systems, tools, ideas, tasks, goals, results
- will not mention people often except as impersonal pronouns (i.e. "they", or "you")
- people become objects, parts of a process

Examples

Person: *"Mr. Richler was ecstatic with my report. I was quite happy with it too."*

Mainly Person:	*"Mr. Richler was ecstatic with my report. I was happy too because it meant quite a breakthrough for the whole company."*
Equally Person And Thing:	*"Mr. Richler was ecstatic with my report. It was quite a breakthrough for the company."*
Mainly Thing:	*"My report meant quite a breakthrough for the company. My boss liked it too."*
Thing:	*"My report meant quite a breakthrough for the company."*

Other Questions:

I recently discovered a test question that will allow you to verify when you are not sure:

"Imagine that you are working very hard to finish a piece of very important work that has to be done in thirty minutes. A colleague whom you really like and respect walks in at that moment, appearing quite upset and wants to talk right now about a personal crisis. What do you do?"

Either the person may choose to complete the task (Thing), drop everything to comfort the person (Person) or waver between the two, (Equally Person and Thing).

Alternately you could ask the person: "Tell me about a perfect day at work." The person will either tell you about tasks and things, or people and feelings.

Here is another example of someone who is Equally Person and Thing:

SRC:	Simon, what is it you liked about helping that person solve a problem?
Simon:	The problem is fixed. And the person is important.
Note:	Simon is paying attention, both to getting a solution and to the person.

When you ask someone to tell you about a work situation that met their Criteria, and then ask them what they liked about it, they will usually reveal the element that has the most importance for them. The exception is when your interviewee knows the LAB Profile® and therefore also knows what you are listening for. "Naive" subjects just give you their Pattern.

Influencing Language

Just experiencing how great it is to use just the right words will help you achieve your goals.

Person

- use people's names; feelings; thoughts; experiencing; this will feel good; for you; for others; the people; our team; our group

Thing

- things; systems; objects; tasks; objectives; process; get the job done; focus on the task at hand; the goal; the results

Good and Bad People?

Having a Person Pattern is not an indication that you are either a "good" or a "bad" person. For example, if someone's profession consists of defrauding others, they are likely to be totally focused on the emotions of other people. They will wind and weave emotions while spinning their web.

In fine dining establishments, the maître d'hôtel treats all the patrons basically like objects, placing them in their seats while calling for service. But his job is to make sure that these *objects* are happy. The best example of that kind of Thing Pattern, for me, is on commercial airplanes. The flight attendants move down the aisle with the cart between them and you can see they are having a real conversation with each other. They're saying: "And you know what else I heard about him?" Then they plaster on a fake smile and bend down to one of the relatively immobile objects in a seat. "Would you care for a coffee?" You get your coffee and then they can return to their tête-à-tête.

Politicians sometimes also refer to people as objects. They talk about *the electorate*. What is the electorate? It is you and I, folks. But to some, it is an object, a thing, to be tracked and manipulated on social media, as in the 2016 US Presidential Election, when Cambridge Analytica used Facebook data to determine relevant personality traits and churn out "messaging" to create support for or alienate segments of the electorate from the candidate.

The finance and banking sectors also commonly refer to their clients as things; using the term "wallet share" or "Share of Wallet" (SOW), to talk about how much of a customer's business they have.

Recruitment

At work, some jobs are organized to focus on accomplishing specific tasks and need a mainly Thing employee. However, professional recruiters are increasingly looking for people who also care enough about people and feelings to communicate, establish rapport, and solve conflicts.

Some positions require a mainly Person orientation. Customer service and reception are good examples. They also need to have an External Pattern, as their customers' feelings must come first. One of the administrative employees with whom I worked in a French training company had a strong Person Pattern and was very fond of me. When I would ask her to do something, she frequently would drop everything and attend to me right away. I often had to tell her that it was not urgent and could be done the following week. She would also *not* do someone else's work right away, when she did not like them. In this case, she was also attending to their feelings.

Person salespeople may have a hard time asking for a close. They are having a lovely time communing with their prospective customers and do not want to end it by focusing on the task at hand. Person managers run meetings that can get off topic for long stretches to discuss personal war stories. "That reminds me of the time...." Thing managers will sometimes not recognize feelings and may hurt or embarrass others, and then say, "Feelings have no place at work." In informal social situations, you can often easily recognize the Person people. They are the ones who continue talking to you as you are trying to leave. Sometimes they are loathe to break rapport and end your visit.

Many people choose coaching or work in human services because they care deeply about how people feel. Sometimes they forget that the task is to help people become independent and then move on to their next *case*. When they have a high Person Pattern, they risk becoming overly preoccupied with the emotions of their clients and their relationship, and may suffer from burnout, (especially if they also have Away From and the Feeling Stress Response, which many do). For their own long-term well-being, these professionals need to create boundaries between themselves and their clients, to focus more on the task at hand (without neglecting their clients' feelings).

Some people have said to me, "This material is very new for me. I don't feel comfortable." Since I tend to be more focused on the task at hand, my inside response usually goes like this: "So, are you being paid to feel comfortable?" However, as a professional, I usually respond by saying, "You know, discomfort is an interesting feeling, because it is a sign that you're stretching. And if you're doing something new that you're not used to, chances are you'll feel uncomfortable. Are you OK with that?" In my mind (with my mainly Thing Pattern), making people feel at ease is a *means to accomplishing* the goal of learning.

Leadership and management styles are often characterized by how much focus is on tasks or relationships and when it is best to do more of one or the other. The styles have various names such as authoritative, consultative, coaching style, and so on. You can probably place any management style as being somewhere on the continuum between Person and Thing.

It can still be tough for women in a male work environment. Women are often still perceived as too emotional. When certain men (and some women too!) hear a lot of Person-type language and see Person behavior, particularly from women, they dismiss their ideas as too soft. On the other hand, when women use mainly Thing language, while it seems more credible, they are often perceived as "too hard". It can be tough to find the right balance, which is why I developed the Advanced Business Influence[1] program for women leaders and managers.

Miscommunications between Thing and Person people can happen even over simple things and I have plenty of examples of this. When I was attending a course on Neuro-linguistic Programming in Paris and had lunch with a friend. As I was recounting a funny disaster that had occurred, Suzanne stopped me to ask: "But how did you feel?" "Alright, I guess," I replied, and continued on with the next in the series of mishaps. She did not respond to the funny events, but rather, "But how did they *feel*?" she wanted to know. "I don't know how they felt," I said, starting to become annoyed, "but this is what they did." The two monologues continued. "That must have been difficult for you." "Yeah, I suppose, but what happened then was...." On another occasion, a friend recounted how her husband asked her to take a picture of him with their new car. He was dismayed that it was impossible to see the car as she had taken the picture with him as the central focal point. Can you guess the Patterns in these situations?

Sales and Marketing

Person people will buy something for the experience, how it will make them feel. Hair coloring and other personal products and services are sold this way. "You're worth it", from L'Oréal. People who have all the things they need may prefer to have an experience as a gift. My niece gave us the present of a family cooking class where seven of us, chose a menu and spent an evening learning how to cook with a professional chef. And then eating together, of course!

To sell to Thing buyers, focus their attention on the product or service and the benefits. Think about the technophiles in your life who have to have the latest devices. When my business partner Andreas

Plienegger and I developed the digital LAB Profile® for Sales platform[2], Andreas realized that a better way to talk about Person and Thing in sales would be to ask potential clients about their "Impact Preference" and listen for whether the person talks about people or things.

The design of your website, products, services and even business cards should reflect the Person or Thing preference of your target market. If your market is a caring, sharing group of folks, make your font choices be irregular and quirky, along with round, friendly graphics. Conversely if your market wants just the facts, use regular fonts sans serif and more square designs. What does your business card look like?

Summary

Organization

Question: *Tell me about a (work) situation that was (Criteria). What did you like about it?*

Person: Concentrate on feelings, thoughts, relationships. They become *the task.*

Thing: Focus on task, systems, ideas, tools, things. Getting the job done is the most important thing.

Distribution at Work:

      15% Mainly Person

      30% Equally Person and Thing

      55% Mainly Thing

      (in the work Context, from Rodger Bailey)

Influencing Language:

Person: use people's names; feelings; thoughts; feel good; people like

Thing: things; systems; the thing is; the goal is; process; task;

[1] see the Institute for Influence (bit.ly/AdvancedBusinessInfluence), Advanced Business Influence Program

[2] for digital LAB Profile® for Sales Training, bit.ly/SalesTrainerPlatform

Chapter 16
Rule Structure: Guidelines for Yourself and Others

> *What are the rules for behavior that people apply to themselves and others?*

Rule Structure will give you information regarding the ability or willingness to manage oneself and others. There are four Patterns in this category:

My/My: My Rules for Me, My Rules for You

My/My people have rules for themselves and for others in specific contexts. They are willing to communicate their rules to others. Because they believe that people are similar, they think that what is good for themselves will also suit other people. They will say things such as: "If I were you, I would. . .." A large majority of people at work have this Pattern and probably in other Contexts as well.

My/.: My Rules for Me, I Don't Care

The My/. (period) people have rules for themselves and do not care about others. They do not necessarily harbor malicious intent toward others; it is simply not their problem or concern. These people often get on with what they need to do without thinking about others. Sometimes they are called selfish by others because they simply did not consider anyone else.

I was often awakened in the middle of the night in my sixth floor Paris apartment by people who I believe had this Pattern. They would honk loudly at two o'clock in the morning, in a residential district, surrounded by hundreds of people who had, presumably, been sleeping.

No/My: No Rules or Don't Know Rules for Me, My Rules for You

No/My people do not know or do not have guidelines for themselves, but once given the rules, are quite willing to pass them on to others. As a result, they may have difficulty providing direction for themselves or making decisions. Instead, they may get stuck and not know what to do.

My/Your: My Rules for Me, Your Rules for You

People with a My/Your Pattern know the rules and policies to follow at work but are reluctant or unable to communicate them to others. They operate from a "different strokes for different folks" perspective. Because they believe everyone is different, they may consider it arrogant to tell others what to do. As a result, other people are often unclear as to their expectations.

These are the people who can understand both sides of an argument, as annoying as this may seem to those of us who take strong positions.

Distribution %	
(in the work Context, from Rodger Bailey)	
My/My	75%
My/.	3%
No/My	7%
My/Your	15%

Identification

You will need to ask these two questions and notice whether the person answers both or one only, as follows:

Questions:

WHAT IS A GOOD WAY FOR YOU TO INCREASE YOUR SUCCESS? (at work)**?**

- listen for the answer

WHAT IS A GOOD WAY FOR SOMEONE ELSE TO INCREASE THEIR SUCCESS? (at work)

To identify these Patterns, you will need to compare the answers to these questions. When someone does not know, they will hesitate a long time and respond with a questioning tone:

My/My:

- Some kind of answer to both questions or answers both questions easily. (The answer to each question may not be the same.)

My/.:

- Clear response to question one. Indicates lack of interest for question two.

No/My:

- Doesn't know the answer to question one. Has rules for question two.

My/Your:

- Has rules for question one. Doesn't know or wouldn't presume to say for question two.

Examples

My/My:	*"1. Work harder. Be more organized."*
	"2. Be prepared. Know what you want. Work hard."
My/.:	*"1. Be more organized."*
	"2. Not my problem."
No/My:	*"1. Uhm, ah ...Not sure."*
	"2. Be organized."
My/Your:	*"1. Work harder. Be more organized."*
	"2. Everybody's different."

Influencing Language

If I were you, I would simply pay attention to what the person does because, after all, everyone is different, right? The following are phrases to use when speaking to the people who have these Patterns.

My/My:

- "You would do that if you were him? You know what you want and what would work for the others, you can apply what you think to the situation with the group." (these phrases reflect that the person decides for themselves and others)

My/.:

- (For this group, I suggest using the language that you would use for Internals, with a twist) "You're sure about this and it doesn't matter about the others, this may be in your best interest, never mind what *they* think."

No/My:

- "Now that you've been informed about what's expected, you can pass that along, wait until you hear from the boss and then let everyone know, would you tell the group what the rules are from our guideline book? what would George do?"

My/Your:

- "You know what you should do and you want to leave it up to the others to decide for themselves, you have your own unique way and recognize that each person is different, everyone is different."

Recruitment and People Management

People with the My/My Pattern are well-suited for people management positions, provided they have the other requisite Patterns: Proactive and Reactive, mainly Internal, mainly General, Other, Choice, and so on, (and the knowledge and skill, of course). They can clearly state what they expect of their people and know and understand the rules by which they guide their own behavior. If a job or a particular function demands that someone impart expertise to others, the My/My Pattern is best. You would need to be able to tell others what to do.

In situations where a manager has an extreme My/My Pattern, and particularly when combined with Internal, they can cause problems within the team. In an organization for which I had done a large training program, the director decided that all the staff were to go through video-based training. His rationale was that this training had done him a world of good and would therefore accomplish the same thing for the staff. In my opinion, not everyone (at that level) was ready for that kind of experience.

When a manager has the My/Your Pattern, they may create some anxiety, especially if the team is inexperienced, because they don't *tell* others what they expect. But they are great for mature teams who know what they need to do. When it is important to discover the Criteria, values, goals, and so on, of someone and then work with those, a My/Your Pattern is useful. My/Your people make good mediators and negotiators because they can understand each party's views while maintaining their mediator's neutrality. Much of today's training in listening and questioning skills for coaches, facilitators, trainers, and therapists aims to create a My/Your Pattern.

Sales people who have a My/My Pattern can do well, provided they also have the other desirable Patterns for their work (Proactive, some External, mainly Procedures, Choice, Proximity, etc.), because they will ask for the sale. If they have an extremely My/My Pattern, they may go overboard about telling others what to do. My/Your sales people may be reluctant to ask for the sale or make suggestions.

So Why Does Middle Management Get the Squeeze?

The Pattern often found in middle management in large, hierarchical organizations is No/My. These people do not typically set the rules for their team; they find out what the rules are and pass them on.

Since the economic meltdowns of the early 1990s, the Dotcom crash in 2000, the financial crisis of 2008, the oil-price collapse in 2016, etc., etc., organizations have been going through many contortions: downsizing, "re-engineering" their processes, re-organizing, flattening the hierarchy, and each time it seems, pushing out middle-level managers, among others. Middle managers are often perceived as adding little value to many processes, since they are deemed to be (incorrectly in my opinion) merely policy and procedure *relay mechanisms*. (This is probably a Thing view of the world.)

The role that middle management plays as people facilitators and developers has been undervalued, when organizations want to cut heads. As a result of this process of elimination, a large group of people with a No/My Pattern suddenly find themselves looking for work, some for the first time in their lives. What can we predict about these people? It is difficult for them. They haven't got many rules for themselves about finding a new career or a new job. Fortunately, there are many job sites and connecting forums (LinkedIn, Xing, etc.) that can be of help.

Telling Yourself What to Do

I had a career coaching client with the No/My Pattern. I asked her, "Do you have trouble sometimes making decisions?" "Oh yes!" she said, "When they concern myself." I asked her to imagine that she was over there in another chair and then had her tell herself what to do. That solved a lot of problems for her. She had no problem telling other people what she expected but she had difficulty deciding what she expected from herself in the work Context. This issue of difficulty making decisions can be even worse if someone has External, Options and No/My in the same Context.

My/. people do best where they can concentrate on the job to be done and not on others' needs. This kind of work is increasingly difficult to find, as many companies insist that their people communicate and coordinate their activities. These people sometimes take the "It's my way or the highway" approach and, if also Proactive and Internal, will bulldoze their way through whatever is going on around them.

I worked with the owner of a small environmental firm who had this combination. He had frightened most of his staff to the extent that they were convinced a pink slip was waiting for them at the end of each day.

Intimate Relationships

It is possible to have a My/My Pattern at work and My/Your one in a relationship. Since My/Your people do not usually state what they expect from their partner in a marriage, it may be useful for them to switch into My/My from time to time just to let the other person know what they want or do not want. If someone stays in a My/Your mode and consequently doesn't let their partner know what they like or dislike, it can cause long-term resentments. I know couples who do not talk about important issues, such as how to help or not help their adult children in crises, or planning finances and retirement. When I asked why they don't discuss such things as a couple, they just looked at me helplessly. Similarly, people who spend most of their time in a My/My mode in their marriage may want to shift into My/Your to learn how their partner perceives the situation.

I believe that by knowing the different Patterns, you can start to choose which one would be the most appropriate at a given time.

Raising Kids

In the Context of raising children, do you find out from your children what they want, understanding them to be who they are, as well as telling them what you expect? In parenting, it is often appropriate to be in a My/My mode. It is also fitting at other times to use My/Your. One of the goals of parenting is to foster children's growth and development.

Helicopter Parenting, a mode of parenting from birth through to early adulthood where parents supervise, direct, coach, control, and attempt to prevent failure or other negative experiences for their children is an extreme example of My/My, combined with Internal and Procedures in the Context of being a parent. (I know the right way that my child should do something). It is however increasingly common and seems to be related to the rise in mental health issues in university students.[1] If we add in the loneliness factor, mentioned in the Style chapter, it seems as though smart phones and parenting methods aren't helping children mature into adults.

According to a study quoted in the New York Times, the parents of ordinarily creative children had an average of 6 rules, while the parents of highly creative children only had one.[2] Fewer rules, telling your kids what to do and how to do it produces more creative kids. But they are probably harder to manage!

Summary

Rule Structure

Question: ***What is a good way for you to increase your success (at work)? What is a good way for someone else to increase their success (at work)?***

My/My: My rules for me. My rules for you. Able to tell others what they expect.

My/.: My rules for me. I don't care about others.

No/My: Don't know rules for me. My rules for you. Typical middle management pattern.

My/Your: My rules for me. Your rules for you. Hesitant to tell others what to do.

Distribution at Work:

75% My/My

3% My/.

7% No/My.

15% My/Your

(in the work Context, from Rodger Bailey)

Summary

Influencing Language:

My/My: "You would do that if you were him? You know what you want and what would work for the others, apply what you think to the situation with thegroup." (these phrases reflect that the person decides for themselves and others)

My/.:   For this group, I suggest using the language that you would use for Internals. "You're sure about this and it doesn't matter about the others, this may be in your best interest, it doesn't matter what *they* think."

No/My: "Now that you've been informed about what's expected, you can pass that along, wait until you hear from the boss and then let everyone know, would you tell the group what the rules are from our guideline book, what would George do?"

My/Your: "You know what you should do and you want to leave it up to the others to decide for themselves, you have your own unique way and recognize that each person is different, everyone is different."

---

[1] bit.ly/KidsOfHelicopterParents

[2] DACEY, J. S. (1989), Discriminating Characteristics of the Families of Highly Creative Adolescents. The Journal of Creative Behavior, 23: 263–271. doi: 10.1002/j.2162-6057.1989.tb00700.x, quoted in the New York Times, 2016, 0131.

Chapter 17
Convincer Channel:
How People Gather Information

What type of information does a person need to gather, in order to start the process of being convinced?

The information you will glean from the last two categories in the LAB Profile® is especially important for sales people. The Convincer Channel category and the next one, the Convincer Mode, deal with how a person gets convinced about something. Until someone is convinced, they will not take the appropriate actions. At the moment they become truly convinced about something, they are most likely to buy the product or service, or to perform the task at hand.

For each given Context, people generally have a Pattern about how they get convinced. There are two phases in this process. First, people will *gather information in a specific sensory channel*, (Convincer Channel), and then they will *treat that information in some way* (Convincer Mode).

Channel Patterns

See: They need to visually "see" a product, service or idea.

Hear: They need an oral presentation or to hear something.

Read: They need to read something.

Do: They have to do something.

Distribution %
(in the work Context, from Rodger Bailey)

See	55%
Hear	30%
Read	3%
Do	12%

Identification

Questions:

HOW DO YOU KNOW THAT SOMEONE ELSE IS GOOD AT THEIR WORK?

or

HOW DO YOU KNOW THAT ... (a car) IS WORTH ... (buying)?

- **See:** have to see some evidence
- **Hear:** will listen or hear what someone will say
- **Read:** read reports, etc.
- **Do:** have to work with someone to know

Examples

See:	*"Just by watching them."*
Hear:	*"When they explain their decisions you can judge their rationale and thinking process."*
Read:	*"I read their reports."*
Do:	*"I have to work with them to get a feel for how they work."*

Sometimes people will have more than one answer to this question. For example, they may need to both *see* and *hear* evidence.

Applications

When you wish to convince someone about something, in a sales situation for example, or when assigning a task, you can simply match their Convincer Channel. If you know what kind (Channel) of information they need in that Context, simply give them the information in that form. If you don't know the preferred Channel, try using See. Our culture is wired for images and movies. I teach people my Influencing and Persuasion Principle, whenever I am teaching LAB Profile®:

"In order to get people to go somewhere with you, you need to meet them where they are and not just pretend they are already where you want them to be."

Most people cannot remember the principle, but even decades later they remember the bus stop, which is an image you can hold in your mind's eye – the whole idea about going to someone's bus stop.

Examples

See:	*"I would like to show you a sample."*
Hear:	*"Sounds alright, doesn't it? Is there anything else you need to discuss?"*
Read:	*"The figures in the reports are good."*
Do:	*"You'll want to work with it for a bit to decide."*

Influencing Language

You can show a person what you are talking about between the lines, just the same way that they do it. Here is some sensory: based vocabulary for the above Patterns:

See

- see, look at it this way, show, perspective, image, clear, clarify, light, dark, shiny, colorful, visualize, light up, vague, foggy, horizon, flash, get a look at, picture it, see it in action, view it, etc.

Hear

- hear, talk, listen, wonder, say, question, ask, dialogue, ring, noise, rhythm, in tune, harmonious, musical, tone, discord, symphony, shout, discuss, hear about, tell yourself, etc.

Read

- read the report, go through the text, scan the page, read through, read in detail

Do

- feel, touch, grasp, gather, in contact with, connect, concrete, pressure, sensitive, solid, closed, open, soft, link, hot, cold, warm, try it out, make sense, work with it, grapple with it, try it on, test it out, etc.

Summary

Convincer Channel

Question: *How do you know that someone else is good at their work?*

See: Needs to see evidence

Hear: Needs an oral presentation or to hear something.

Read: Needs to read something.

Do: Needs to do something with the evidence.

Distribution at Work:

55% See

30% Hear

3% Read

12% Do

(in the work Context, from Rodger Bailey)

Influencing Language:

Match the sensory channel (see, hear, read, do) with your language.

Chapter 18
Convincer Mode: Clinching the Deal

> *What does a person do with the information previously gathered in order to become convinced?*

After a person has gathered the information in a specific sensory Channel, they will need to treat it in some way in order to become *convinced* about it. This treatment is called the Convincer Mode.

There are four Patterns:

Number of Examples

Number of Examples people need to have the data a certain number of times to be convinced, or to learn something.

Automatic

People with an Automatic Pattern, take a small amount of information and decide immediately based on what they imagine the rest to be. They jump to conclusions and, once decided, do not easily change their minds. They will often give the benefit of the doubt.

Consistent

Believe it or not, Consistent people are never completely convinced. Every day is a new day and they need to re-evaluate every time. I call this the *Scarlett O'Hara* Pattern, because "Tomorrow is another day."

Period of Time

Period of Time people need to gather information for a certain duration before their conviction is triggered.

Distribution % (in the work Context, from Rodger Bailey)	
Number of Examples	52%
Automatic	8%
Consistent	15%
Period of Time	25%

Identification

Question:

HOW MANY TIMES DO THEY HAVE TO DEMONSTRATE THIS (see, hear, read, do) **BEFORE YOU ARE CONVINCED?**

Number of examples

- will state a specific number of times

Automatic

- one example or assume people are good
- give the benefit of the doubt

Consistent

- never really convinced
- judge each time

Period of Time

- will talk about a duration or period of time they need

The question, as designed, asks for a specific number of times. People will either be able to answer that question or it will, at first, flummox them. Then you will know, by the process of elimination, that the Pattern is *not* Number of Examples.

Examples

Number of Examples:	*"Two or three times."*
Automatic:	*"I can tell right away."*
Consistent:	*"You have to judge each piece of work."*
Period of time:	*"Over a couple of months."*

Here are some sample dialogues, to show you how to test to make sure:

SRC:	Gillian, how do you know that an equal of yours is good at their job?
Gillian:	I just need to see and hear them once.
SRC:	Once?
Gillian:	Yeah, I can tell right away.

There's a hint here. Sometimes you will get the answer to both the Channel and Mode questions when you ask the first one. Gillian needs to see and hear, and has an Automatic Convincer Mode.

SRC:	Jim, how do you know someone else is good at their job?
Jim:	I'll see what they've accomplished and hear good things about them.
SRC:	How many times do you have to see and hear that to be convinced that they have done a good job?
Jim:	Two or three times.
SRC:	(Let's test to be sure.) So if you saw and heard that twice, would you be totally convinced that they're good at their job?

Jim:	Maybe.
SRC:	If you saw and heard that three times, would you be totally convinced?
Jim:	Yes. (nodding his head)

Jim needs to see and hear; Number of Examples: 3

SRC:	Natasha, how do you know someone else is good at their job?
Natasha:	I would want to work with them for a while.
SRC:	How many times do you have to work with them?
Natasha:	Uh, I don't know. How long?

Natasha's Channel is Do; she also revealed her Period of Time Pattern while answering to the first question, confirming it in her second answer. Now we need to find out how long she needs to get convinced:

SRC:	How long would you have to work with someone to be convinced that they are good at their job?
Natasha:	Oh, a couple of weeks.
SRC:	So if you worked with someone for a couple of weeks, you would be convinced?
Natasha:	Yes.
SRC:	Adam, how do you know that a colleague of yours is good at their job?
Adam:	I read their monthly reports.
SRC:	How many times would you have to read someone's monthly reports to be convinced that she or he is good?
Adam:	Well every report is different. You could do a good job on one and not on the next. You have to read each one.

Adam needs to read (Channel) and has a Consistent Pattern for his Convincer Mode. He is never completely convinced once and for all; he judges each time.

Applications

Most of the population (52%) has a Number of Examples Pattern (in the Context of Work), which means that they need to have the data a certain number of times to be convinced. Old advertising dogma stated that if you repeated a message six times, or ten times depending on the author within a given time period, most people would get the message and act upon it. Online advertisers seem to believe that if you flood potential customers with ads, follow them wherever they go on the internet and show them ads for the same product or service, eventually people will crack and buy their stuff. And the online ad Gurus each believe they have the magic formula to get people to buy your stuff: "If you get this ONE THING right...."

In the personal development field, there was a now debunked belief, that 21 days is enough to change a habit. It apparently depends on what kind of habit one is trying to change, but what is interesting in LAB Profile® terms is that the research and discussions about habit-changing are about Period of Time rather than Number of Examples.

Learning

Let's take education as a Context for a moment. A child is learning addition or subtraction at school and needs to repeat the sums twelve times to be convinced that she has learned it. The chances are that during school hours she will never get the number of examples she needs to convince herself that she can add or subtract. Lessons are usually designed with a certain number of repetitions of skill sets. If a teacher can detect how a student having difficulty gets convinced that she knows how to add, then exercises can be adapted to provide the necessary repetition.

This information can also be useful for parents to help their children with school work. "How would you know that someone can read well?" "When they can get all the words right away." (Channel: Do) "How many times would they have to get all the words right away for you to be *sure* that they can read well?" "Ummm, lots of times." "Lots? If someone could read all the words right away three times would you be sure?" "Hmm, I'm not sure." "Well, let's say they read all the words five times right away; would you be sure then?" "Yeah, of course." Then, as a parent, you can make sure that, at each stage of reading, the child counts the number of times up to five that they got the words. Once the child gets the *proof* they need, they will believe that they can do it and will read with more confidence.

You will sometimes need to discuss the proof with the child. If getting *all* the words or *always* getting the right answer is unrealistic, then maybe you could help them use a more attainable proof.

If a child has Consistent Pattern (never completely convinced) in the Context of learning, you will notice that she will need to get convinced that she knows something *each* time she does that activity. You might want to point out that this time is like *each other time*, in that the child was able to do it, once again.

Tough Customers

People with an Automatic Pattern tend to take a small amount of information and decide immediately based on what they extrapolate. In other words, they hallucinate the rest, then they decide. They are the sort of people who jump to conclusions or make snap decisions. If you are trying to convince an Automatic person of something and they say no in the first breath, do not bother going back to try to reconvince them. They only rarely change their minds.

Consistent people take nothing for granted. Combined with Away From, this Pattern is ideal in tasks that involve checking for mistakes or in any kind of quality control. You would not want Joe to think that, since he "knows" Charleen performs well, he does not really need to check.

As customers, Consistent people are the most difficult to deal with. You will need to re-establish your credibility each time you serve them. They may love your service one day and hate it the next and love it again the following day. They appear skeptical and just will not get convinced. Use the same Influencing Language as for an Internal person, paying attention to match their Convincer Channel. "I suggest you try it out before you decide" (Do, Consistent), or "Look it over and tell me what you think" (See, Consistent). This group is the most likely to return items that they have bought, or to change their minds on something they have agreed to in a negotiation.

I was working with the Marketing Department of a Pharmaceutical company once a month, to teach them LAB Profile® and help design their marketing initiatives for the sales reps and the doctors with whom the reps would be speaking. On the first day, Tammy walked in, looking miserable, slammed her files down on the table, slumped into her chair and grumbled about wasting her time here when she had many other things to get done. By the end of the day, she was very enthusiastic about the work and its applications. In our second workday together, (a month later), she came in looking miserable, slammed her files down on the table and began grumbling again. "Strange," I thought, as I had the impression she had been convinced this work was worthwhile. And by the end of the day, her enthusiasm had reappeared. When the same thing occurred on the third session, I realized that she had a Consistent Convincer Mode, and I just needed to re-establish rapport and credibility with her. Even today, she keeps in touch with me and wherever she is working, looks for opportunities to have me come in and consult with her team.

Period of Time people need to have information over a set duration before they get convinced. Your customer may tell you that she needs to discuss (Hear) your product for a couple months. You can either wait for that period or phone her a few weeks later and say that you have been so busy, it feels like a couple of months have gone by. There have been several participants in my LAB Profile® Consultant/Trainer Certification with this Pattern. For several days, they are reticent to join in activities, they look skeptical, or put up an Invisibility Force Field around themselves. And then suddenly they pop up, participate enthusiastically and laugh with self-recognition when we talk about the Period of Time Convincer Mode.

I worked with a small business owner who was having difficulty finding the right team members for several of the highly-skilled positions he wanted to fill. His process was fine, which involved a probationary period where the candidates would be given assignments to do. It turned out the issue was the business owner's Period of Time Convincer Mode. He was giving people three to six months to perform, even when he wasn't happy with the first or second piece of work. After much discussion about this Convincer Pattern, he made himself say yes or no after one or two projects with a much shorter time frame. And he agreed to test out more than one candidate at the same time (they all work remotely). This has enabled him to eliminate people who cannot do the work and has helped him find the right people much more quickly.

Influencing Language

Each time you are with people, you can give them the benefit of the doubt that they will consistently take the time they need to make up their minds, at least a couple of times.

(Remember to also match the Convincer Channel)

Number of Examples:

- (Use the number)

Automatic:

- You can assume; benefit of the doubt; decide fast; right now

Consistent:

- try it; each time you use it; every time; consistent performance; don't take my word

Period of Time:

- (match the period of time) a couple weeks, an hour or so, 10 days

Summary

Convincer Mode

Question: *How many times do they have to demonstrate (see, hear, read, do) this for you to be convinced (that they are good at their work)?*

Number of Examples: They need to have the data a given number of times to be convinced.

Automatic: They take a small amount of information and get convinced immediately. They hardly ever change their minds.

Consistent: They are never completely convinced. Every day is a new day and they need to get reconvinced.

Period of Time: They need to gather the information for a certain duration before their conviction is triggered.

Distribution at Work:

52% Number of Examples

8% Automatic

15% Consistent

25% Period of Time

(in the work Context, from Rodger Bailey)

Influencing Language:

Number of Examples: use their number

Automatic: assume; benefit of the doubt

Consistent: try it; each time you use it; daily; every time; use Internal Influencing Language

Period of Time: match the period of time

Chapter 19
The LAB Profile® Worksheet: Productivity Patterns

On the following page is the second half of the worksheet to assist you in profiling someone's Productivity Patterns. I have again included the indicators for each to help you practice recognizing the Patterns.

You can find a complete profiling sheet for both the Motivation and Productivity Patterns in the Summaries section at the back of the book.

LAB Profile® Worksheet: Productivity Patterns

Name: _____	Company: _____
Profiler: _____	Position: _____
Date: _____	Context: _____

Questions	Categories	Patterns: Indicators
(no questions for Scope and Attention Direction)	**SCOPE** _____	**Specific:** *details, sequences, exactly*
	_____	**General:** *overview, big picture, random order*
	ATTENTION DIRECTION _____	**Self:** *short monotone responses*
	_____	**Other:** *animated, expressive, automatic responses*
Tell me about a (work situation) that gave you trouble.	**STRESS RESPONSE** _____	**Feeling:** *goes in and stays in feelings*
	_____	**Choice:** *goes in and out of feelings*
	_____	**Thinking:** *doesn't go into feelings*
Tell me about a (work situation) that was (Criteria).	**STYLE** _____	**Independent:** *alone, I, sole responsibility*
	_____	**Proximity:** *in control, others around*
(wait for answer)	_____	**Cooperative:** *we, team, share responsibility*
What did you like about it?	**ORGANIZATION** _____	**Person:** *people, feelings, reactions*
	_____	**Thing:** *tools, tasks, ideas*
What is a good way for you to increase your success at *(your work)*?	**RULE STRUCTURE** _____	**My/My:** *My rules for me/My rules for you*
What is a good way for someone else to increase their success at (their work)?	_____	**My/. (period):** *My rules for me/ Who cares?*
	_____	**No/My:** *No rules for me/My rules for you*
	_____	**My/Your:** *My rules for me/Your rules for you*
How do you know that someone else *(an equal of yours)* is good at their *(work)*?	**CONVINCER** _____	See ____ **# of Examples:** *give number*
	_____	Hear ____ **Automatic:** *benefit of the doubt*
	_____	Read ____ **Consistent:** *not completely convinced*
How many times do you have to *(see, hear, read, do)* that to be convinced they are good?	_____	Do ____ **Period of Time:** *give time period*

Part 4: Applications

Chapter 20
How to Complete a LAB Profile®

The completion of the LAB Profile® has 2 stages:

    A. Asking the Questions

    B. Guess and Test (to validate step A)

A. Asking the Questions

At this stage, you ask the LAB Profile® questions and mark how many indicators you see/hear for each Pattern. You don't have to write down what they answer (except for the Criteria question). For the rest of the Patterns, just make a mark, each time you see/hear an indicator of a Pattern. You are not as interested in WHAT people are saying, as HOW they say it.

Here are the steps:

1. Write the name, company name, etc. Choose a Context and write it down. Refer to this Context before you ask each question to make sure they stay within that context (E.g. "With regards to your work as a Project Manager, why is that important?").

2. Ask the questions and make a mark each time you see/hear an indicator of a Pattern. You may end up having 3 marks for Options and 1 for Procedures, etc.

3. There aren't any questions to ask for Proactive/Reactive and General/Specific, and Self/Other. Watch and pay attention to the non-verbal signs to detect these Patterns.

B. Guess and Test

The Guess and Test phase also ensures that you understood correctly, helps correct for any bias and makes the whole process more accurate and objective. After you have finished the questionnaire, and have your first round of marks, it's time to test what you got by giving feedback to the person and noticing their response:

1. The first step is making sure you are at ease describing the behaviors of each of the LAB Profile® Patterns. To master that, I suggest you practice describing each Pattern, as many times or for as long as you need, to become comfortable with that.

Example:

"Toward: when you have a Toward Pattern you are focused on achieving a goal. If you don't have a goal, it is hard to get motivated or to get started. And you don't like having to deal with problems."

2. Then, to give someone feedback, start with the Context and, using statements, describe the behaviors associated with the Patterns you marked. Watch the person react as you are giving them the statements. People will instinctively agree or correct what you have said. Their reaction, either nodding in confirmation, looking confused or negating the description etc., will enable you to confirm or change what you thought was the Pattern. If you are still not sure after offering the person your statement, ask them to give you an example. Listen for examples of the Pattern language in their example.

Example:

"When you are at work (Context), you have what is called a Toward Motivation Pattern. This means you tend to be focused on achieving a goal. If you don't have a goal, it is hard to get motivated or to get started. And you don't like having to deal with problems."

Remember to keep on specifying the Context. Otherwise, they might slip into a different Context and their Patterns may be different there. **Use statements rather than questions** to do the guessing and testing. It's ok to have a questioning tone, as long as you are making statements in your sentence structure.

Example:

"When you are working as a Project Manager (Context reminder), *you like to prevent problems from occurring."* (Away From)

Here are some great statement starters that you can use, to avoid asking questions in the Guess and Test stage:

In X Context,

- it seems to me that you like ....
- I have the impression that you ....
- I suspect that you like ...
- what motivates you is ...

Note: You can correct your scoring, based on the feedback you get in this phase.

You may wish to **watch the demonstration videos** to see how I do it.[1] You can download my **LAB Profile® Cheat Sheet**[2] so that you will have all the questions and language to listen for, right in your hand, and not have to remember everything.

---

[1] Demonstration videos of asking the LAB Profile® Questions and doing the Guess and Test to test for accuracy: bit.ly/LabProfileDemoVideo1; bit.ly/LabProfileDemoVideo2; bit.ly/LabProfileDemoVideo3; bit.ly/LabProfileDemoVideo4

[2] I designed the LAB Profile® Cheat Sheet to help you with the questions and answers, in case you don't remember them all: bit.ly/LabProfileCheatSheet

Chapter 21
Applications

In this section, I have included examples of different applications for the LAB Profile®. You will find lots of hints and subtleties on the uses of the questions, the Combination Patterns and on the Influencing Language.

The following topics will be covered:

- Understanding and Working with Combination Patterns
- Influencing Strategies and Techniques
- The LAB Profile® of Conflict
- Conversational Coaching with the LAB Profile®
- Career Coaching and Personal Profiles
- Corporate Culture Diagnosis and Change Measurement
- Recruiting Employees Who Perform
- Building a High-Performance Team
- Negotiating
- Understand and Speak to Your Market
- Education and Learning
- Default Profiles
- LAB Profile® Inventions and Tools

Chapter 22
The Next Step: Understanding and Working with Pattern Combinations

Since the publication of the previous editions of *Words That Change Minds*, and translation of the book into multiple languages, thousands and thousands of people worldwide have been using the LAB Profile® to understand their own and other peoples' motivations. I have been engaged by companies to identify the unconscious Motivation Patterns and Triggers of clients, as well as to train coaches, trainers and organizational leaders to use the LAB Profile®. They have learned how to improve their communication, get better results in persuasion and recruit people who "fit".

But.

The LAB Profile® in its very basic form shows you how to pay attention to one Pattern at a time. Both unfortunately and fortunately, human beings are more complicated than that. To truly understand the source of behavior and what motives them, you need to take into account complex sequences of Contexts, each having combinations of several LAB Profile® Patterns.

While it is useful to know that someone has an Internal Pattern while at work, this knowledge is insufficient to understand, predict and influence their behavior. They are Internal with regards to whom? What Criteria motivate them? Do they need to follow a Procedure or explore Options? Do they focus on tasks or relationships at work? (Thing and Person) Someone who has the Combination of Internal, Options and Thing at Work will have a strong preference for having much flexibility in their tasks.

If they have Proactive and Towards Patterns as well as Internal, Options and Thing at work, then it is very likely that they will jump into doing many activities at once, without thinking about the consequences or taking into account any feedback on lack of efficiency of starting so many things at once.

One reason I also wrote, *Words That Change Customers' Minds* was to demonstrate how to work with LAB Profile® Combination Patterns specifically in the sales and service Contexts.

For my clients who offer products and services to other businesses (B2B), I have helped them decode the Combination Patterns in each step of the Buying Cycle typically used by their prospective customers. From this analysis, we created the appropriate marketing language at each step and identified the Buying Process to adapt to each prospective client to accompany in their own, unique way.

The big discovery from this kind of work is that there are indeed, certain Pattern Combinations that work for different kinds of groups, even very large groups. Once you can find out what they have in common, you can then direct your communication based on these common Combinations.

When you know what the Combination Patterns of your group of prospects are, you can increase your sales and reduce the time it takes to make a sale. For my mutual fund client who sells investment strategies to "high net worth individuals," we discovered that one group of clients first preferred to evaluate the options for themselves, so as to avoid losing money. (Internal, Options and Away From). Then, after having checked out the options for themselves, they wanted to be told how to proceed to obtain their financial targets. (External, Procedures, Toward). These clients had 2 separate Contexts in their process, each with its own Pattern Combination.

How to identify Pattern Combinations

Once you have someone's LAB Profile® for a given Context, here are the steps to take to determine which Patterns interact with other Patterns to create a behavior or an attitude.

1. Briefly review the behaviors associated with each separate Pattern,
2. Ask myself if each Pattern would add to or counteract the behavior of the other Patterns,

3. *Look at what the overall Patterns seem to add up to.*

Example:

Toward and Internal
Toward: Needs a goal to get into action, focuses on the goal.
Internal: Judges for self, based on what they think is important.

This person knows what they want and is difficult to persuade otherwise.

Example:

Away From, External, Other, Feeling, Person
Away From: notices what is or what might be going wrong.
External: needs feedback from outside, is influenced by what others are thinking & doing.
Other: notices and responds to non-verbal cues from other people.
Feeling: gets upset when there is trouble and stays in negative feelings for a long time.
Person: organizes time to pay attention to people, feelings & experiences.

This person notices when others are upset or have problems because they are paying attention, is easily upset by these problems, and stays upset by them.

Now, to understand how one Pattern could reduce some of the above behavior, let's substitute the Thing Pattern for Person:
Thing: focuses on tasks, things to be done.

This would somewhat counteract the tendency to take on other people's negative states. They would focus more on the problem than being upset for the other person and may be more likely to find a way to solve it and stay more focused on that.

Looking for the Combination Patterns in Someone's Profile

Particularly when you are recruiting, it is useful to look at the Combination Patterns of your candidates to help make more accurate predictions about how they are likely to perform in a given position. Knowing their Combinations is also helpful when you want to influence someone.

Here is the LAB Profile® of a Sales Director at Work:

Motivation Patterns

Level		
√√		Proactive
√		Reactive
Criteria		
success, results, improve methods, find better strategies		
Direction		
√√		Toward
√		Away From
Source		
√√		Internal
_____		External
Reason		
√		Options
√√		Procedures
Decision Factors		
_____		Sameness
√		Sameness with Exception
_____		Difference
_____		Sameness with Exception & Difference

Productivity Patterns

Scope

√		Specific
√√		General

Attention Direction

		Self
√		Other

Stress Response

		Feeling
√		Choice
		Thinking

Style

√		Independent
√√		Proximity
		Cooperative

Organization

		Person
√√		Thing

Rule Structure

√		My/My
		My/. (period)
		No/My
		My/Your

Convincer

√	See	3		No. of Examples
	Hear			Automatic
	Read			Consistent
	Do			Period of Time

At first glance, this Sales Director has several Patterns which could come together to create a behavior:

Mainly Proactive, Towards, Internal, Procedure, Sameness with Exception and Thing.

They would probably tend to jump into action to reach their goals, knowing that this is the right thing to do, without listening to what others think. They probably have little patience when things are late or with obstacles, because they are proactively focused on their goals and want them done right away. To persuade or motivate this Director it is in our best interest to suggest (Language of Suggestion for Internals) the method (Procedures + Thing) to achieve their goals faster (Towards, Thing + Proactive).

"May I suggest that you consider (Internal) having your sales team use the LAB Profile® questionnaire (Procedure + Thing) during their initial meetings to speed up the needs analysis and create rapport (Towards, Thing + Proactive)?"

Here is the LAB Profile® of a Human Resources Director:

Motivation Patterns

Level
√_____   Proactive
√_____   Reactive

Criteria
create a performance culture, find great tools for the team,
make a difference to the people and to the business

Direction
√_____   Toward
√√_____   Away From

Source
√√_____   Internal
√_____   External

Reason
√√_____   Options
√_____   Procedures

Decision Factors
_____   Sameness
√_____   Sameness with Exception
√√_____   Difference
_____   Sameness with Exception & Difference

Productivity Patterns

Scope			
√	Specific		
√√	General		

Attention Direction

_____	Self		
√	Other		

Stress Response

_____	Feeling		
√	Choice		
_____	Thinking		

Style

_____	Independent		
√√	Proximity		
_____	Cooperative		

Organization

√	Person		
√	Thing		

Rule Structure

√	My/My		
_____	My/. (period)		
_____	No/My		
_____	My/Your		

Convincer

√	See	2	No. of Examples
√	Hear	_____	Automatic
_____	Read	_____	Consistent
_____	Do	_____	Period of Time

Here is one Combination that enables us to understand, predict and influence this HR Director:

Mainly Away From, Mainly Internal, Options and Difference

When they notice an issue or problem, chances are they will be motivated to explore the possibilities of creating a change. They also have another interesting Combination:

Proactive/Reactive, Mainly Internal, Proximity and Person/Thing

With this Combination, they may consult with others before making a decision for themselves. If they had an Independent Pattern instead of Proximity, they would have less tendency to consult. To persuade a person with both these Combinations, make a suggestion (Language of Suggestion for Internals) about the choices (Options) to avoid, prevent or resolve an issue (Away From) or to change (Difference) something.

> *"You might wish (Language of Suggestion for Internals) to avoid (Away From) these choices (Options) if you want to change (Difference) the results (Thing) and whom it affects (Person)."*

LAB Profile® Combination Patterns for Behaviors

Being able to work with LAB Profile® Combinations can enable you to understand, and therefore influence complex behaviors. Below are a couple of examples.

Profile of Cheaters: The Volkswagen Emissions Scandal

In 2015, the news broke that Volkswagen had fixed the emissions control software in their diesel cars to perform well during inspections and tests, but to violate American pollution standards under normal driving conditions.

The investigation showed that the decision to cheat had been made as early as 2005. In a New York Times article[1], VW executives described the thinking and behaviors around the decision to do this:

- the company's **ambitions** in the United States collided with US air quality rules (Criterion of "ambition" Toward, and Internal)
- "In 2007, Volkswagen executives declared their **determination to overtake Toyota as the largest carmaker in the world and were eager for any competitive edge.**" (Criteria, Internal, Toward)
- intense internal debate about what kind of emissions technology to use (Internal and Options)
- tolerance for breaking the rules (Options)

- "a chain of errors that were allowed to happen" (Internal and Procedures, once the decisions were made, they decided (allowed) to follow through - errors indeed!)

If these descriptions are accurate, then the Profile of the cheaters would be:

Criteria: ambition, overtake Toyota as world's largest car maker
Toward (that goal)
Internal (making the decisions based on what is important to themselves)
Options (breaking the rules) and **Procedures** (in implementing the prior decisions to break the rules).

This could be a Profile of many cheaters; have **Criteria** about succeeding or winning at all costs, with a Combination of **Toward** (focusing on the goal and not looking out for what is wrong with what you are doing), **Internal** (convincing oneself and deciding based on one's own Criteria), **Options** (motivated to break the rules) and lastly **Procedures** (for the step by step implementation). This Combination of Patterns does not tell you that someone *will* cheat, only that they are *more likely* to cheat than someone who has different Criteria with the same Internal with Procedures Patterns.

Profile of the Radicalization Process

Most people do not become "radicalized." However, it can happen when certain conditions arise in the environment and in the person them self. These conditions can be described and therefore can be decoded into LAB Profile® Patterns. David Brooks, in an opinion piece in the New York Times[2], discussed Eric Hoffer's thesis from his classic work: *The True Believer: Thoughts on the Nature of Mass Movements.* According to Hoffer, the prime objective of mass movements is to get the individual to sacrifice them self. This is most likely to happen when traditional, strong social structures have fallen apart, and the individuals concerned are frustrated; unable to achieve their dreams or even their "normal" ambitions, and they have lost faith in being able to succeed.

Then, the successful mass movement can convince them that the cause of their frustration is from an outside source. The past is glorified; the present vilified. The next step is promoting the belief that a radical change is needed, to become a vividly described future utopian world, more real than the current reality, made possible by an "infallible leader". This leader decides everything as the individual and their experience of reality is diminished. Hoffer says: "For men to plunge headlong into an undertaking of vast change they must be intensely discontented yet not destitute, and they must have the feeling that by the possession of some potent doctrine, infallible leader or some new technique they have access to a source of irresistible power. They must also have an extravagant conception of the prospects and potentialities of the future. Finally, they must be wholly ignorant of the difficulties involved in their vast undertaking. Experience is a handicap."

If this is correct, the Context, in LAB Profile® terms, is about a crumbling social order (**broken Procedures and Sameness**), the blame is on someone else (**External and Reactive**), with a leader who will make everything Different (**External to leader, Difference**), plus a focus on a glorious **Past** and **Future**.

The individual feels extremely frustrated with their current situation (**Reactive, Away From, and Feeling**), needs the social structure they had before which no longer works (**Procedure, Sameness, Person and Thing**), and doesn't have the solution in themselves (**External**). This combination of **Reactive, Away From, Feeling, External**, needing **Procedure and Sameness**, makes them long for an **External** solution or person who will bring the right answer. When the leader or ideology appears, these individuals are ripe for the picking.

The above description does not completely explain their willingness to jump into action to kill or die for the cause because, even though they are **External to the leader**, they are still in **Reactive** mode. I suspect that an analysis of the LAB Profile® Patterns using an objective technology such as my Libretta® software could identify if the language used by such a 'radical', had switched into indicators that the person was ready to act.

The LAB Profile® Patterns for Changing a Habit

Many people believe that changing a habit is hard. Maybe, or maybe not. A habit, a habitual behavior is about being in Procedures, Sameness, and Internal. I decide to do the same thing, in the same way, over and over. What does one need to do to change a habit? Because of the Combination Patterns in a habit, it is probably easier to create a new habit, than break an old habit.

According to a study quoted in the Scientific American[3], heavy drinkers aged 19 to 25 who got text messages before and after each weekend reminding them of their plans to reduce their alcohol intake, reduced their drinking significantly more, than those who did not. This study among others, indicates that **External** measures help people adopt a new habit, at least at the beginning. I suspect that when people are unsuccessful at adopting a new habit, it could be because they don't get the **External support** and they do not follow a systematic **Procedure**. (Procedure and Sameness). No Procedure usually means no commitment to the new habit.

An interesting study[4] used two strategies to get people to start and keep going to the gym. For the first four weeks, employees were given $10 per gym visit to a maximum of three visits. At the end of the four weeks, the payments stopped, but some employees were offered a "commitment contract" where they could put aside their own money which would be given to them only if they went to the gym regularly for the following two months, otherwise it would go to charity. **This group was 20% more likely to work out regularly than the group not offered this contract, <u>three years after the end</u> of the three-month experiment.**

In LAB Profile® terms, the kick-start motivation came from External and Toward. An external source rewarded the target behavior. For the maintenance part of the experiment, it was a combination of Internal and External, along with the Toward. I decide to put the money aside for myself, and then the external authority decides if I get the money based on if I have completed the target activity.

Imagine if you added in the Procedure and Sameness, how much easier it would be to create a new habit, especially if it were something you wanted to do, or gave you a result you wanted. As we saw in the chapter on Toward and Away From, an Away From motivation can get you started in a new direction because you can't stand the current situation any longer ("my jeans shrunk"), but it isn't motivating enough over the longer term.

How Self-Help "Gurus" Get You to Buy

I wrote an article and developed a keynote speech entitled *Sex, Diets and Success*, which received much positive feedback. It decodes the sequence of LAB Profile® Pattern Combinations used by the "Merchants of Success" to get people to buy. I also explain how these same Patterns set most people up to fail, then blame themselves and encourage them to buy the next self-help product in the hopes that this will be the one that will "do it for them." When you are invited to dream of vast wealth, big mansions, fancy cars, etc., you are invited to shift into Reactive, Options and See Patterns, which is great for dreaming but not for getting something done! The article also shows you how to distinguish between those Merchants of Success and the personal and professional Partners in Progress who can actually help you.[5]

In the Applications chapters, I will be covering other ways to use LAB Profile® Context and Pattern combinations to understand and influence outcomes, solve problems and help people to improve results and I will demonstrate how to do this.

How many Patterns can you find in the sentence above?

[1] VW Says Emissions Cheating Was Not a One-Time Error; by Jack Ewing: bit.ly/EmissionsCheating

[2] How ISIS Makes Radicals, by David Brooks: bit.ly/HowIsisMakesRadicals; Eric Hoffer; The True Believer: Thoughts on the Nature of Mass Movements

[3] bit.ly/TextRemindersCutBingeDrinking

[4] A study by lead author Heather Royer, quoted in, Josh Barro; How to Make Yourself Go to the Gym: bit.ly/HowToMakeYourselfGoToTheGym, January 10, 2015

[5] Here is the link to my article and intro to my keynote, entitled Sex, Diets and Success: bit.ly/SexDietsandSuccess

Chapter 23
Influencing Strategies and Techniques

Now that you know the individual LAB Profile® Patterns and see how they work in Combinations, it's very helpful to be able to have specific influencing strategies and techniques to really *up your impact* every day. This chapter gives you several ways to influence and then shows you how to use them, including recapping some of the techniques from earlier chapters. Any time you need to influence, this is your reference for both inspiration and technique.

The Bus Stop

The Influencing and Persuasion Principle states:

> *To get people to go somewhere with you, you need to meet them where they are and not just pretend they are already where you want them to be. Go to their bus stop, and from their bus stop, invite them to let the bus take them where you want them to be.*

Going to someone's bus stop implies imagining what it is like to be them, in their situation, experiencing what they are living, and operating from their LAB Profile® Patterns in this situation. In tense or conflictual situations, it may take some time and personal work to get there.

I recently set myself an overall personal goal to be a better person, by getting in touch with how others are experiencing a situation before I react (go to their bus stop). I noticed that in tense situations, I had to go through the steps of being annoyed, feeling rejected, believing the other person was completely unreasonable, and working through that until I got to the point of having some calm and insight. Then it was much easier to go to the other person's bus stop.

In practice, what does it mean to go to someone's bus stop? Is there a process (Procedure)? In order to have someone be willing to get on your bus and go somewhere, you need to pick them up at their bus stop. Here is the formula:

Match, Match, Match, Lead

That means matching their Patterns at least three times before leading them to what you want. For example, if you would like someone to finish a report by Tuesday and they have an Away From and Internal Pattern Combination, you could say:

*"Since you mentioned that it is important to you (**Internal**) to avoid making mistakes (**Away From**), because you don't like (**Internal and Away From**) having to redo work over again, and that it isn't like you (**Internal and Away From**) to miss a deadline, I just wanted to let you know (**Language for Externals**) that the report is due to go out on Tuesday (**Toward**).*

The Language of Suggestion vs. Command Language

I like to assume that everyone is Internal to me, unless there is proof that they are in External Mode with me. That means I operate as if I haven't yet established credibility *in their eyes*, and they are evaluating for themselves whatever I am saying and doing and don't want me to *tell* them what to do. When I have succeeded at establishing credibility, the other person indicates this by becoming more External to me; believing what I say, accepting recommendations, etc. However, if I use "should" too often or "Command Language," they can easily shift back into Internal. Starting with the Language of Suggestion, using a confident tone of voice and body language enables you to go to the bus stop and speak the right language for an Internal. Avoid using Command Language, such as "here's what you should do," unless you are truly in command or have impeccable credibility. Since so many people wanted more information about this, I created an online training called **"Boost Your Credibility"**[1].

The Suggestion Model©

To review from Chapter 5, the Suggestion Model© is a powerful way to get people to take your idea seriously. This technique uses language for **Internal, Away From, Toward** with a little bit of **External** encouragement at the end. I suggest you use it whenever you want to recommend something because it reduces resistance, enables people to see the positive benefit of your suggestion and is easy to do.

There are 4 steps:

1. Make the suggestion (Using the Language of Suggestion for Internals)
2. State what problem it avoids or solves (Away From)
3. State the benefit (Toward)
4. Overall why it's easy to do (for Externals)

Example:

"**I believe** *this version of the software makes the most sense right now, because* **it doesn't have the issues** *the other ones have, plus* **it integrates well** *with the other software you are using, and it will be* **fairly easy** *to implement."*

The Universal Opener: The 4Mat System

When someone does the old standard introduction to a presentation: "First I'm going to tell you what I'm going to tell you. Then I'm going to tell you. And lastly, I'll tell you what I told you," I cringe in my seat and look for an escape hatch to get out of the room!

Every five to fifteen seconds there is a competition for attention in presentations, between the presenter and the audience's phones, computers and other devices. Every five to fifteen seconds they are deciding which is the most interesting, which has the most pull on their attention. If you want to be effective, you need to win that competition.

I adapted the 4Mat System from Bernice McCarthy's work[2]. It is based on the same Jungian typology as the Myers-Briggs Type Indicator. When you want to get people's attention and stop them from wandering, this four-step method will do it. Notice the 4Mat covers different LAB Profile® Patterns in each step, and if you use the Language of Suggestion in some of the steps, it works well for Internals.

1. **Why** your topic is important to your audience. (Options, Away From and/or Toward)
2. **What** is the topic/content (Thing)
3. **How** – the steps (Procedures)
4. **Where Else** is your topic useful to people (Options)

Example:

People are more skeptical today and it's hard to get their attention. (why)
The 4Mat is a technique to open a presentation or a conversation. (what)
It has 4 steps. (how)
You can use it anytime you want to make someone interested in what you are about to say. (where else)

The 4-Step Motivation Method©

I developed this method for my **HusbandMotivator™ app**[3] to give people a motivating method based on someone's previously determined LAB Profile® Patterns, but it can be used in many situations. You can see it is based on the 4Mat above, but with two twists; it is customized for the person with whom you are speaking (that is why the app is so useful with just about any Context), and the last step gives it the juice to improve relationships.

1. **Why** – either Toward or Away From
2. **What** – in language for Internals or Externals

3. **How** – choices (Options) or steps (Procedures)
4. **Appreciation** – why I love and appreciate you

Example:

Talking to your spouse
You wanted to avoid spending all day on home repairs, (Why – Away From)
So, I suggest that we prioritize the things that need to get done, (What – for Internal)
The first step could be eliminating what's not essential, then … (How – Procedures)
It's great that we can talk about this and get it out of the way. (Appreciation)

Another Example:

Manager to team member
You were looking to impress your clients in your presentation, (Why – Toward)
So, they will appreciate it if you can give them some solutions, (What – External to the clients)
Let's look at what the options are. (How – Options)
I am very happy that you are getting input to make sure this presentation works. (Appreciation)

How to Sell to Internals

My coaching client Brenda, the owner of a web design and online ad management company, had done an analysis of the current web strategy for one of her prospects. She had unearthed valuable information but had no way to present it. Her prospective customer, a business owner, had been difficult to deal with. He didn't like being told what to do and was a bit Macho. In LAB Profile® terms, he had an Internal Pattern.

Many people get stuck thinking about "what should I say next?" when they are preparing to present something. But if you don't present vital information in a way that matches your prospect's buying process, chances are there will be no sale.

Here is an easy to follow process, especially for dealing with highly Internal prospects, that will make them feel comfortable and motivated, and therefore more likely to buy. As you know, people won't buy (or buy into an idea) unless how you present it strikes a chord with them.

Here's the formula I gave her:

Fact -> Problem -> Solution -> Benefit -> As you know ....

Let's decode the formula that works for highly Internal prospects (or even your clients!):

Fact: Start with the information you have researched or that is commonly known and agreed. In Brenda's case:

"I researched the traffic coming to your site and there is an average of 10 searches per month for your key terms."

Note: Avoid judging this information and make sure it is purely factual.

Problem: What problem(s) does this fact cause for the person?

"This means that people who need your services are likely using other search terms and not finding your company, so you are missing some business that should be coming your way."

Solution: What is the proposed solution?

"I suggest (Language of Suggestion for Internals, rather than Command Language such as "you should") having us identify the highest frequency, most likely search terms for companies looking for what you provide."

Benefit: What is the positive result that your prospect can expect from the solution?

"This will get more people coming to your site who actually need your services and can in turn increase your business."

As you know: Invite the person to internally verify something that relates to the problem. This is irresistible for clients who are in Internal mode and reminds them of the problem they need to fix (Away From). This triggers the start of the process which leads to the end result - buying in:

"As you know, most people only click on the very top results for their searches, so if your site doesn't come up at the top for the search terms they are using, it is unlikely they will find your company."

The Macho Test©

Just for review as we already covered this earlier, to make sure that even the most Macho of people will listen to your idea, here again is the Macho Test© from the chapter on Source: Internal and External:

When you are writing something, preparing a presentation and you want to make sure to be listened to and taken seriously without the other people feeling threatened, first prepare your draft.

Then, ask yourself if you have implied or stated the following:

1. There is something they don't already know,
2. I am telling them what to do,
3. They have a problem and I have the solution,
4. They are not perfect in some way, and/or
5. I am better than they are in some way.

If any of the above are stated or implied, it does not pass the Macho Test! You may wish to rephrase as follows:

1. As you probably know…. (then state the thing you suspect they do not know)
2. Use the language of suggestion: You may wish to consider…

3. I understand that other organizations have had this issue and what some of them have done is… How have you solved this problem? (implies they have already solved all the problems)
4. With your experience and knowledge in this area….
5. Your role is…. My role is… (establishing different yet equal roles)

The Bad News Formula©

As the song goes, "You can't, always get, whatcha want". Sometimes you can't do what others want either, but you can let them know in a way that reduces their distress and it is relatively easy to do, and maintains good relationships. First make sure you have established a good level of rapport with the person. Then use the Bad News Formula©:

If you think you have no good news, find some! Good news for the other person I mean. I suggest writing it out before using it, at least for the first few times.

I was hired by a young and growing fleet management software company to help their executives develop their Customer Philosophy[4] and then train all their team members in California, Atlanta, Toronto and even New Zealand in customer service strategies. They found me because I was in a documentary called "Customer Dis-Service," that was shown around Canada on CBC and around the world on MSNBC. The reason they needed my help was that they were acquiring companies so quickly that integrating them had an impact on their ability to service their current customers.

Among other strategies, I taught them the Bad News Formula© to help manage customer expectations. Three months after I completed the assignment, I still hadn't received my payment. I wrote a short email to Philip in Accounts Payable (whom I knew from the training sessions) and received this in return:

> Dear Shelle,
> I know you haven't received your check yet, but I'm seeing the VP of finance this week and I'll put your invoice in front of him and I'll let you know as soon as I can that your bill will be paid.
> I read his email and thought "That's fine." A few seconds later it hit me!

Wait a minute! I wrote him back: "I taught you how to do that!" And he replied with a smiley face. Even when you know the Bad News Formula©, it still works.

The 3-2-1 Away From – Toward Sandwich for Highly Away From People

Some people get stuck in an unhappy rut, thinking only about everything that is going wrong (Away From and Reactive), miserable but unable to find the energy or motivation to get unstuck. And some people are not unhappy, but they prefer to look for and find the problems (Away From) in whatever is happening. In Germany, this would show up when someone would tell me: "Das geht nicht," which usually meant "that will never work in Germany." Even some of my friends there would take great delight in telling me what was wrong with my projects.

Using a variation of the "Match, Match, Match, Lead" formula, the 3-2-1 Away From-Toward Sandwich starts at the other person's bus stop to get them motivated to move forward.

Here's the formula:

3 Away From Statements, *segue,*
2 Toward Statements, *link,*
1 Away From statement (to reassure them).

Example (with a coaching client stuck in a rut)

You said that you don't like anything about your life right now, you want to get out of your job, and you're tired of being alone all day. (3 Away Froms)

That's why, (segue to link the next part)

I suggest we spend time identifying the things you do want, so that you can put a plan in place to make them happen, (2 Towards)

so that (link*) you don't have to continue to be in this situation.* (1 Away From)

Example: (with someone who sees what is wrong with the team's project)

You have pointed out areas that are problematic, the negative consequences of those issues, and why we want to avoid them. (3 Away Froms)

That's why (segue)

I would like the team to look at what our objectives should be and what results we want from accomplishing our objectives, (2 Towards)

otherwise (link*) we will be left with just the parts that don't work.* (1 Away From)

The above strategies and techniques give you options for different people and situations, with clear steps so they are not so challenging to use, even when you don't have much time to prepare. For even more strategies with demonstrations in real time, please check out *Presenting Ideas to Skeptical People*[5], and *Words That Change Customer's Minds*[6].

[1] Check out my free online training: Boost Your Credibility: bit.ly/BoostYourCredibility

[2] McCarthy, Bernice; *The 4Mat System: Teaching to Learning Styles with Right/Left Mode Techniques.* Excel, Inc. Illinois, 1981

[3] HusbandMotivator™ app available in Android and iOS: bit.ly/HusbandMotivatorAPP

[4] For more information on how to develop your Customer Philosophy, please see my book, Words That Change Customers' Minds

[5] Presenting Ideas to Skeptical People MP3, with a real-time demonstration of how to respond to a skeptic: bit.ly/SkepticalPeople

[6] Strategies for dealing with upset customers; Words That Change Customers' Minds: bit.ly/WTCCM

Chapter 24
The LAB Profile® of Conflict

In my consulting work, I help clients decode complex communication problems and develop strategies for resolving them. Businesses, large organizations, and families (not to mention national legislatures) often have complicated interactions, filled with "history", competing needs and different LAB Profile® Patterns.

The LAB Profile® can help you understand and choose how to communicate to resolve these conflicts. There is a generic LAB Profile® structure in conflict:

Each party to the conflict goes into **Internal** and **Away From** vis-à-vis the other party. This is not about someone's personality; it is the nature of the conflict Context. Each party knows within them self what is good or bad and tends to only hear things they disagree with coming from the other person. Think about when you had a conflict with someone. Were you convinced that you were right, and that the other person was wrong about something?

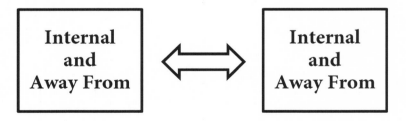

Beyond this Combination, there are different types of conflict. Often in organizations, there are battles between people with Options versus Procedures preferences, General versus Specific, Proactive and Towards versus Reactive and Away From, Thing versus Person.

What do you do?[1]

First of all, pick a time to talk when you are both calm – not in the heat of battle. Once you have created a relaxed atmosphere and framed the conversation using language for Internal and Away From, ask the other person what is important to them about the issue. This will enable them to explain their Criteria for the situation.

"We seem to be having a disagreement about the next steps and I thought if we had a chance to talk about it, we could prevent further issues between us. (Framing in Away From language). What do you think? (Language for Internals)

"What is important to you about our next steps?" (Criteria question)

Demonstrate your understanding by playing back the key words and phrases and giving an example.

"It's important to you not to waste time or resources, and to get things done as quickly as possible, including, deciding about the budget by the end of this week?"

Then you can talk about what is important to you, and together begin to look for strategies that embody both sets of needs. The key is to set the stage by meeting the other person at their bus stop and using the Language of Suggestion for Internals and Away From.

---

[1] To get the complete process for conflict resolution and negotiation, check out my one-hour audio program, Only Pick a Fight When You Can Win: bit.ly/OnlyPickaFight

Chapter 25
Conversational Coaching© with the LAB Profile®

Coaching and mentoring are about helping people find the means to become who they truly can and want to be, and it is up to them to define what that is. There are many methods for doing this. I have focused on helping clients identify their success strategies and helping them solve problems through understanding their LAB Profile® Patterns. That is why I developed the Conversational Coaching© methodology and the MP3 with the demonstration[1].

The key to the Conversational Coaching© process can be found in paraphrasing the famous quote which is often attributed to Einstein: People don't create solutions with the same Patterns as they created them. I discovered that when people are in a stuck state, they are in a typical set of LAB Profile® Patterns and a very different set for when they are in a solution state.

If coaches can understand what unconsciously motivates their clients, they can help them reach their goals more quickly. Since we know from the LAB Profile® that only about 40% of people are actually motivated by goals at work, I suspect that that number is much lower in the Context of working with a coach. The trigger for many people to seek a coach is usually an issue or problem they want to solve or prevent, rather than a goal they are pursuing.

Individuals seeking coaching are often not entirely ready to think about their goals because they are preoccupied with the issues and the things with which they are dissatisfied. It is important therefore to understand and respect this motivation when coaching someone. The LAB Profile® gives you the language to match someone's motivation.

Since much coaching also happens outside of the official "coaching session," in the hallway, on a phone call, or as a 'by the way' at the end of a meeting, it is useful to have an informal way to help people solve problems. This is also when I use this conversational approach – to help someone solve an issue.

Essentially, what the LAB Profile® (and NLP) add to coaching and mentoring is Pattern detection and utilization.

The steps in the Conversational Coaching© Process are:

1. Get in state
2. Establish framework: Rapport and Credibility
3. Get permission and anchor resources
4. Agree on "problem" and outcome
5. Present State - Desired State in LAB Profile® Patterns
6. Intervention
7. Ecology Check and Sanity Check
8. Future pacing

You will notice that these steps are similar to the standard NLP-type intervention:

1. Rapport and credibility
2. Anchor resources
3. Agree on "problem" and outcome
4. Intervention (any developmental process)
5. Ecology Check
6. Future pacing - test for commitment and ease of accomplishment

But there are also some significant differences in between these approaches!

1. Get in State

Since this method is an informal kind of coaching, it is especially important to get oneself in an appropriate state to be of help to someone while maintaining the casual conversation aspect. (Opinion alert: I find that in a casual conversation, many people are more relaxed and can easily take in pertinent information, than in some formal coaching situations.)

I have an Anchor[2] I call "Coaching Shelle", since my goal is to engage the following in myself before I start any actual coaching:

- a feeling of calm,
- a mild caring about the other person (i.e. not overly invested in their problem and solution),
- alert
- grounded

I call this my *state of grace* and it helps me listen, converse and do what I need to do to be of help.

2. Establish Framework and create rapport & credibility

The second step is to establish the framework (why we are here) and create rapport & credibility. It is important at this point, early in the conversation to ensure that the person actually believes there is a solution, and that they could in fact make it work, and that you are indeed the right person to help them.

I call this step *creating faith*, since as of yet there is no solution in sight! Here is something I might say: "I'm really glad you came to me about this --- no point in letting this continue like this." (this presupposes there is a solution)

3. Get Permission and Anchor Resources

Now is also a good time to check that the person *actually wants help* with the issue (inside of merely wanting to moan about it). Get their permission to work with them, make suggestions, etc. "You really want to create solutions for this?" Then help the person access a resourceful state. An open mind yields better results!

Some clients are more difficult to work with than others and some are more stuck than others. Inertia can be a powerful force and people get used to having problems or being unhappy, appearing to have little appetite or energy for heavy lifting to get out of a negative situation.

If your client is pessimistic or skeptical, your coaching and mentoring will take much longer than if you have a willing person who knows that they need to explore and develop strategies. Here is what I do, from my audio program Presenting Ideas to Skeptical People[3]:

Pre-empt possible objections your client may have by taking an educated guess about the objections your client may have about the possibility of having a solution and state these objections before the client does:

"It may seem that because the problem has gone on so long, it may be hard to solve."

Secondly, hint that there could be a positive result for the coaching or to a particular problem:

"I suspect there may just be a solution to this."

Mention examples where your clients can check in with their own experience and confirm what you are saying for themselves. This also helps establish your credibility and enable them to begin to believe that it is possible to solve their issue. Here is an example:

"Have you ever noticed that when some people get convinced of something; it can be very difficult to get them to consider something else? (Pause, wait for your client to reflect and acknowledge the statement.) And have you ever noticed that when you begin to believe there is a possibility or a hope, it is easier to find a solution? And when you don't know what you want, you rarely get it?"

Notice how these examples invite you to confirm or deny what was said, allowing the person to decide for them self whether or not they agree.

This will enable them to feel understood, because you demonstrated that you grasp why it has been hard for them, as well as expressing hope. Then they can let go and move beyond this into a more resourceful state. Remember: Stay in rapport with the person but keep a distance from their problem. You don't want to be in the hole with the client. Your job is to help them by offering a ladder, so they can climb out of the hole.

Some people don't want to be told what to do, (Internal), and they would object strenuously if a coach were too enthusiastic or definitive in helping them access a more resourceful state (or during other parts of the coaching conversation). When working with a client who remains skeptical or resists what you say, you may find it helpful to think about this person as someone who needs to decide for themselves rather than someone who wants to be either directed or given feedback from the outside. For a client in Internal mode, establishing your credibility is more important than rapport.

You can use the Language of Suggestion to make sure you have impact:

- only you can decide,
- here's a suggestion you may wish to consider,
- may I offer something you may wish to think about.
- what would you think about....?

Many coaches typically use this kind of language already with their clients. However, if you were to use those same phrases with clients with External Pattern, they might become confused. This language makes no sense for people in an External mode. They need some outside guidance or feedback to know if what they're doing is the right thing. Use such phrases as:

- (person) ... *will appreciate this,*
- *when you do that others will notice,*
- *the results will show you.*

If someone is very External, and you have high credibility in their eyes, you could simply tell them what to do. But that defeats the usual goals of coaching and mentoring, does it not?

Why is it important to notice if your client is in an Internal or External mode when coaching? When someone is in Internal mode, they need you to establish credibility, so they can work with you effectively. If you do not, they are likely to resist your process or your suggestions.

Think about the most difficult clients with whom you have worked, and perhaps even your closest family members.

If they are External to you, they will probably believe you when you tell them something and take in instructions and follow your process. *Rapport is more important to them than credibility.*

4. Agree on Problem and Outcome

Using the NLP Outcome Strategy questions, you can listen for both the desired outcome and the present state, what the problem is, and what having the solution will be like.

With careful listening, you hear which LAB Profile® Patterns are present for someone when they are having an issue or a challenge, and which Patterns they use when talking about their "desired state".

The NLP Outcome Strategy

Questions	Conditions for a well-formed outcome
What do you want?	STATED POSITIVELY what you want instead of what you don't want
Who? When? Where?	SPECIFIC CONTEXT test: one clear image
How will you know you've got it?	VERIFIABLE what you will see, hear, feel
Who does your objective depend on? What resources do you have that will enable you to get your objective? How does what's happening now, indicate what you could do now?	ATTAINABLE you are able to initiate and maintain your objective yourself

What is important about your objective? How does it reflect who you want to be?	WORTH THE TROUBLE your objective is sufficiently motivating so you'll actually do it
Is this what you really want?	it respects your values
What would happen if you got what you wanted?	ECOLOGY your objective respects the whole system you function in.
What do you get out of the present situation that you want to be sure to keep? What do you risk losing? What would be the consequences on your environment (colleagues, department, family, job, future etc.) of getting what you want?	your objective preserves the desirable aspects of the present situation.

5. Present State - Desired State in LAB Profile® Patterns

Here is the Conversational Coaching© grid I use:

	Present State (problem)	Desired State (outcome)
Problem- Outcome		
Criteria		
LAB Profile® Patterns		
Other		

This is a process that takes skill and practice. There is a demonstration and a debrief of this process in my one-hour MP3 **Conversational Coaching with the LAB Profile®**. Essentially you listen for the Patterns as they talk about what has been bothering them and what they want instead.

Once you can determine the LAB Profile® differences between how the person is experiencing the problem (present state), and what it will be like when they have a solution (desired state), you can help the client get into the desired state mode. This will enable them to access solutions and find insights to help them with the issue at hand more easily.

The "Stuck" State

When people cannot solve a problem, often they get stuck, going over and over the same territory without being able to shift out of it. Through years of teaching and using the LAB Profile®, I discovered that there can often be a generic combination of Patterns when a person is in this stuck mode:

Reactive: thinking rather than doing something,
Away From: dwelling on the problems and the negative consequences
Options (sometimes): may have too many Options and not know the Procedure (how) to advance,
Feeling: stuck in a negative emotional state with difficulty coming out of it.

If you hear all or some of these Patterns as your client is talking, they may well be in a stuck mode. And if you can identify the Patterns for when they imagine having found a solution, it will truly help them get out of the hole they are in.

6. Intervention

In the Conversational Coaching© Model, the only real intervention consists of overlapping the language of the present state Patterns into the desired outcome Patterns. This may need to be repeated a few times. This is a skill and takes some mastery of the LAB Profile® Pattern language.

"So you've been thinking about all the ways (Options) *things were out your control* (External) *and seemed to happen to you* (Reactive) *and how much you disliked that and want to get Away From that situation* (Away From) *and of course thinking about it now* (still Reactive), *you realize that* (slightly Internal), *number one* (start of a Procedure), *you make your own decisions one way or another* (more Internal with a bit of Options), *two, that once you know what is important to you, you generally know how to proceed* (Internal and Procedures). *Lastly, just jumping in to get started figuring out what you want, isn't so hard at all.* (Proactive, Procedures and a little Away From)*"*

This very abbreviated verbal Pattern-overlapping is an example of how to start from the Patterns in a given problem present-state (in this case Reactive, Away From, External and Options) and overlapping into the desired state Patterns that were previously uncovered. (In this case Proactive, Internal and Procedures.) It is **desirable here just to use Patterns and not suggest a concrete solution**, since the person can probably figure it out them self as long as they are operating from the Patterns of their desired outcome.

Often the person looks confused once you have overlapped the Patterns and you can see that they are processing, questioning, and reframing all at once. Just wait. They will often come back to you with new insights, a solution in mind, or a way to fix the problem. Be careful not to give the solution, just get the person to shift into the Patterns they have when in the solution mode.

Another example, if my client had Reactive, Away From and Internal Patterns in the current problem state and had indicated that they would be more External in the solution, I might say something like this:

"So you know (Internal) *what has been happening to you* (Reactive) *that you don't like* (Internal and Away From), *and as you think about it and decide for yourself* (Reactive and Internal) *what you don't want any more* (Away From), *you then may begin to notice* (still somewhat Reactive) *what others are doing* (a little bit External) *that might work* (still a little Reactive and Internal), *and even get feedback and suggestions* (External) *that are helpful in this kind of situation, and see the reactions you get* (External) *that help you adapt* (External) *to what you need to be doing* (Reactive and Proactive)."

After letting your client consider what you said, find out what they are thinking now. Listen to see if they have shifted Patterns and if they have come up with a solution. My client who was in External when talking about his desired state, said this after the intervention:

"I am not necessarily the one who has all the ideas. I have tried stuff that didn't work, but I bet that my brother Michael can help with this. He's really good at this kind of thing and I really value his opinion. I'm gonna ask him about this."

More Choice Is Better? Better for Whom?

Many coaches and mentors strive to help their clients have more choice in their lives. This can either be beneficial or overwhelming, depending on whether this matches another important Motivation Pattern. I often talk about the "**Options Dilemma**", which consists of having too many choices and no process for deciding; often causing the feeling of overwhelm.

Psychologist Barry Schwartz spoke about this in his book *The Paradox of Choice*. He said: "the paradox is that choice is at the heart of the freedom and opportunity to be cherished, yet the number of options we face every day is overwhelming."

Procedures and Options

If your client is suffering from feeling overwhelmed, chances are they need a step-by-step procedure to get out of it rather than continuing to have to consider more options for possibilities and more choices. If they are in an Options mode, but clearly need a procedure to move ahead, you can help by talking about the difficulty of having too many choices (matching the client's issue) with no step-by-step procedure to follow. Then gradually switch to a more Procedures-type language such as step one, step two, step three and help your client to identify the process they need. The key here is to help them finish and complete something, rather than wandering off in another direction without seeing it to completion. Once a client is in a Procedural mode, they are more likely to be motivated to finish and complete what they started.

Clients who stay in an Options mode tend to start something else rather than complete and finish what they have begun. This could be a big issue for them in their lives and possibly one of the reasons why they have sought you out as a coach or mentor. Many creative people have this issue. They have the ability to conceive creative ways to come up with an idea or find ways around issues but lack the stamina or the ability to stay motivated over a longer period of time to complete and finish what they start (and get the benefit from that).

7. Ecology Check and Sanity Check

Then check the "ecology" of the solution they come up with. (Are there any possible negative consequences for the solution?). The Sanity Check asks; even if there are no negative consequences, *is this solution a good idea*? Does it actually make sense?

8. Future Pace

As in a typical NLP intervention, we test to see if the solution will actually work and be applied by asking the person to imagine the future and notice what happens.

The "Done" Frame

When you are Future Pacing, it can be very useful to know if your client will actually go out and do what they said they would do. A particular combination of LAB Profile® Patterns determines if the client is done with an issue, when they have solved it. This is how you know they are **committed to a solution or action**?

Here are the LAB Profile® Patterns to listen for:

- **Proactive**
- **Toward**
- **Internal**
- **Procedures**

In other words, this person will get into action to move towards their goal (Proactive, Towards), knowing inside themselves (Internal) what it is they want to do, and they have a step-by-step process (Procedures) for using that they are committed to completing. I have noticed that when I hear this kind of language from a client, they are much more likely to follow through and get the results they really want.

Coaching practices and methods continue to evolve. It can be very helpful to master more than one coaching structure for different people and situations. This Conversational Coaching© process works well remotely as well as in person and you can record your session, not only for your client, but to review how you worked and picked up and used your client's LAB Profile® Pattern Combinations.

---

[1] To hear a demonstration and a debrief of the Conversational Coaching© method: bit.ly/ConversationalCoaching

[2] An Anchor is an NLP technique associating a particular internal response with some external or internal trigger so that the response may be quickly accessed. I touch my left index to my left thumb to call up my "Coaching Shelle" state.

[3] Learn the 4 steps for working with skeptical people, and hear a live demonstration with a real skeptic, in my MP3 Presenting Ideas to Skeptical People: bit.ly/SkepticalPeople

Chapter 26
Career Coaching and Personal Profiles

When people come to me for career advice and coaching, we usually start by doing a LAB Profile®. Also, managers have asked me to profile their employees to determine their strengths and weaknesses, either for the job they are presently doing, possible promotion, or transfer.

If you would like to have your own LAB Profile® in the Context of your work, go to bit.ly/TheLabProfile to do a free online LAB Profile®.

Remember to clearly establish the Context with the person being profiled. Since most of the people interviewed do not know much about the LAB Profile®, I usually include, in their report, the LAB Profile® Summary, found near the end of this book.

Here are two examples of LAB Profile® reports for career coaching:

LAB Profile® Report: Bill X

Context: Work

Motivation Patterns

The following Patterns describe those things that will trigger Bill's motivation.

Mainly Reactive with some Proactive

Bill is more likely to think and consider than to jump into action. He is mostly motivated by situations where he gets to understand, analyze, and think. He may wait for others to initiate and feel more comfortable responding.

Criteria

The following words and phrases are his hot buttons about work. He will be motivated when he thinks of or hears them:

personal and professional satisfaction, sense of purpose, sense of passion, sense of excitement, sense of accomplishment, part of

something larger, provides a purpose for my life, sense that I am empowering people and organization.

Mainly Away From

His motivation is usually triggered to move away from bad situations. He is primarily energized when there is a problem to be solved, a situation to be avoided, gotten rid of, or not have happen. He is a natural trouble shooter. He will need to refocus on his goals at regular intervals to avoid being sidetracked.

Mainly External

In situations where he must decide for himself, he can and will, but he doesn't have a particular need to be the one who decides. His motivation is triggered when he gets feedback, either from other people or from results. In the absence of such feedback he will become demotivated. He may accept information as instructions.

Mainly Options

Bill is usually motivated to develop new options, alternatives, possibilities. He often has difficulty *following* procedures, but is usually good at *developing* procedures. When asked to simply follow a procedure, he may try to fix the procedure. Breaking the rules is irresistible to Bill.

Sameness with Exception and Difference

He likes his work situation to change often. When he is sure that he knows his job, he is happy doing that job for a couple of years. For some aspects of his work life he likes to do a job for five to seven years; for other aspects he likes one to two years. His task clock seems to average at about three years.

Productivity Patterns

The following Patterns describe the work environment that Bill needs, the kind of tasks that suit him, his response to stress, and how he gets convinced about something.

Mainly General

Bill usually makes sense of his work as an overview and prefers to work on the big picture, but he can work with detailed sequences for extended periods if necessary.

Other

He accepts the emotional content of his communications with others. He has automatic reflex responses to the behavior of people, which facilitates interpersonal communication. He makes sense of communication with others based on the nonverbal part of the communication.

Proximity with some Independent

Bill usually likes to work with others around and involved. To be most productive, he needs to have his own clear territory of responsibility. For some aspects of his work he wants to be totally alone, without interruption.

Thing with some Person

At work, Bill concentrates on the task at hand. While he recognizes the importance of feelings, given the choice, he will focus on the job to be done.

Stress Response: Choice with some Feeling

Bill initially reacts to job pressures emotionally and may stay in emotional feelings longer than necessary. He is usually able to adapt to stressful situations and will respond based on his own belief of appropriateness. He is best suited to tasks where empathizing with others is an asset.

Rule Structure: My/My

Bill expects others to work the way he works. He has no difficulty telling others at work what he expects. He is well suited to people-management tasks because of this trait.

Convincer Channels: Seeing, Hearing, and Feeling

He is primarily convinced about projects or ideas by seeing the evidence or observing the product or process. He is also convinced by hearing or discussing it. To be fully convinced, he also needs to "get a sense" of something, a feeling.

Convincer Mode: Number of Examples

Bill is convinced by three to four examples. This is the number of times he needs to see, hear, and feel something to be convinced. Fewer than this number leaves him unconvinced.

Ideal Work Situation

The following points describe Bill's ideal work:
- time to reflect, analyze, and understand, with some time for initiating
- problem-solving and troubleshooting
- feedback in terms of results or by significant others
- possibility to create options, design new procedures; less apt to follow procedures himself
- evolution and revolution; wide variety of tasks and major change about every three years
- prefers to work on overviews, rather than detail
- with own territory of responsibility, others around; some time totally alone
- concentrate on ideas, tasks, systems, and some feelings

- avoid high-stress work

Suggestions

Bill needs to refocus on his goals at regular intervals. This will help him to assess his present activities as to whether they bring him closer to his goals and reflect his deeply held values.

Since Bill has an aptitude to create alternatives and to reflect at an overview level, he will need to team up with someone who is more Proactive and more Procedures and detail-oriented to complete and finish the ideas he will develop. To succeed at an endeavor, he will need to divide what he has to do into steps and follow them.

High-stress work with looming deadlines, for example, will not be healthy for him over the long term.

The checklist and suggestions at the end of the report can be used by the client when evaluating choices.

Depending on the profile of the client, you can either suggest options or give them a procedure for finding work, starting a new career, and so on.

Here is another sample report for a client who was considering moving her part-time business to full-time:

LAB Profile® Report: Claudia Y

Context: Work, present and future

Motivation Patterns

The following Patterns describe those things that will trigger and maintain Claudia's motivation:

Equally Proactive and Reactive

Claudia initiates or waits for others to initiate. She does either with equal ease. She can be energized, while at the same time she can think and not act. Understanding is just as important as action. She is just as likely to consider as to act. She needs her work to provide the opportunity to do both.

To successfully set up and run her own business, Claudia will need to actively engage her Proactive part, particularly to generate new business.

Criteria

The following have a high level of importance for Claudia in her work. They are her *hot buttons*:

always have things to learn, work with words and language, contact with the outside world, team work, well paid.

The experiences represented by these words are what Claudia is looking for in her work.

Toward

Claudia is motivated to move "toward" her goals. She is motivated by goals. She wants to attain, achieve, get, and is so goal-oriented that she may not recognize real or potential problems. She would benefit by having someone with a facility for recognizing problems help her when she is planning.

Mainly Internal with some External

Usually Claudia decides for herself and is motivated when she gets to decide. To a lesser extent she needs feedback from others to check how well she is doing, but generally Claudia knows within herself. She usually takes that information from others and evaluates it by her own standards. In her ideal work situation, she would have the opportunity to judge her work for herself, using feedback from others as input.

Mainly Options with some Procedures

Claudia is usually motivated to develop new options and find other ways of doing things. She is very creative. She may have difficulty completing procedures, because her main motivation is to develop alternatives. If Claudia runs her own business, it will be important for her to make sure that procedures are completed and that her ideas are taken to their logical conclusion before starting on a new project.

Sameness with Exception

She likes her work situation to progress and evolve. Claudia likes to do the same work for about five to seven years. She can accept changes once a year, provided they are not too drastic. This is an excellent Pattern for building a business, as Claudia will stick with the setup and development phases, provided she is doing activities she enjoys.

Productivity Patterns

The following Patterns describe the work environment Claudia needs, the kind of tasks that suit her, her response to stress, and how she gets convinced about something.

Mainly General and some Specific

Claudia prefers to think about her work in an overview. She can work with specific details for extended periods. As a manager or coordinator of other people's work, she must remember to let other people focus on the how while she manages the general overview. She can see the big picture at work but deal with details when she has to.

Other

Claudia is sensitive to the nonverbal behavior of others, such as voice tone, facial expression, body posture, and so on. She has automatic reflex responses to the behavior of people. She makes sense of the communications with others based on the nonverbal part of the communication.

Stress Response: Feeling with some Choice

Claudia initially reacts to job pressures emotionally and tends to stay in feelings longer than necessary. She is usually able to adapt to stressful situations and will respond based on her own belief of appropriateness. She is best suited to tasks where empathizing with others is an asset.

Proximity

Claudia likes to work with other people around. She likes to be the boss or to have a boss, as long as her territory of responsibility and authority is clear. Her productivity will suffer if she has to work totally alone or if she has to share the responsibility with others.

Mainly Person with some Thing

While at work, Claudia focuses mainly on people's needs. This means she will be responsive to clients' and her boss' feelings. She can also be task-focused. At times she may drop the task to take care of someone's personal feelings. At these times, she may need to remember the goals and decide on priorities, which she has the ability to do.

Rule Structure: My rules for me / My rules for you

She expects others to work the way that she works. She understands the rules and unwritten policies of the workplace and she has no difficulty telling others what those rules are, an essential quality for management.

Convincer Channel: See and Hear

Claudia needs to hear and see evidence when getting convinced about something. To a lesser extent she needs to do something with the product or person to input the necessary data to start the process of being convinced.

Convincer Mode: Period of Time

Claudia needs to hear, see, and do something consistently with the evidence for a period of six months before she is convinced. Less than this amount of time will leave her unconvinced.

Ideal Work Situation

In summary, Claudia needs the following elements in her work:
- opportunity to take the initiative and to reflect
- work toward goals (she needs to have elaborated specific goals or she will be demotivated)
- work that she can judge for herself with input from others
- opportunity to develop systems, procedures, and ideas
- progression and personal growth in five to seven-year cycles
- concentrate on the big picture with a bit of detail work
- have the responsibility and authority with others involved
- rapport and empathy with others

Things for Claudia to Consider when Deciding on Developing Her Business:

- be proactive about prospecting for clients
- have someone help during the planning stage who can easily perceive potential and actual problems. Explain their role clearly to them
- make sure that the procedures needed to make the business a success will be taken care of
- evaluate the business ideas and make sure that each plan is completed
- plan for incorporating growth and development in the work she does

THE KEYS TO PERSONAL PROFILES

1. Decide on the Context and the purpose of the Profile.
2. Adapt the questions to the Context.
3. Describe the Patterns using layperson's language for the Patterns, when giving feedback to the person.
4. Make sure to include the ramifications of any relevant combinations; For example, with Away From combined with Person, you can predict that your client will drop whatever he or she is doing to take care of others' needs.
5. Test your diagnosis by asking the alternate questions when you are not sure.

Working Independently

Many people make the leap from being an employee to working for themselves, being a digital nomad, starting a business, or buying an already operating business. Countless others dream of doing so. In the United States 6.3% of the workforce was self-employed in 2017, while in Canada, 8.3%, in Germany 10.2%, in the UK 15.4% and in Mexico 31.5 % in the same year.[1]

According to Statistics Canada, fewer than 30% of people becoming self-employed stayed self-employed up to five years, while under half of new business owners lasted that long.[2] Working for yourself is very different than being an employee and takes different LAB Profile® Pattern Combinations. Even though there are many different reasons *why* people choose to become self-employed, they need to be able to have several skills to succeed:

- certain values, beliefs and attitudes (e.g. action orientation, desire for independence, initiative, creativity etc.)
- 'soft' skills including interpersonal communication and networking skills (I call these the 'harder skills')
- realistic awareness of the risks and benefits of self-employment

285

- functional business skills (financial, HR management, market research)
- enough subject-matter expertise
- relevant business knowledge (legislative, taxation, sources of finance etc.)[3]

If we were to identify the LAB Profile® Patterns for the above skills needed to succeed, they would be:

- Mainly Proactive
- Criteria: Success, Achieving My Goals, (plus many individual Criteria)
- Mainly Toward
- Mainly Internal
- Mainly Procedures with a good dose of Options for problem-solving & developing new solutions
- Sameness with Exception and Difference
- Mainly General, with the ability to focus on Specifics when needed
- Other
- Choice
- Mainly Independent with some Proximity
- Mainly Thing with a good dose of Person
- My/My

Someone who is self-employed needs to get out and make it happen, not just think about it. (Proactive, Thing, Toward) They need to decide where to put their time and energy and make the right strategic decision (Internal and General). Less successful people do everything themselves, even the low value work, because they lose sight of the big picture and the strategy. (Specific, Procedures) They need to commit to and complete the right activities, not just do the next thing on the list. (Procedures, mainly General) And they need to find ways around issues and be able to pivot when needed. (Options and some Away From) They need to negotiate and manage relationships (General,

Other, Person, Thing, Choice) And they need to be able to work alone, by themselves for long periods of time! (Independent, Thing)

Not everyone has this kind of flexibility, the ability to prioritize and make decisions, is able to manage relationships and work alone without getting overwhelmed by everything there is to do.

Of course, **one of the big secrets about succeeding at being self-employed** is that what you are doing is SO important that you are willing to do whatever it takes (even the hyper-boring stuff that you do have to do) to make it work. That is about your highly-held Criteria and values.

It also appears that self-employed people are only half as likely to participate in work-related training and education, though they may be learning in less formal ways. I believe that learning about how to do things better or think more productively is key. If you are self-employed or are running a business, how can you continually learn and grow?

Considering Taking the Plunge to Go Out on Your Own?

If you are thinking about quitting your job to work for yourself, rank yourself from 1 to 5 on the following questions:

1. Can I work for long periods on my own?
2. Do I need to go out there and just do it?
3. Am I strategic enough to make good decisions about where to spend my time, energy, money?
4. Am I good at motivating and negotiating with others?
5. Do I complete what I start?
6. Can I find ways around problems?
7. Am I a quick learner who seeks input and applies it?
8. Is my project so important that I would do even the most yucky work to succeed?

If you are not sure what your LAB Profile® Patterns are, you can take my online LAB Profile® Test.[4]

[1] check here for many other OECD countries: bit.ly/SelfEmploymentRate
[2] bit.ly/StatCanGc
[3] bit.ly/SkillsForSelfEmployment
[4] bit.ly/TheLabProfile

Chapter 27
Corporate Culture Diagnosis
and Change Measurement

There is a very simple, unscientific way to figure out the culture of an organization in LAB Profile® terms: ask the people who work there. In my experience, I have been surprised by the high degree of consensus among employees and managers about the profile of their company. While groups with whom I have conducted team building operations usually begin on agreeing about nothing, except that they have problems, they will instinctively know whether the organization has mainly Options or Procedures, Internal or External, Toward or Away From, Difference or Sameness with Exception, and so on.

At the IBM International Education Centre in La Hulpe, Belgium, the managers of management development from each country did a Present State - Desired State analysis of the LAB Profile® of the corporation. They affirmed that the company had an Internal pattern, trying to shift to External, from Procedures to adding Options, and from Sameness with Exception to adding some Difference. This analysis enabled them to understand exactly what kind of attitudes their programs should be encouraging. We then worked on some of the strategies they were using and could use to those ends. (But that is another book.)

To accomplish the analysis, I simply described the attributes of each pattern and asked the participants where they thought IBM was. The process took about three hours and was achieved by consensus.

Culture Diagnosis Process Overview

1. Convene a group of people who are a representative sample from the team/organization.
2. Describe the behaviors of each Pattern and ask the group which Patterns fit: "how things are around here." (*Hint: Make statements, not questions*)
3. Get people to generate examples of each behavior.
4. Check agreement and exceptions.

Have them come up with a sentence or word that describes each behavior (Pattern) and anchor.

I also did this with a large group of city leaders; business leaders, politicians, volunteer leaders from service organizations, in St-Louis, Missouri. They worked in groups at their tables and we managed to do it with consensus. Here are some sample statements I made for them to discuss at their tables. Can you guess which LAB Profile® Patterns are contained in the statements?

People here don't care what outsiders think of them or their city......
or
People here are sensitive to the reputation this city has elsewhere.

People here like to explore possibilities, alternatives and adore breaking the rules...
or
They prefer to follow the normal procedures for getting things done.

People here get really excited by changes and new things....
or
People here like steady progress......
or
People like to be here because there is a lot one can always count on.

You can also use the LAB Profile® to measure the effectiveness of organizational change operations. Do a *before* corporate-culture diagnosis with a random group of people from the organization. Implement the desired changes with the appropriate strategies, paying attention to match your language to the Decision Factors patterns (Sameness, Difference, etc.) that are prevalent in the organization. About six months to a year after you have put the major changes in place, pick a different random group of employees. Have them describe the present culture using the LAB Profile® descriptions. The *effective* changes should show up by changes in the LAB Profile® patterns.

Organizational Change Process Overview

1. Determine the Desired State. What behaviors, values and beliefs, identity and vision does the organization wish to have? Profile the desired state in LAB Profile® terms.

2. Diagnose the Present State. What are the behaviors, values and beliefs, identity and vision of the organization and its employees in LAB Profile® terms?

3. Design and deliver change messages using appropriate communication/change strategies with the appropriate influencing language, starting by matching the present state of the organization.

4. Measure the impact by convening a group of people who are a representative sample from the team/organization to do a LAB Profile® analysis. Changes which "stuck" will show up in the Profile. (Several months after completion of change process.)

Chapter 28
Recruiting Employees Who Perform

An engineering and manufacturing company had advertised for a production manager. They received *300 applicants* and, out of that group, found *only one good candidate.* I was asked to profile the position and the senior management team to whom the successful candidate would report. I wrote their next ad with the appropriate Influencing Language, designed to attract the right people and discourage the ones who wouldn't fit. They received *100* applications and *eight good candidates.*

The LAB Profile® can help you attract good candidates and evaluate your shortlist for the person with the best fit. (It does not measure knowledge and skills.) It is well-known that using intuition and some traditional interview questions such as "Tell me about yourself," or "Why would you like to work here?" lead interviewers to make poor decisions based on their personal biases. Industrial psychologist Scott Highhouse, who specializes in hiring and interviewing, said in that job interviews: *"Expert interviewers, experienced interviewers in H.R. are actually worse than a layperson who uses structured questions that are job related and behavioral in nature."*[1]

The LAB Profile® of Qualities

When you are recruiting, it can be very useful to identify the qualities you want to find in a candidate. By using the following process, you can then identify which LAB Profile® Pattern Combinations are in a quality or attitude. Of course, some LAB Profile® Patterns will be essential to exhibit that quality and some Patterns come from individual differences. Here is how to distinguish:

Process: GUESS and TEST

1. Clearly define the behavior of the quality.

2. Identify the Pattern(s) which are necessary to do / to have that quality.
3. Test by giving an example to see if the Pattern fits.
4. Can one still do *that* with the opposite Pattern? Yes? Individual Difference. No? Must be a part of the quality.

Let's say that you wish to recruit someone who is "Diplomatic", which in this case means that they are able to notice when others are pleased and displeased and capable of preventing and solving interpersonal issues and creating great relationships. Which LAB Profile® Patterns would have to be there for someone to succeed at this?

Proactive? Reactive?
Toward? Away From?
External? Internal?
Procedures? Options?
Sameness? Sameness w Ex? Difference?
Specific? General?
Person? Thing?
My/My? My/Your?

My evaluation would be more Reactive than Proactive, Mainly Away From, a mix of Internal and External, Mainly General, Mainly Person and a combination of My/Your and My/My.

Job Profiles

To profile a position, you will need certain information about the job itself, the environment, and the culture that the successful candidate will be working in.

For the position itself, you will need to understand what the specific *tasks* are and the *responsibilities* that the person will hold. The following elements will help you determine the profile of a job and whether it demands that the person doing that role:

- just go and do it / think about it / think and do (Proactive-Reactive)?

- manage priorities, attain goals / identify and solve problems (Toward-Away From)?
- decide by oneself, hold standards / adapt to feedback (Internal-External)?
- follow procedures / design them (Procedures-Options)?
- revolution, frequent change / evolution / maintain standards (Difference-Sameness with Exception-Sameness)?
- big picture / detail (General-Specific)?
- rapport with others (Other, Choice)?
- high / medium / low stress (Stress Response: Feelings-Choice-Thinking)?
- work alone / in charge of own territory with others around / together as a group (Independent-Proximity-Cooperative)?
- focus on feelings / tasks to be accomplished (Person-Thing)?
- communicate rules and own expectations / transmit received rules / just get it done / understand both sides (My/My - No/My - My/.- My/Your)?
- check for errors, quality control (Consistent and Away From)?

Here is the job description for the Production Manager mentioned above. This company designs and builds equipment for the manufacture of different kinds of plastic film:

Production Manager – Job Description

Manufacturing Production Management:

- Balance plant production levels with sales requirements.
- Manage plant workforce through supervisors.
- Determine manpower and material requirements.
- Carry out studies on unit (trade category) loading, capacity analysis, and performance.
- Monitor production reports and investigate causes of errors in production, shipping and data entry. Release work orders to departments in accordance with master schedule. Devise

detailed production plans and schedule machine setups for trials and shipping. Develop standard costing systems.

- Ensure that shipments are properly done:
  - completeness of order
  - correctly crated/packaged/protected for shipment so that damage will not occur during shipment
  - necessary assembly/electrical installation drawings are included
  - shipping costs
  - quality control
- Interface with Engineering to establish priorities for jobs to be released.

Materials and Inventory Management:

- Responsible for all WIP and stock.
- Order and time deliveries from suppliers to coordinate with production requirements.
- Maintain optimal inventory levels.
- Coordinate and direct all activities relating to physical inventory audits.
- Oversee bills of materials, determine production standards and part number.
- Implement automated materials / inventory control system when feasible. Coordinate / oversee purchasing department.
- Negotiate prices / terms with major suppliers.
- Select / establish new suppliers.
- Bring new ways / methods to make the purchasing function more effective and make sure that it changes to reflect the current environment.

Government Compliance:

Overall responsibility for compliance with applicable government regulations with the plant. This would include:

- OHSA-Safety compliance and due diligence
- Workers' Compensation
- Hazardous waste removal
- WHMIS compliance
- Evaluations
- Discrimination

Facilities Maintenance:

Prepare annual budgets for supplies, spare parts, and accessories. Establish procedure for equipment selection, operation, maintenance, and replacement. Using the above job description, and having profiled the senior management team to whom the Production Manager would report, I came up with an ideal LAB Profile® for this position. I have included it here to show how I write job profiles.

Production Manager – Job Analysis

The following characteristics are to be preferred, based on the job description and the relationship with the directors.

Motivation Patterns Mainly Proactive with some Reactive

The job requires a high level of energy and the ability to initiate; to a lesser extent the person must be able to analyze and reflect.

Mainly Away From with a little bit of Toward

The successful Production Manager needs to be constantly troubleshooting, inspecting for errors, and making corrections. The directors will need to be goal-focused, with an eye on managing priorities.

Internal

The Production Manager will have to set standards and evaluate against these standards. To fully assume the workload, he/she will need to know internally when things are good or bad, and not have to rely on the constant feedback of the directors. To work well with the directors, they must agree on a set of standards and how they will be evaluated, and then let the Production Manager get on with it.

Mainly Procedures with some Options

The Production Manager will need to be motivated by following procedures most of the time. He/she must be the sort of person who is compelled to complete and finish what he/she has started. To a lesser extent he/she will have to develop new procedures.

Sameness with Exception and Difference

The Production Manager will need to manage improvements and progression over time *and* be able to introduce new procedures and systems. He/she must also be able to handle a wide variety of tasks simultaneously.

Productivity Patterns Mainly General with a good dose of Specific

To work effectively the Production Manager needs to always have a handle on the overview. This would allow him/her to delegate when appropriate. However, several of his/her tasks necessitate that he/she handle specific details for extended periods. Normally a person who is equally General and Specific has a difficult time delegating, which could lead to frustration on the part of his/her staff, and burnout over the long term for the person him/ herself.

For this reason, a person who is mainly General is preferable.

Other

The person must be responsive to tone of voice and body language to supervise and communicate with staff and negotiate with suppliers.

Stress Response: Choice

The Production Manager will need to be able to empathize with others and be able to control his/her internal state, to handle the work load without burning out when things go wrong.

Mainly Proximity with some Independent

Most of the tasks require someone who needs and understands the need for having a territory of responsibility while working with others around. For some of the tasks, he/she will need to work/think while completely alone.

Mainly Thing and Some Person

The person must remain focused on the task at hand and be responsive to feelings. Given ambitious production deadlines, the task must take priority over feelings.

Rule Structure: My/My

He/she has to be able to give clear directions.

Convincer: Consistent

Ideally, a person who is "never completely convinced" is the best choice for a position that demands quality control and inspection. This means that he/she will constantly check and not assume that things are okay because they were last week.

Most Important Patterns

Upon analysis of the job description, and taking into consideration the Profile of the three directors, the following Patterns are the most important for the new Production Manager:

Mainly Away From
Internal
Mainly Procedures

I used the following comparison chart to compare each of the short-listed candidates from the first advertisement (that the company wrote), relative to the 'ideal' for the job.

COMPARISON CHART

PROFILE PATTERNS	PRODUCTION MANAGER	BOB	JOHN	MIKHAIL
Proactive-Reactive	Mainly Proactive	Equally Proactive & Reactive	Mainly Proactive	Mainly Proactive
Toward-Away From	Mainly Away From	Mainly Toward	Away From	Mainly Toward
Internal-External	Internal	Mainly External	Internal	Mainly Internal
Options-Procedures	Mainly Procedures	Mainly Procedure	Equally Options & Procedures	Mainly Options
Sameness & Difference	Sameness w/ Exception & some Difference	Sameness & Difference	Sameness w/ Exception	Difference & some Sameness w/ Exception
Specific-General	Mainly General & some Specific	Mainly General	Mainly General	Mainly General
Other	Other	Other	Other	Self & Other
Independent-Proximity-Cooperative	Mainly Proximity, some Independent	Cooperative with some Proximity	Proximity	Mainly Proximity with some Cooperative
Person-Thing	Mainly Thing & some Person	Equally Person & Thing	Mainly Person & some Thing	Mainly Thing
Stress Response	Choice	Choice	Choice	Choice
Rule Structure	My/My	My/Your	My/Your with some My/My	My/My
Convincer	Ideally, Consistent	Consistent	Period of Time	Large Number of Examples, possibly Consistent

Recommendations

In my opinion, regarding the attributes of each candidate (not the skills or knowledge base), John is the most suitable, followed by Bob. I believe that John is the best because of his ability to perceive, predict, prevent, and solve problems and because of his proficiency at making decisions. He is the most likely to relieve the directors of many responsibilities.

Bob is more goal-oriented and may tend to overlook problems. Because he is more External, he is more likely to need feedback on a continuing basis to help him decide.

Attracting Only the Right People: Career Advertising

To demonstrate how to write an advertisement, here are the two ads used for the Production Manager position. This was the advertisement placed by the company before I was asked to profile the position:

PRODUCTION MANAGER

Private fast-growing engineering company manufacturing high-tech quality machinery for worldwide export has immediate opening for decision maker to manage production division.

Production to double within the next year necessitates efficient coordination of rapidly expanding department.

Right candidate must have minimum 10 years related experience. Emphasis on organization, planning, and purchasing. Candidates must have excellent people-management and leadership skills.

Here is the ad I wrote after doing the Profile of the position:

PRODUCTION MANAGER

Immediate opening for a proactive Plant Manager who will grow with this engineering company, which manufactures high-tech quality machinery for worldwide export.

The right candidate will manage the production division, solving technical, people, and government-compliance issues by following procedures and developing new ones when necessary. You will set standards and assure they are consistently met, even under the pressure of ambitious delivery targets. You are highly experienced and skilled in project and people management and purchasing and can prove it.

The first step is to call now for all the information you need.

I suggested that the candidates call, because only Proactive people will actually pick up the phone. Can you identify the specific Influencing Language used in the second ad?

---

[1] Scott Highhouse, discussing interviewer bias on Stephen J. Dubner's Freakonomics Podcast; bit.ly/YourPerceptionOfTime

Chapter 29
Building a High-Performance Team

As a leader or people manager, it is incumbent upon you to assess accurately the strengths of your people. Beyond being aware of their knowledge and skill levels, when you also know their LAB Profile®, you are better placed to redesign or adapt individual task assignments (where you are able to do so).

I have created an online training called *Words That Change Minds for Managing People*[1] to give examples of doing this.

First list the priority activities and desired results for your team and verify that each one is indeed necessary and useful. Using the elements from the Job Profile section, you can list the ideal LAB Profile® Patterns beside each activity, along with the knowledge and skill requirements. Then zoom out to get an overview of the ideal Patterns needed for this position. (This takes practice!)

Then you can profile each of your team members and discuss with them how effective they feel with regards to each of the priorities. You might adjust task assignments based on what needs to be done and the profile of your team member. It is best to do this in a consultative manner, considering their preferences where feasible.

Let's look at the team as a whole. What are the elements in LAB Profile® terms that characterize your team? What are the strengths and weaknesses when you consider the tasks that need to be accomplished? How can you maximize these strengths? How can you reduce, or take advantage of, the weaknesses when pursuing team goals and objectives?

This is an area where there is no one miracle recipe. Your team will first need to decide its vision, mission, and goals (within the larger context of the organization, of course). There are many books on the numerous available methods for doing this. The next step is to assess your resources (including your people) and evaluate where you are now in terms of performance. Any intervention you decide upon will then come as a result of comparing (1) your desired state and your resources with (2) your present state.

I used the LAB Profile® to help the department of pharmaceutical services at a leading-edge university hospital improve their performance. After they had clarified, in both general and specific terms, where they were going, I profiled the entire team and the tasks to be accomplished.

Here is a comparison chart of what I found when comparing three Contexts: the *overall* work of the pharmacists, work in the *dispensary*, and the *clinical* work they do on the wards-with the group profile.

PHARMACIST LAB PROFILE®			
OVERALL JOB	**DISPENSARY WORK**	**CLINICAL WORK**	**PHARMACISTS n=17**
Proactive & Reactive	Mainly Reactive	Proactive & Reactive	Proactive & Reactive
Mainly Away From, some Toward	Away From	Away From	Mainly Away From
Mainly Internal	Internal	Internal & External	Evenly distributed between Internal & External
Procedures to Options (2 to 1)	Mostly Procedures	Options & Procedures	Mainly Options
Sameness w/ Exception & some Difference	Sameness with Exception	Sameness w/ Exception	Mainly Sameness w/ Exception, some with double Pattern
Mainly Specific & some General	Mainly Specific	Mainly Specific	Mainly General
Other	Other	Other	Other
Proximity	Proximity	Proximity	Mainly Proximity
Thing with some Person	Thing	Person & Thing	Evenly distributed Person, Thing & both

Choice	Choice or Thinking	Choice	Mainly Choice
My/My	My/My	Mainly My/My & some My/ Your	My/My

While it is obvious that there are strengths where the group profile matches the job to be done, and possible weaknesses where the Patterns do not match, there are also other performance factors to consider. This particular group holds frequent departmental meetings to discuss how to work with patients, how to introduce and manage new technological developments and how to move the department towards its goals in improvement of quality.

Given that the group has a mainly Away From Pattern, with about half highly Internal and mainly Options, I was able to predict what their meetings were like. A problem would be raised, and solutions suggested; then long-winded disagreements would ensue on what was wrong with the analysis and suggested solutions. Many members of the team were frustrated by the length, frequency, and lack of productiveness of these meetings. We discussed ways to create more effective meetings by taking advantage of the strengths in the team. For example, they would need to discuss and agree on Criteria and standards to be met (Internal). "What do we want instead of the current situation?" They also specified what tangible evidence would demonstrate that standards had been met by asking: "How would we know we had achieved what we wanted?" Then they could explore options for how to get there. The Away From people would have free rein to examine the suggested solutions for problems and fix them. Lastly, the Procedures people on this team could ensure that the resulting tasks would be completed.

Interestingly enough for this group, given that the profile of their job had a good dose of following Procedures, most of the group fell on the Options side of that continuum. This may be an example that illustrates how one needs to take into account the culture of the organization. This hospital is a teaching and research hospital, known for its innovations in health care. Perhaps the institution itself attracts Options people to work there because of its reputation. I questioned the pharmacists about how they view their job, asking them if they saw their day-to-day work as basically following procedures? Many of them answered that each patient is different, with a problem that needs to be solved, as they search for *new options* with their multi-disciplinary team of doctors, nurses, and so on. I would like to be able to profile Pharmacists in other institutions to see if this group is actually different.

They recently hired a more Procedures manager to balance the team. She has contributed greatly by establishing more protocols and ensuring that they are followed. I continue to help them with hiring new staff.

While it is difficult to generalize about how to create a high-performance team, the starting points are a thorough knowledge of your team members and the tasks to be done. Reflect upon the individual attributes of your team members in comparison to the mission, tasks and specific goals. (Am I My/My or what?)

Using the LAB Profile® to do employee and group profiles and comparing the profiles to the tasks that need to be done, will enable you to identify areas that need improvement and areas where your team can go from good to great. You will need to have some Options thinking about this, because no one step-by-step process will fit all cases.

[1] Words That Change Minds for Managing People free online training: bit.ly/WTCM4ManagingPeople

Chapter 30
Negotiating and Bargaining

One of my corporate clients in the auto parts industry was confronted with a looming strike. The relationship with the union - the United Auto Workers (UAW) had recently deteriorated, so they were very concerned and needed to find a way to avoid a strike.

The Bargaining team thought it might be possible to get an agreement with the union reps. The problem was that there wasn't a lot of trust between the people Bargaining on behalf of the Union and the membership: differences in culture, race, and social class. They needed to find a strategy that would also speak directly to the membership. That is what I taught them how to do.

I trained them in the LAB Profile® Strategies for Negotiations. We ran role plays, simulating actual negotiations. It was difficult, and everyone ended the training days tired and with large sweat stains on their shirts. They learned how to use language that would not only speak to the negotiators on the other side, but would also indirectly get a message through to the membership.

What followed was very interesting. They were able to get a deal with the union reps, as expected. But when it went to the membership, it was voted down.

Strangely, two days later several of the union members had gone away, thought about it, and decided it was actually a good deal, and so they instigated a new vote. Not only did the membership approve the deal, they signed the first 5-year agreement in the history of the company. Up until then, there had only been 1- or 2-year agreements. This was the very first time they had ever gotten a 5-year agreement because people realized it really *was* a good deal.

The company's Bargaining team told me afterwards that they were not expecting to be able to avoid a strike. But the strategy worked. Everyone realized it was an excellent deal. And they were very happy that the relationship with the union membership had dramatically improved.

While the LAB Profile® itself is not a protocol for negotiating, it can be used effectively for understanding the needs and communication style of all parties. It will allow you to present your proposals in ways that your partners in negotiation can best accept.

At the risk of making a gross generalization, certain groups or sectors have identifiable cultures that can be understood in LAB Profile® terms. For example, a combination found frequently in union Bargaining units is the following: Reactive, Away From, Internal, Procedures, Sameness, and Consistent. People with this combination will react to management initiatives by noticing what is wrong (from their perspective) with any proposal, decide based on their own standards and Criteria, insist on following the same procedures to the letter, and protest loudly when conditions and demands change.

They tend to ask for identical treatment of workers (Sameness) and therefore will fight the introduction of systems such as merit pay (Difference) and two-tier compensation systems which penalize newer employees. *Fairness* is a word one hears often in this Context. It is a Sameness word. *Fair* usually means the same treatment for everyone.

As a result, to negotiate effectively with a partner having the above combination, give your rationale in terms of the problems for the workers that would be prevented or solved. As they probably have an Internal Pattern, ask them to *consider* information on the disastrous alternatives. Forget about suggesting options. Better: "The *right way*, to avoid treating anyone *unfairly*, would be to..."

Remember that if you are negotiating with people who have a Consistent Pattern, you will need to re-establish rapport and credibility at each contact, whether in person, on the phone, or in writing. I put the Consistent Pattern in perspective for a newly hired general manager. He was taking his company through a turnaround, starting in a situation with historically bad labor-management relations. "In order to convince your workforce that you want to make the company and the workers thrive," I told him, "you will have to prove your good faith many times. You will only need to screw up *once*, in their eyes, to destroy all the goodwill you have been creating" (Consistent).

For union negotiators, I would suggest that your proposals be put in Toward and Internal terms, unless your counterparts have mainly Away From Patterns, listing the concrete benefits for them to consider. Management tends to understand and agree more readily to forward-moving, goal-oriented proposals. Management cultures also may have an Options Pattern and not want to be tied down to following a given procedure, such as a collective agreement.

Preparation Is the Key

To get ready for a negotiation, beyond the normal preparation for negotiating where you identify your aims and what you can live with, getting ready mentally etc., analyze your counterparts in LAB Profile® terms. In cases where you have yet to meet, and cannot pre-establish contact by phone, look at any written communication you have received from them for phrases that resemble the Influencing Language Patterns.

You could plan to ask some of the LAB Profile® questions in your first meeting, such as "Why is that important?" or "How will you know when this negotiation is successful?"

When I am negotiating, I usually assume that the person I am negotiating with has an Internal Pattern in that Context, unless there is proof to the contrary. This assumption allows me to avoid being perceived as disrespectful, and creates a climate where both our views will be honored.

Sometimes you will find that a person has an Internal preference in the Context of the negotiation but an External Pattern to her or his perceived constituency. In this case you will need to use both sets of Influencing Language, while being careful to place each in the correct Context. "Only you can judge if your constituents will approve this," or "Having studied this to the depth you have, when you decide on the right answer, your people will show their appreciation for all the work you've done," or "What do *you* think about the impact this will have?"

It is also imperative to notice shifts in Options and Procedures. As for sales, someone will indicate that they are ready to conclude on an item when they go into Procedures mode and talk about the "next steps". You can test if someone is ready to move forward by asking if they are ready to go to the next step. But don't push this too often or you risk having your counterpart feel bulldozed and then becoming more resistant to your suggestions.

The key to using the LAB Profile® in negotiating situations is to take the necessary preparation time to figure out your counterparts' (and your clients', if you are representing them) main Patterns. Your diagnosis will guide you in how to present or discuss issues with them.

Chapter 31
Understand and Speak to Your Market

Market Research

A mutual fund company had the following problem: They were generating leads for high-value new customers from their investment advice television program, but they were not happy with their closing rate.

Their high-value prospective clients, people who had $2 million or more to invest, would watch the TV program where the CEO handled phone-in inquiries about investing, and after several months of watching, would phone to find out about investing with the company. The issue was that the company had no formal sales process, so customers were somehow lost along the way.

They hired me to conduct LAB Profile® market research. I interviewed prospective clients who phoned the company and said "yes" to investing and prospects who also phoned but didn't end up saying "yes". From these interviews I uncovered what were the key LAB Profile® Motivation Triggers™ for each group. Using that information, I designed a sales process for them and proposed a series of keywords to use on their website and in the television program that they are still using today, 15 years later.

Their closing rate increased by 50%. Because of this, the CEO decided to come and train with me because he wanted to understand what was the difference that actually ... made the difference. He registered for my 10-day LAB Profile® Consultant/Trainer program, but wouldn't commit to doing the whole program (even though he had paid for the whole thing). At the end of each day, we wondered whether he was coming back the next day. In the end he stayed the full 10 days. He really wanted to learn.

Surveying your marketplace can be done simply and inexpensively using the LAB Profile®. You can do it by phoning your sample group.

Adapt the questions for the appropriate Context: toothpaste, using rail service, buying a car, and so on. You may well find, after profiling, that only a few of the categories are relevant for your product or service. You can then design your advertising or sales processes around the Influencing Language for the people most likely to buy.

If your product meets the needs of groups you are not presently reaching, you can switch some of your language and images.

You can also use the LAB Profile® to re-interpret research that you have already completed. For one of the products in the software example, the *innovators* and *early adopters* segments of the market match the Difference Pattern in the LAB Profile®. *Mid and late adopters* together, have generally the same distribution and behaviors as Sameness with Exception people.

The advantage of translating your research into LAB Profile® terms is to determine exactly which Influencing Language will be the most effective in your marketing campaigns and sales literature. A pharmaceutical company that had produced a new drug for stroke patients, asked me to review the market research they had been done previously, but with which they weren't satisfied. They wanted me to do a LAB Profile® analysis of the raw transcripts of the interviews a research company had conducted with emergency room doctors and neurologists. The doctors had been interviewed about how they diagnosed their patients, because the pharma company wanted to know how to promote, label and give instructions on the product. Unfortunately, I had to discard a portion of the transcripts because the interviewers, who were not aware of how their own LAB Profile® preferences, had biased some of the questions and answers.

From the transcripts that were useable, I discovered a marked difference between the diagnostic approach between the emergency room doctors and the neurologists. The emergency room doctors had a very Procedural methodology, while the neurologists tended to have a much more Options approach. This led to me recommending that the pharmaceutical company have two different kinds of labeling on the product, because of the different approach of each group of doctors. The drug was not approved for use in the end.

Finding Your "Ideal Customer"

Marketers need to understand their target market (Thing); their ideal customer (Person). And when you also understand their typical LAB Profile® Patterns, you can test and quickly improve your lead generation and client acquisition. I have developed an online training specifically to help sales and marketing professionals hit their mark.[1]

First define the demographics, values and behaviors of your ideal customer. (For me, an ideal customer has the money to pay for your products/services, loves what you do for them/gets huge personal value and knows it, and tells all their friends, particularly on social media.) Then look at their behaviors and values (Criteria), guess which their main LAB Profile® Patterns are. You can guess and test with online ads to see which language produces the best results for the lowest cost.

I used these Criteria, to help a white-water rafting company in British Columbia identify their ideal clients as:

40+ years old, middle to high income, family with kids 10+ years old, loves nature, adventure and the outdoors, on a road trip in British Columbia. Their main LAB Profile® Drivers would probably be: mainly Proactive, mainly Toward, mainly Internal, Difference and mainly Person. (They could also have some Away From -> Toward; getting Away From everyday life, perhaps avoiding danger, moving Toward an adventure). This knowledge can help you write ads, taglines etc. How about: "Escape the everyday to your adventure in nature." (Yes, it needs work!)

Rodger Bailey, the developer of the LAB Profile®, and I did some consulting for a major software company. They wanted to have a profile of their print advertisements (both media and flyers) to find out who they were reaching, and to test consistency within the advertisements. Specifically, we looked at two elements: the overall visual aspect (that which would first attract a person to look at the ad), and what was contained in the content (mainly text) of the ad.

We examined the ads and found that nine of the fourteen categories were represented. Here is a summary of our findings.

- **Level** (Proactive-Reactive): The ads matched the normal Pattern for the general population at work.
- **Direction** (Toward-Away From): The ads were skewed in the Toward direction.
- **Source** (Internal-External): The ads focused mainly on attracting an Internal audience, although this Pattern was not as clear as some of the others.
- **Reason** (Options-Procedures): The ads represented both Options and Procedures.
- **Decision Factors** (Sameness, Sameness with Exception, Both, Difference): While the ads generally showed a normal distribution (mainly Sameness with Exception), the visual aspects of the ads were much more Difference than the body text. This means that people with a high Difference Pattern would be attracted to the ad and then *not* find what they were looking for in the content.
- **Scope** (General-Specific): While a normal distribution is skewed towards General, the ads contained much more Specific data. Our client and ourselves felt that this overrepresentation of Specific matched the corporate buyer of software fairly closely.
- **Style** (Independent-Proximity-Cooperative): The ads reflected heavy clusters around Proximity and Independent. We suggested that it would be useful to determine if our client's marketplace is actually shaped that way.
- **Organization** (Person-Thing): The ads contained a strong Thing orientation, which was probably appropriate for the Context.
- **Convincer Channel** (See, Hear, Read, Do): For the flyers, the visual aspects used mainly Do, while the text was mainly See

and Read. Once again, what attracted the reader was not to be found in the content.

As a result of this analysis and an analysis of the desired audience, our client was able to determine whether their ads and flyers were reaching their target for the two products we profiled. By using data collected from their 800 information line, they tested whether people with certain Patterns were or were not responding to the ads.

We also demonstrated a startling fact for our client. I put the ads into two piles stating that one group had been written by one person and that the other group was written by someone else. This was verified by the account executive of their advertising company. We had clearly demonstrated that the writing was more influenced by the writer's profile than by the ability to reach a certain audience.

We would have liked to do more work with them to help specify the ideal Influencing Language for each of the products, based on re-interpreting market research already done into LAB Profile® terms. Unfortunately for us, our client, needing high Options and Difference at work, had left the marketing-director position and had moved on within the company. He now works for a competitor, in a different city.

Online

In online sales and marketing, the landscape keeps changing, as the platforms constantly adjust their algorithms for showing people content and ads, and processes that worked for years suddenly offend or create indifference in specific target markets. You need specialists with expertise, and they need to be experimenting continually to improve conversion rates and sales. How can the LAB Profile® be of help in this environment of ever-shifting ground swells and earthquakes?

You need to know your audience, and not only their story, situation, needs and wants, but also create a trusting relationship with them and be able to meet their needs. A LAB Profile® analysis of them, their situation, and their process for making decisions is incredibly helpful regardless of the current method for selling online.

When we researched and developed the Advanced Business Influence Program[2], we realized that one of our target markets, new managers, would probably be mainly Proactive and mainly Internal in making the decision about taking this program. They would be the ones deciding to take the program, without asking for permission. However, in the Context of being at work as a new manager, they were likely to have a Combination of Person and External, because they had not yet developed the confidence and skills of more senior manager and were sensitive to what others say and do. Our other individual target for this program is the more senior manager or director. We knew that this group of managers would probably be more Internal and slightly more Thing in their work. Our third market is organizations and we also profiled the typical organizational culture in LAB Profile® terms. These analyses enabled us to create and test our materials, emails, ads, landing pages and sales processes.

Successful online campaigns need the potential customer to willingly get into a Procedure that they are motivated to complete. Even if you attract your clients with Options, they still need to "go to the next step" to make a purchase. This is where Period of Time and Number of Examples are relevant. How many times (or for how long) do your potential clients need to get value from you or your ideas to know that they need your product or services? Many people post videos, and events hoping they will "go viral" and get lots of attention. From my analysis of viral videos, I noticed there was usually a story about people. To succeed, the story needs to be both Procedural and Person in LAB Profile® terms. Of course, stories are Procedures (they have a beginning, middle and end). But people have to CARE! That's why the Person element is so important.

---

[1] Words That Change Minds for Sales and Marketing, free online training: bit.ly/WTCM4SalesMarketing

[2] Advanced Business Influence Program: bit.ly/AdvancedBusinessInfluence

Chapter 32
Education and Learning

It is not my intention to criticize public-school education in this section, but rather to provide some food for thought.

Why are educational programs designed the way they are? It is usually because the authors believe they have discovered the *best way* to learn a subject. Often, they are right about large percentages of the groups they hope to reach, but what about the smaller percentage of students for whom this is not true?

My comments are about these *other* students, for whom a given model does not work, and who therefore are more likely to drop out of school, quit online programs, not finish continuing education courses, etc. In the work I have done with educators on the topic of reducing the number of dropouts in secondary school, we discussed strategies for keeping kids interested *throughout the school cycle*.

My advice to individual teachers in primary or secondary school would be to first identify the pupils who are not engaged by class activities. Secondly, profile them to discover what will trigger and maintain their motivation. Once the individual's motivation Patterns are known, you can then adapt activities to suit their needs, using the resources and methods available, and inventing some when necessary. Lastly, you will notice a marked improvement in the participation and performance of these previously hard-to-reach students.

For example, Options students may have difficulty following the prescribed procedure, and as a result may become frustrated or disruptive in the classroom. These students are more likely to stay motivated and focused if they are given more choice and the possibility to develop their own process. Procedures students may have difficulty knowing how to start an open task. They would appreciate having a procedure to follow to get started. In each case you would need to make sure to use the Influencing Language that matches the student's Pattern. "Think of all the possible ways to do this!" (Options); "Here are the first steps to get started" (Procedures).

You can also design or use activities to encourage flexibility in the LAB Profile® Categories, following and completing Procedures as well as developing Options.

For Internal learners to stay motivated they need to make their own decisions. You can get them to evaluate their own work. When making suggestions to this group, you might want to use phrases such as: *"You might want to consider,"* or *"Can I make a suggestion for you to think about?"* External students will need lots of feedback to know how well they are doing. To encourage the development of both Internal and External Patterns, you can provide a balance in activities: self-evaluation (Internal) and adapting to feedback received (External). You will be able to see and hear who responds best to which Patterns merely by observing the students' reactions to the tasks.

Much of someone's ability to use what they have learned is dependent on the *level of confidence* they have about having mastered it. When someone's Convincer Patterns have been satisfied, they are more likely to use the material or do the activity more confidently.

If a child needs six or seven repetitions of a skill to be convinced they know it, it is unlikely that they will get enough repetition in the course of a school day. My suggestion to teachers, when they notice a child feels unsure of what they have learned, is to ask the Convincer Channel and Mode questions. "How do you know when someone else is good at addition?" "How many times do you have to see them do it right (or hear that they got the right answer, or do the work with them, etc.) for you to be convinced that they are good at addition?" Then you can assign homework based on the Number of repetitions or Period of Time needed. If the student has a Consistent Convincer Mode, (never completely convinced), you will find that they know they can do it one day and may be unsure the next. Remind them of the previous times when they knew they could do it.

In school Contexts the LAB Profile® is useful in two ways. First, it can be used to diagnose and plan for students who are not doing well with the programs in vogue. Second, it can help teachers understand what Patterns they are unconsciously encouraging or discouraging as a matter of course.

Adult Learners

Learning is a Context in and of itself. The act of *learning* something is about taking in new material and acquiring it for oneself, while *using* what one has previously learned requires a different set of behaviors. As you can probably deduce, this process is a sequence of Contexts: Take in something new in External; evaluate it in Internal; use it and determine the results in Internal and External and probably a good dose of Procedures.

For someone to learn something *new*, they need to be in an External mode. If someone is attempting to take in something new while remaining in Internal mode, the new material will find itself banging up against previously held standards and Criteria within the person. As a result, the ability to actually acquire the new material is limited. In some adult education courses, the learners are asked to put aside for a while what they already know about a topic, to facilitate taking in a new way of thinking about it. They are invited to reinstate their critical thinking caps once they have mastered the material. However, I personally hate being told to leave my knowledge and experience at the door when I take a course, especially since it took me so long to acquire it.

You might wish to consider a more elegant way to help your students shift into an External mode for the *learning* part of the activities. Simply establish your credibility, so that your students become External *to you*. This credibility is particularly important for adult learners, as any corporate trainer will tell you.

The Solution for Short Attention Spans

There is so much competition for attention, while attention spans seem to be getting shorter. With demands to be ever more productive, to respond to texts and apps within seconds, many people are in a constant state of pressure and feeling overwhelmed. Plus, people have become so used to small bites of information, short tweets, swiping pictures left or right, up or down in nano seconds, that long sentences (such as this one) are harder for many people to read. This makes it more challenging to learn, integrate, apply and remember new skills and information.

The solution needs to match the way people go about their activities or else they tend to keep putting off learning because it is too great an effort. There is a large dropout rate on e-learning because people are not motivated by the topic or format, don't have the time, don't schedule the learning time in their calendar, there are no consequences for dropping out, they find it boring and so on.

That is why micro-learning formats, and gamification with high levels of interactivity were developed. When done well, these formats work in part because they address the needs of several LAB Profile® Patterns. To get and keep people interested, the learning needs to be in short doses, of course, but they need to get people hooked into a Procedure, because then the learner is motivated to complete the process. Stories are a great way to get people into a Procedure. (Stories have a beginning, a middle and the end.... a Procedure). Stories are a combination of Procedure and Person. But any way of getting the learner engaged in any fun Procedure will do.

There also needs to be an element of newness (Difference) to keep people attentive. Movement is a way to create Difference, as movement is not static (same). This is particularly important when people are learning on their phones, because the screen is so small in comparison to all the things moving about in the environment around the phone. And because we are talking about learning, feedback on your performance is important (External), as much as the clicks and likes that give us hits of dopamine.[1]

For these reasons I created several programs using the Micro-training format. Short time frames, fun and games (as well as seriousness too!), feedback, lots of newness. The Advanced Business Influence program[2] is for women leaders and managers who want to increase their impact, without taking time off work. The LAB Profile® for Sales digital training[3] enables sales professionals to learn LAB Profile® skills directly applied to their work. These programs blend interactivity and personal contact with highly engaging, short digital streams of practical information with an emphasis on applying the skills immediately in whatever is going on in the learner's life.

But as our engagement with technology continues to evolve, so must learning formats and methods.

---

[1] Molly Soat; Social Media Triggers a Dopamine High: bit.ly/MarketingsEthicalLine and Trevor Haynes; Dopamine, Smartphones & You: A battle for your time: bit.ly/ABattleForYourTime; May 1, 2018
[2] For more information on the Advanced Business Influence program, see Institute for Influence: bit.ly/AdvancedBusinessInfluence
[3] For more information on LAB Profile® for Sales in Micro-Training format and to get a demo course bit.ly/SalesTrainerPlatform

Chapter 33
Default Profiles

Defaults are the standardized settings on your computer and other devices. They are what your device *assumes,* unless you give instructions to the contrary. You can also use the LAB Profile® Patterns to make educated guesses about people and situations that you may not have been able to research in advance. What Patterns are likely to be operating *unless* you get proof to the contrary?

For example, when I begin a presentation to a group of people whom I do not yet know, I find it useful to guess that the members of the group may be skeptical and will likely have the following Patterns:

- **Internal** to me: They are each wondering: "Who the hell is this woman and what makes her think she has something of value to offer to me?"

- **Away From** with regard to what I am presenting: They will notice faux pas, any inappropriate remarks, or examples that are not relevant to them.

- **Consistent**: They will like me when I say or do something they agree with and dislike me should I step out of line, with regard to their expectations. They decide with each idea or sentence. This is the group of people who fact-check you with their phones before you reach the end of your sentence.

Although these kinds of assumptions may seem negative at first glance, in fact they help me prepare. If I assume that a group has an Internal Pattern (at least at the beginning) then I do two things right at the start of my presentation: I take steps to establish my credibility and I use Internal Influencing Language. "I will be presenting some information for you to consider in your work. I invite you to compare it to your own experience and decide what you think."

For the Away From Pattern I suggest: "You know your working environment better than I do. We will have the opportunity to adapt these ideas to your milieu. I'm sure you'll notice which parts are appropriate and which *aren't.*" To deal with the Consistent Pattern, I constantly monitor the individuals in the group to notice signs of disagreement, confusion, and concern. I make sure to use Influencing Language for Internal and avoid making definite statements. I will invite someone with a concerned face to tell me what they are thinking, so that I can respond to it. For the complete four-part formula for skeptical people, check out my MP3 Presenting Ideas to Skeptical People.[1]

Once you know the behaviors associated with the LAB Profile® Patterns, you can predict the Default Profile for many situations. You can identify which Patterns are *safe* to assume unless you get evidence to the contrary. I use the word "safe" intentionally: If you had unconsciously assumed the opposite Pattern would a disaster result?

For example, you might assume (outside of your awareness) that a group to whom you were to present had an External Pattern to you, just because they hired you. As a result, when you begin your presentation, you might forget to establish credibility, presupposing that they believed everything you say. Under these circumstances, it is quite likely that you will be attacked on a substantive issue by a member of the group.

Aruna, a student and client of mine, had to do a presentation for her company in a large, packed amphitheater, standing at the bottom in the light, looking up at the rows of seats of people, mainly in the dark. As she was about to start, an unseen man sitting way up at the top yelled out: "Hey Aruna, you're just as beautiful as you used to be 20 years ago." And everybody laughed. Of course. And not only that, because they all worked for the same company, they were probably thinking: "WOW! Did they have an affair 20 years ago?", "Why is he saying that?", "Did he sleep with her?", "What kind of relationship did they have?" They were certainly no longer thinking about Aruna's topic.

Many women who have been sabotaged in this jovial manner are taken aback and feel embarrassed. They end up just laughing because everybody else is laughing. Huge mistake! Because now everyone is distracted, and she may have just lost credibility by not handling the situation. It looks like Mr. Joker has just pulled the rug out from under her feet. Some people may even start feeling sorry for her! But Aruna didn't make this mistake. She had been my student for many years and didn't fall into the trap. She knew exactly what to do when somebody throws you a "Banana Peel," implying: "Here, darling, slip on this!"

She followed what I taught her about how to handle a "Banana Peel," by throwing it right back to the person who threw it at her. And she was brilliant! Aruna said: "Gee Peter, unfortunately I can't say the same for you." Everyone laughed, and she immediately regained credibility and did a great presentation. Later, she told me: "if I hadn't known how to respond to a Banana Peel, I probably would have fallen in the trap of laughing and lost credibility."

Proving your case means both establishing your credibility and providing information to support your points. This will address the Internal and Away From Patterns in your audience.

In sales situations, you can develop Default Profiles for your prospects and customers. Let's say you are a computer consultant. Perhaps many of your customers have an External Pattern to you. They come to you for expertise and might run away if you asked them what they thought the best solution was.

The marketing group for a large pharmaceutical company presents their new marketing strategies quarterly to the sales representatives. We did Default Profiles for both the sales reps and the end customers: physicians. The marketing group felt that the sales reps had the following Profile when they were in the field, working their territories:

Mainly Proactive; Toward (focused on the sale); **External** (to physicians); **Procedures and Sameness with Exception.**

They also thought that the sales reps had a different profile when dealing with Head Office and the Marketing Group:

Mainly Proactive; Away From (picking holes in marketing strategies); **Internal** (we know the field better than those guys at Head Office); **Procedures and Sameness with Exception** (don't keep totally changing what we are supposed to do).

As a result of this analysis, the marketing group listed Influencing Language to use and to avoid in their presentations. They also redesigned their strategies to take into account the two different Profiles of the sales reps (for two different Contexts) and the customers' (physicians') Profile.

If you are a therapist or coach, you can assume that your clients have an Away From motivation when they come to you for help. You might consider using Away From Influencing Language in your promotional materials and when working with them. "You've decided that you are fed up enough with this problem to want to get rid of it, once and for all."

Default Profiles are an example of a Generalization. They are useful if you make sure to pay attention and adapt to the exceptions.

---

[1] My MP3 Presenting Ideas to Skeptical People: bit.ly/SkepticalPeople

Chapter 34
LAB Profile® Inventions and Tools

Since the development of the LAB Profile®, several more exciting tools, applications and software have been developed.

LAB Profile®-Based, Automated Questionnaires Online

My newest development! Discover your **LAB Profile® at work *FOR FREE*** at bit.ly/TheLabProfile. If you would like to do many profiles automatically, without interviewing each person there are three LAB Profile® online questionnaires that can be used with large groups:

iWAM

bit.ly/iWAMQuestionnaire

The **Inventory for Work Attitude & Motivation** (iWAM) is a questionnaire used for job-related activities, such as recruitment, coaching and training projects. It is based on metaprograms, a model of cognitive thinking styles (48 parameters are measured and explained). The iWAM Management Report identifies a person's motivational and attitude preferences in the job context and predicts how this person will behave in various job types, such as administrative, customer contact or managerial tasks. The iWAM Attitude Sorter predicts key motivational preferences and development areas. The questionnaire can be administered over the Internet or as a pen-and-paper test. The iWAM is currently available in more than 15 languages. Test administration takes 25 to 45 minutes. Check out our Research page to learn about the background of the test, and the thorough research that our products are based on.

Identity-Compass

bit.ly/IdentityCompassTool

The Identity Compass® is an innovative personnel selection tool which uses an inventory of "thinking structures". It registers how people think and make decisions in typical work situations. It points out what motivates employees, what their values are and what their career goals are. The Identity Compass® gives clear guidance on which employees are likely to perform best in which situations and how improvement can best be achieved. Available in 19 languages.

Mind-Sonar

bit.ly/MindSonar

MindSonar is a web-based psychological system, measuring NLP Meta Programs (thinking styles) and criteria (what someone finds important). Meta Programs are the building blocks of the way people think and have a strong influence on how you behave and your emotional response to a given situation.

Libretta® Software from Shelle Rose Charvet bit.ly/weongozi

Libretta® is a tool that *automates the detection of LAB Profile® Patterns* and *evaluates whether or not you have matched someone's Patterns* in your communications. It also *collects LAB Profile® big data about what is motivating large groups of people*, such as customers, software users etc.

Developed with leading Computational Linguistics scientists, Libretta® has two US patents for scientifically determine the Patterns inside text. It is software that can be imbedded anywhere to read an unlimited number of streams at once. Currently it is a plug-in for Outlook 365, available on MAC and Windows.

Libretta® Applications

1. Add NEW Big Data Analytics to show what motivates your customers

Ideal for analytics platforms when you want to provide NEW information that no one else is capturing. Libretta® pinpoints the key Motivation Patterns for each customer or group of customers and ensures that your outbound messages use the correct type of language to engage people and create relationships.

2. Increase your Outbound Marketing Response Rate

Identify the key Motivation Patterns driving your audience. Libretta® tests your texts to make sure the language fits your customers' buying process.

3. Reach a Diverse Audience with your online advertising

Stop losing clicks from interested customers. Use several Motivation Patterns simultaneously in online and mobile advertising to increase CTR & make sure no one is left out.

4. Optimize Click Through and Conversion Rates

Customize mobile and online ads by matching your ad to each customer's dominant Motivation Patterns.

5. Find out what is going on with your employees.

No questionnaires needed. Our **Libretta® Corporate Culture and Mood Analytics™** enable you to discover the Motivation Patterns for your whole organization by using our Libretta® for Email. You can do it monthly to measure how events affect Corporate Culture and Mood.

6. Get your employees to use email strategically and stop making mistakes.

Our **Libretta® for Email** enables each employee to find out what is motivating the person who sent you an email, get tips for responding, and evaluate the fit of your response before you send it. Avoid inadvertently using language that doesn't fit the other person! For more information on Libretta®, check out bit.ly/weongozi and test it out for yourself.

Mobile App HusbandMotivator™ by Shelle Rose Charvet
bit.ly/HusbandMotivatorAPP

Available on iOS and Android

Joke Alert:

"Have you tried using sex and food to persuade your husband, and he still won't do what you want?"

Yes I am of course, joking. But if you had my HusbandMotivator™ app all that would be unnecessary.

As you know, someone's LAB Profile® Patterns can change according to the Context. So this app asks you to choose from seven Contexts: Activities, Household Chores, Intimate Relationship, Family, Work/Career, Health and Finances. Each of these Contexts has several choices for Sub Contexts so you can choose exactly the subject about which you want to motivate someone. HusbandMotivator™ can be used over and over for different Contexts.

And I know what you're thinking: "What about a WifeMotivator App? Or a BossMotivator, CustomerMotivator, TeenagerMotivator, etc?" Great idea! We're working on it.

Part 5:
Appendices

Chapter 35
Summaries and Useful Bits

In this section you will find:

- LAB Profile® Patterns summaries and distribution figures that you can include in reports you give people
- An Influencing Language summary to help you plan what to say or write
- Research Abstracts and other references
- Resources, Tools, Learning Programs for Mastery, etc.
- LAB Profile® Worksheets to use when profiling people

I hope you have as much fun as I have using *Words That Change Minds*.

Chapter 36
LAB Profile® Patterns Summary

Motivation Patterns

How a person triggers their interest and, conversely, what will demotivate them. Each Pattern is described below in its extreme form:

LEVEL: Does the person take the initiative or wait for others?

Proactive: Acts with little or no consideration. Motivated by doing.

Reactive: Motivated to wait, analyze, consider and react.

CRITERIA: These words are a person's labels for goodness, rightness, and appropriateness in a given context. They incite a positive physical and emotional reaction.

DIRECTION: Is a person's motivational energy centered on goals or problems to be dealt with or avoided?

Toward: They are motivated to achieve or attain goals. They may have trouble recognizing problems. They are good at managing priorities.

Away From: They focus on what may be and is going wrong. They are motivated to solve problems and have trouble keeping focused on goals.

SOURCE: Does the person stay motivated by judgments from external sources or by using their own internal standards?

Internal: They decide based on their own internal standards. They like to evaluate outside information by judging it against their own standards.

External: They need outside feedback to know how well they are doing. They are motivated by impact, feedback and results.

REASON: Does the person continually look for alternatives or prefer to follow established procedures?

Options: They are compelled to develop and create procedures and systems and like to bend or break rules. They may have difficulty following set procedures.

Procedures: They prefer to follow the right step-by-step process and once started are motivated to complete. They may get stuck when they have no procedure to follow.

DECISION FACTORS: How does a person react to change, and what frequency of change do they need?

Sameness: They are motivated when things stay the same. They will provoke change about every 15 to 25 years.

Sameness with Exception: They prefer situations to evolve slowly over time. They want major change every 5 to 7 years.

Difference: They want change to be constant and drastic. Major change every 1 to 2 years.

Difference and Sameness with Exception: They like both evolution and revolution. Major change averages every 3 years.

Productivity Patterns

How people treat information; the type of tasks; the environment they need to be most productive; how they go about making decisions:

SCOPE: How large a picture is the person able to work with?

Specific: Details and sequences. They tend not to see the overview.

General: Overview, big picture. Can handle details for short periods.

ATTENTION DIRECTION: Does the person pay attention to the nonverbal behavior of others or attend to their own internal experience?

Self: Attends to own experience. Doesn't notice others' behavior or voice tone.

Other: Has Automatic reflex responses to nonverbal behavior.

STRESS RESPONSE: How does a person react to the normal stresses of a given Context?

Feeling: Emotional responses to normal levels of stress. Stays in feelings. Not suited for high-stress work.

Choice: Can move in and out of feelings voluntarily. Good at empathy.

Thinking: Does not go into feelings at normal levels of stress. Less apt to establish rapport or show empathy.

STYLE: What kind of human environment allows the person to be most productive?

Independent: Alone with sole responsibility.

Proximity: In control of own territory with others around.

Cooperative: Together with others in a team, sharing responsibility.

ORGANIZATION: Does the person concentrate more on people, thoughts, feelings and experiences or on tasks, ideas, systems, or tools?

Person: Centered on people, relationships, feelings experiences and thoughts. They become the *task*.
Thing: Centered on tasks, systems, ideas, tools. Getting the job done is the most important thing.

RULE STRUCTURE: Does a person have rules for themselves and others?

My/My: My rules for me. My rules for you. Able to tell others what they expect.
My/.: My rules for me. I don't care about you.
No/My: Don't know rules for me. My rules for you. Typical middle management Pattern.
My/Your: My rules for me. Your rules for you. Can see both perspectives but hesitant to tell others what to do.

CONVINCER CHANNEL: What type of information does a person need to start the process of getting convinced about something?

See: See evidence.

Hear: Oral presentation or hear something.

Read: Read a report.

Do: Do something.

CONVINCER

MODE: What has to happen to the information or evidence previously gathered to make a person become "convinced" of something?

Number of Examples: They need to have the data a certain number of times to be convinced.

Automatic: They take a small amount of information and get convinced immediately based on what they extrapolate. They hardly ever change their minds.

Consistent: They are never completely convinced. Every day is a new day and they need to get reconvinced.

Period of time: They need to gather information for a certain duration before their conviction is triggered.

PATTERN DISTRIBUTION

From Rodger Bailey, in the Context of work, the Language and Behavior Patterns have the following distribution:

LEVEL

Mainly Proactive	Equally Proactive & Reactive	Mainly Reactive
15%–20%	60%–65%	15%–20%

DIRECTION

Mainly Toward	Equally Toward & Away From	Mainly Away From
40%	20%	40%

SOURCE

Mainly Internal	Equally Internal & External	Mainly External
40%	20%	40%

REASON

Mainly Options	Equally Options & Procedures	Mainly Procedures
40%	20%	40%

DECISION FACTORS

Sameness	Sameness with Exception	Difference	Sameness with Exception & Difference
5%	65%	20%	10%

SCOPE

Mainly Specific	Equally Specific & General	Mainly General
15%	20%	60%

ATTENTION

Self	Other
7%	93%

STRESS RESPONSE

Feeling	Choice	Thinking
15%	70%	15%

STYLE

Independent	Proximity	Cooperative
20%	60%	20%

ORGANIZATION

Mainly Person	Equally Person & Thing	Mainly Thing
15%	30%	55%

RULE STRUCTURE

My/My	My/.	No/My	My/Your
75%	3%	7%	15%

CONVINCER CHANNEL

See	Hear	Read	Do
55%	30%	3%	12%

CONVINCER MODE

Number of Examples	Automatic	Consistent	Period of Time
52%	8%	15%	25%

Chapter 37
Influencing Language Summary
Motivation Patterns

LEVEL

Proactive: do it; go for it; jump in; now; get it done; don't wait

Reactive: understand; think about; wait; analyze; consider; might; could; would; the important thing is to…

DIRECTION

Toward: the benefits are; attain; obtain; have; get; include; this would achieve

Away From: avoid; steer clear of; not have; get rid of; exclude; get Away From, not have to worry about

SOURCE

External: so-and-so thinks; the impact will be; the feedback you'll get; the approval you'll get; others will notice; give references; results will show you

Internal: only you can decide; you know it's up to you; what do you think; you might want to consider, I wanted to run something by you to get your input

REASON

Options: break the rules just for them; opportunity; here are the choices; options; alternatives; possibilities, what else

Procedures: speak in procedures: first; then; after which; the right way; here's how to do it; tried and true; tell them about the procedures they will get to use, first step

DECISION FACTORS

Sameness: same as; in common; as you always do; like before; unchanged; as you know, we've always done this

Sameness with Exception: more; better; less; same except; evolving; progress; gradual improvement; develop

Difference: new; totally different; completely changed; switch; shift; unique; revolutionary; brand new; one of a kind

Sameness with Exception and Difference: it's better and quite new; the new improvements; a unique development; new upgrade

Productivity Patterns

SCOPE

Specific:	exactly; precisely; specifically (and give lots of details in sequence)
General:	the big picture; essentially; the important thing is; in general; concepts

ATTENTION DIRECTION

Self:	(keep communication focused on the content and use Language for Internals; only you can decide; would you like to see the report, so you can decide; what is important to you; since X is important, I suggest
Other:	(influenced by the depth of rapport, so mirror and match their nonverbal behavior; Since X is important…. (check for agreement), then….; you can be comfortable with this; look over here (point to something)

STRESS RESPONSE

Feeling:	it's a major event; intense experience and you don't forget it; exciting; mind-boggling; wonderful
Choice:	empathy; appropriate; makes good sense and feels right
Thinking:	clear thinking; logical; rational; cold reality; hard facts; statistics

STYLE

Independent:	do it alone; by yourself; you alone; without interruption; total responsibility and control
Proximity:	you'll be in charge with others involved; you'll direct; lead; your responsibility is X; theirs is Y; this is your project and coordinate with X
Cooperative:	us; we; together, all of us; team; group; share responsibility; do it together; let's

ORGANIZATION

Person:	(use people's names); our relationship will be; what are your thoughts; it will feel good; people like this; our people need this; the folks will be impacted
Thing:	things; systems; process; task; the job is; goal; organization; company; accomplishments, results

RULE STRUCTURE

My/My: you know what you want; when it's clear to you; what goes for the goose goes for the gander; the fruit doesn't fall far from the tree.

My/.: (use Language for Internals) only you can decide; here's a suggestion; this may be in your best interests.

No/My: (can use Language for Externals) even if you aren't sure; this is what to do; here is how to handle that; what would someone else do in the situation?

My/Your: different strokes for different folks; not everyone is the same; each to his own; you will need to work out what is best for each party.

CONVINCER CHANNEL

See: see this; take a look; it's pretty clear; the light at the end of the tunnel; writing on the wall

Hear: here's what they are saying; the online chatter; rumor has it; something to cheer about

Read: I read this; I can send you some documentation on this; you can read about it; the report says; review the literature

Do: let's work this out; try it on for size; feel them out; get a grip on this; let's work with it

CONVINCER MODE

Number of Examples: (use their number); 3 times is a charm, twice should do it, look this over 2 or 3 times; would you like to see another example

Automatic: assume; benefit of the doubt, you'll right away; as soon as you see it, you'll know

Consistent: try it; each time you use it; daily; every time; consistent; each and every time

Period of Time: (match period of time); it changes over time; in a couple of weeks; you will eventually know; after all this time, it will be alright; The LAB Profile® Worksheet

Chapter 38
The LAB Profile® Worksheet: Motivation Patterns

Name: _____ Company: _____

Profiler: _____ Position: _____

Date: _____ Context: _____

Questions	Categories	Patterns: Indicators
(no question for Level)	LEVEL _____ _____	**Proactive:** *action, do it, short, crisp sentences* **Reactive:** *try, think about it, could, wait*
What do you want in your (work)**?**	CRITERIA	
Why is that (criteria) important? (ask up to 3 times)	DIRECTION _____ _____	**Toward:** *attain, gain, achieve, get, include* **Away From:** *avoid, exclude, recognize problems*
How do you know you have done a good job at … ?	SOURCE _____ _____	**Internal:** *knows within self* **External:** *told by others, facts and figures*
Why did you choose (your current work)**?**	REASON _____ _____	**Options:** *criteria, choice, possibilities, variety* **Procedures:** *story, how, necessity, didn't choose*
What is the relationship between (your work this year and last year)**?**	DECISION FACTORS _____ _____ _____ _____	**Sameness:** *same, no change* **Sameness with Exception:** *more/ better, comparisons* **Difference:** *change, new, unique* **Sameness with Exception & Difference:** *new and comparisons*

LAB Profile® Worksheet: Productivity Patterns

Name: _____   Company: _____

Profiler: _____   Position: _____

Date: _____   Context: _____

Questions	Categories	Patterns: Indicators
(no questions for Scope and Attention Direction)	**SCOPE** _____ _____	 **Specific:** *details, sequences, exactly* **General:** *overview, big picture, random order*
	ATTENTION DIRECTION _____ _____	 **Self:** *short monotone responses* **Other:** *animated, expressive, automatic responses*
Tell me about a (work situation) that gave you trouble.	**STRESS RESPONSE** _____ _____ _____	 **Feeling:** *goes in and stays in feelings* **Choice:** *goes in and out of feelings* **Thinking:** *doesn't go into feelings*
Tell me about a (work situation) that was (Criteria). (wait for answer)	**STYLE** _____ _____ _____	 **Independent:** *alone, I, sole responsibility* **Proximity:** *in control, others around* **Cooperative:** *we, team, share responsibility*
What did you like about it?	**ORGANIZATION** _____ _____	 **Person:** *people, feelings, reactions* **Thing:** *tools, tasks, ideas*
What is a good way for you to increase your success at *(your work)*? What is a good way for someone else to increase their success at (their work)?	**RULE STRUCTURE** _____ _____ _____ _____	 **My/My:** *My rules for me/My rules for you* **My/. (period):** *My rules for me/ Who cares?* **No/My:** *No rules for me/My rules for you* **My/Your:** *My rules for me/Your rules for you*
How do you know that someone else *(an equal of yours)* is good at their *(work)*? How many times do you have to *(see, hear, read, do)* that to be convinced they are good?	**CONVINCER** _____ _____ _____ _____	 **See** ___ **# of Examples:** *give number* **Hear** ___ **Automatic:** *benefit of the doubt* **Read** ___ **Consistent:** *not completely convinced* **Do** ___ **Period of Time:** *give time period*

The LAB Profile® Worksheet: Motivation Patterns

Name: _____   Company: _____

Profiler: _____   Position: _____

Date: _____   Context: _____

Questions	Categories	Patterns: Indicators
(no question for Level)	**LEVEL** _____ _____	Proactive Reactive
What do you want in your (work)**?**	**CRITERIA**	
Why is that (criteria) important? (ask up to 3 times)	**DIRECTION** _____ _____	Toward Away From
How do you know you have done a good job at ... ?	**SOURCE** _____ _____	Internal External
Why did you choose (your current work)**?**	**REASON** _____ _____	Options Procedures
What is the relationship between (your work this year and last year)**?**	**DECISION FACTORS** _____ _____ _____ _____	Sameness Sameness with Exception Difference Sameness with Exception & Difference

344

LAB Profile® Worksheet: Productivity Patterns

Name: _____   Company: _____

Profiler: _____   Position: _____

Date: _____   Context: _____

Questions	Categories	Patterns: Indicators
(no questions for Scope and Attention Direction)	**SCOPE** _____ Specific _____ General	
	ATTENTION DIRECTION _____ Self _____ Other	
Tell me about a (work situation) that gave you trouble.	**STRESS RESPONSE** _____ Feeling _____ Choice _____ Thinking	
Tell me about a (work situation) that was (Criteria). (wait for answer)	**STYLE** _____ Independent _____ Proximity _____ Cooperative	
What did you like about it?	**ORGANIZATION** _____ Person _____ Thing	
What is a good way for you to increase your success at (your work)? What is a good way for someone else to increase their success at (their work)?	**RULE STRUCTURE** _____ My/My _____ My/. (period) _____ No/My _____ My/Your	
How do you know that someone else (an equal of yours) is good at their (work)? How many times do you have to (see, hear, read, do) that to be convinced they are good?	**CONVINCER** _____ See ___ # of Examples _____ Hear ___ Automatic _____ Read ___ Consistent _____ Do ___ Period of Time	

Chapter 39
Research and Research Abstracts

Since the publication of the first and second editions of *Words That Change Minds,* it has been cited by many others to support their own research and applications[1]. As far as I know, at least three master's theses have been done on Meta Programs or LAB Profile®, of which two are mentioned below. One thesis on the topic of high-school dropouts in Montréal by Lillianne Laplante, found that the majority of the students in the study who dropped out had an External Pattern with regards to school[2]. Many other articles have been published, using the LAB Profile®[3]. Below are the two original master's theses.

LAB Profile® Inter-Judge Reliability,
by Étienne Godin, Université de Moncton

Inter-judge reliability of the LAB Profile® was verified in two separate studies using the Statistic Kappa (Cohen, 1986)[4]. In the first one, conducted in 1993, the data analyzed were obtained from recorded interviews with thirty-four subjects. During the second study in 1995, eighty-four people were interviewed in the Context of career decision making.

For each of these studies, analysis showed a statistically significant reliability coefficient for eleven of the thirteen categories covered by the LAB Profile®. In both 1993 and 1995 the Stress Response category did not obtain a significant result, possibly because the judges worked from audio recordings of the interviews, and therefore could not take into account the nonverbal communication of the subjects. For the 1993 study, the Scope category was also not significantly reliable. In 1995, the Level category did not give a significant result.

For each of the above-mentioned categories, there are no specific questions in the LAB Profile® to elicit the patterns. In such cases, inter-judge reliability depends on the level of training and experience of the judges.

In summary, in both studies, ten of the LAB Profile® categories obtained a statistically significant reliability coefficient: Direction, Source, Reason, Decision Factors, Attention Direction, Style, Organization, Rule Structure, Convincer Channel, and Convincer Mode. These two studies demonstrate that it is possible to obtain inter-judge reliability for the LAB Profile® categories that use specific questions to elicit the patterns, and that one can train judges who will get the same results from data obtained from the LAB Profile® answers.

Cohen, J. (1960). "A coefficient of agreement for nominal scales." *Educational and Psychological Measurement*, 20(1), 37-46.

Godin, É. (1997). *Inter-Judge Reliability of the LAB Profile®*. manuscript, Université de Moncton, Moncton, N.B., Canada

The LAB Profile® and Career Indecision,
by Micheline Sirois, Université de Moncton

An exploratory study was done with sixty-one students aged between 17 and 24. The purpose of the study was to determine whether the LAB Profile® would show differences between students who were able to make career decisions that they were comfortable with (n=41), and students who were indecisive and uncomfortable with their indecisiveness (n=20) with regard to career decisions. The students completed the Professional Decision Profile (Jones, 1986) and went through LAB Profile® interviews.

The ordinal data from the LAB Profile® interviews underwent an inter-judge reliability test (Godin and Sirois, 1995). Reliability was statistically significant for nine of the eleven categories used in this study.

The frequency distributions of the two groups were different on the following eight LAB Profile® categories: Level, Direction, Reason, Decision Factors, Scope, Stress Response, Rule Structure, and Convincer Mode. From an analysis using McCullagh's regression model for ordinal data, these results were significant with a 95 percent confidence interval. However, in the Level and Stress Response categories, there was insufficient inter-judge reliability to have complete confidence in these results. There were no significant differences in the following three categories: Source, Style, and Organization.

While the results do not indicate that any of the categories fit one or the other group exclusively, they do show tendencies for each group. For example, while there was a high percentage of subjects in both groups having the Away From pattern, the percentage was slightly higher for the group who were indecisive and uncomfortable with their indecisiveness. Similarly, there was a slightly greater tendency to have the Sameness pattern, as well as a slightly smaller tendency to have the Difference pattern in the indecisive and uncomfortable group than with the decisive and comfortable group. However, these patterns were found within both groups. Also, all the people who had a Toward pattern were in the group who were able to make career decisions that they were comfortable with.

These findings, among others, have prompted the researchers to suggest that further studies on the LAB Profile® and career indecision also include other elements. Apart from profiling the subjects, researchers should probably also include in their data whether the subjects have found in their environment the resources that meet their needs, as identified from the LAB Profile®. For example, if individuals need to follow a procedure, were they able to find a suitable one from their environment? If so, how much more likely is it that they will be in the decisive and comfortable group?

Another aspect that might also be researched would be whether one can help the indecisive and uncomfortable people become more decisive by a judicious use of the appropriate Influencing Language.

Godin, É. and Sirois, M. (1995). *Inter-Judge Reliability in 83 LAB Profile® Interviews.*

Unedited document, Université de Moncton, Moncton, N.B., Canada.

Jones, L.K. (1986). *The Career Decision Profile.* North Carolina: Lawrence K. Jones (instrument).

McCullagh, P. (1980) *Regression Models for Ordinal Data*. J.R. Statist. Soc. B. 42(2), 109-142.

Sirois, M. (1997). *Comparative Study of the LAB Profile® Patterns in Groups of Decided and Undecided Individuals With Regards to Career Decision-Making*. Unpublished Master's Thesis, Université de Moncton, Moncton, N.B., Canada.

I appreciate all the work that Micheline and Étienne contributed toward legitimizing the LAB Profile® and also wish to thank Dr. Lorraine Bourque, who directed this NLP research and gave them much encouragement. Thanks also to Dr. Réal Allard, who co-directed Micheline's thesis and provided many insightful questions and comments.

We spent many hours discussing the theoretical aspects relating to career decision and the LAB Profile®, as well as the implications of the findings and the nature of the tools used to measure decisiveness and indecisiveness. We developed hypotheses on possible combination patterns that might make a person less or more decisive in the Context studied. After much debate and statistical analyses, we all felt that, while one could measure decisiveness (using Jones' test), perhaps decisiveness is actually a function of having one's needs met, whatever those needs may be.

But this remains to be proven. Anyone interested?

---

[1] To find other English-language publications that have cited Words That Change Minds: bit.ly/ScholarGoogleWTCM and bit.ly/ScholarWTCM

[2] Lillianne Laplante, La motivation chez les jeune décrocheurs et caractéristiques des métaprogrammes du Profil LAB : Une étude exploratoire. (Motivation of Young Dropouts and Meta Program Patterns from the LAB Profile®: An Exploratory Study) Masters Thesis, Université de Montréal, November 2008

[3] For other articles, please contact me directly; shelle@instituteforinfluence.com

[4] The Statistic Kappa was introduced to measure nominal scale agreement between a fixed pair of raters (p. 378, *Psychological Bulletin*, 1971, Vol. 76, No. 5).

Chapter 40
Resources

Want to go further? Here is a list of websites, organizations, programs, and learning materials so that you can explore ways to use LAB Profile® in your work and life.

LAB Profile® Free Demonstration Videos

How to do a Profile and test it using the Guess and Test Methodology:
- bit.ly/LabProfileDemoVideo1
- bit.ly/LabProfileDemoVideo2
- bit.ly/LabProfileDemoVideo3
- bit.ly/LabProfileDemoVideo4

LAB Profile® Free Cheat Sheet: bit.ly/LabProfileCheatSheet

LAB Profile® Proposal Template: bit.ly/LabProfileProposalTemplate

Institute for Influence

For leaders and managers who want to increase their impact. The Institute for Influence has several programs to help you master the LAB Profile® in your communication every day:
bit.ly/InstituteForInfluence

LAB Profile® for Digital Sales Training

Most customers' buying process is unique to themselves. That's why learning to detect and work with the LAB Profile® Triggers can make all the difference. My student and partner Andreas Plienegger and I created an online company to enable sales trainers to offer digital and blended LAB Profile® for Sales training. For information and a free demo course, check out bit.ly/SalesTrainerPlatform. For organizations who want to have their sales professionals learn how to use LAB Profile®

with high-quality digital training, please contact me directly at shelle@salestrainerplatform.com.

Free Online Trainings to increase your impact and solve communication problems

1. Boost your Credibility and Impact: bit.ly/BoostYourCredibility
2. 10 Hidden Differences Between Men and Women: bit.ly/10HiddenDifferences
3. Words That Change Minds for Managing People: bit.ly/WTCM4ManagingPeople
4. Words That Change Minds for Sales and Marketing: bit.ly/WTCM4SalesMarketing
5. Words That Change Minds for Customer Relations: bit.ly/WTCM4CustomerRelations
6. Words That Change Minds for Trainers, Speakers, Coaches and Consultants: bit.ly/WTCM4Trainers

Shelle's YouTube Channel, for insightful quick hits to make your day: bit.ly/YoutubeSRC

Quizzes for your own self-discovery

- Take a FREE LAB Profile®: bit.ly/TheLabProfile
- The Macho Factor Quiz: bit.ly/MachoTest
- The Credibility Quiz: bit.ly/CredibilityQuizIFI
- The Male & Female Model Quiz: bit.ly/MaleorFemaleModelQuiz

Mobile App HusbandMotivator
bit.ly/HusbandMotivatorAPP

Easy Listening Audio Programs - listen while in the car, out for a walk or a run

1. Presenting Ideas to Skeptical People: bit.ly/SkepticalPeople

2. Building Long Term Relationship with Clients: bit.ly/LongtermRelationship
3. Only Pick a Fight When You Can Win: bit.ly/OnlyPickaFight
4. Influencing & Persuading People: bit.ly/InfluencingAndPersuading
5. Increase Sales in Tough Times: bit.ly/SalesInToughTimes
6. Ending Stage Fright: bit.ly/EndingStageFright
7. Irresistible Presentations: bit.ly/IrresistiblePresentations

Shelle's Patented Libretta® Software – to automatically detect and use LAB Profile® Patterns in email and customer relationship management bit.ly/weongozi

Consulting, Training and Keynote Presentations on Influencing
contact Shelle directly at shelle@instituteforinfluence.com

Chapter 41
What Else?

Words That Change Minds is the fruit of my experience using and playing with the LAB Profile® in many different Contexts. It can help you jump in and communicate better, as well as giving you information to understand what happens when people communicate. You can achieve many of your goals quicker, while at the same time preventing and solving communication problems.

As you use these tools, you will notice for yourself what a difference it makes, and others will surely notice too! The possibilities are endless for communicating in just the right way. You can make a big difference, improve what is already good, and maintain relationships that are important to you.

Whether you use the material in this book in great detail or just focus on the big picture, you will understand what is said to you and notice behaviors in new ways. This material can raise many passions and provide for rational thought. Whether you are working alone, with others around, or together in group harmony, you can feel great about what you accomplish.

If I were you, I would take these tools for myself and use them to guide me and help me understand how others are different. You will see, hear, and feel the improvements that working with the LAB Profile® will instantly provide, over and over again, consistently, for as long as you want.

While I have explored applications and ideas, I am sure that there are *many other ways* to use this tool. So, I put the question to you:

"Now that you know how to understand, predict, and influence people's behavior by finding out what will trigger and maintain their motivation, what else would you like to do with it?"

I look forward to hearing from you.

Shelle Rose Charvet

Chapter 42
LAB Profile® Specialist Certification

If you like LAB Profile® and you would like to learn it in depth and then use it in business…

I've created a 6-Month MBA-level experience for you called Advanced Business Influence, where I literally break down the complete Linguistic and Motivational system and walk you through how to incorporate it in your work, step by step.

This Certificate allows you to consult with clients and help them find the Words That Change Minds in their business, for their recruitment processes, for their marketing processes, for management or in customer experience.

Use this link to get a $270 discount:

bit.ly/Advanced-Business-Influence-book2019

Index

Made in the USA
Middletown, DE
28 February 2020